True Beginner's Mind

Fresh Encounters with Zen

Compiled and with a Foreword by
Peg Syverson, Ph.D.

APPAMADA

True Beginner's Mind: Fresh Encounters with Zen is the first book in the *Liberating Intimacy* series, which is dedicated to the relational heart of Zen and the voices of lay Zen students and their teachers.

Designed and typeset by Ben Syverson in Adrian Frutiger's Univers

First Edition, April 2011
ISBN 978-0-615-42559-7

Published by

APPAMADA

913 E. 38th St
Austin, TX 78705
http://appamada.org

Contents

Foreword
Peg Syverson

Nearly all of the vast literature about Zen is written by Zen masters, Zen teachers, or scholars. Sometimes readers are given a bit of biographical background about the master's early training, but the outcome is never in question. What we have are, for the most part, the success stories of Zen training and practice. Often these books are intended as teachings themselves. Every so often, a solitary account of a Zen student appears, usually self-deprecating and hilarious, but generally these books, too, are the record of those highly motivated to study Zen.

Anyone familiar with Zen teaching and practice knows, however, that there are many more Zen students than Zen teachers, and that there are even more people who encounter Zen only to struggle and founder, and ultimately abandon practice altogether. We know very little about how Zen teachings and practices are experienced by students who begin with little or no background or knowledge of Zen. So this book should be of interest both to Zen teachers who are interested in the often unvoiced uncertainties, doubts, and struggles of their students, and also to Zen students who wonder about the uncertainties, doubts, and struggles they can barely name, that may be shared by others.

In the fall of 2010, twenty-one college students at the University of Texas enrolled in a class titled Non-argumentative

Rhetoric in Zen. With no prior experience of Zen, and for the most part no experience of meditation, they were encountering the ancient teachings and practices of Zen for the first time. This book is a record of their experiences, told in their own words.

The class was created by Peg Syverson, a professor in the Department of Rhetoric and Writing, an ordained Zen priest, and the Director and Resident Teacher for Appamada, a contemporary Zen center in Austin, Texas. The class was explicitly presented not as a religious studies course, or a philosophy course, but a course that looks closely at how language is used in Zen teachings. The Zen tradition is well-known for its unconventional rhetorical approaches—the use of contradiction, negation, surprise, story, silence, and gesture—even language denying language. The language of Zen tends to deconstruct conventional logic, argument, and persuasion. Despite these unpredictable, puzzling rhetorical features, Zen teachings are profoundly transformational.

In the class, students were first introduced to foundational teachings and influential teachers, followed by a look at how meditation practice impacts the brain, and concluding with a text that challenges many of the tacit assumptions about Zen held even among Zen practitioners and scholars, Dale Wright's masterful *Philosophical Meditations on Zen Buddhism.* You can see the full list of texts assigned and recommended below.

Each class began with 15 minutes of stillness and silence, followed by five minutes of personal freewriting that was private to the student. The rest of the class was structured around one major writing project and three kinds of inquiry, inquiry into rhetoric and writing, inquiry into the texts we were reading, and inquiry into the practice and traditions of Zen. In this way, students determined the direction of the class as it unfolded. The product of these inquiries forms the basis of the chapters of this book.

Each student also posed an "unquiz" question over the course of the semester. These questions reflected a student's current question, based on the reading, meditation practice, and anything else related to the class. Two questions were posted online each week, and the other students in the class responded to these questions. We have included at the end of this book the list of unquiz questions and one response chosen by the student who originally posed the question. Students documented their observations about their experiences in a Learning Record, which gathers evidence of student learning and helps students analyze and evaluate it. More information about the Learning Record can be found at www.learningrecord.org.

The questions raised by students are questions encountered by Zen students everywhere. What is nonduality? Without desire, or attachment to goals, how will I be motivated to accomplish anything? How can meditation help me be a better person? How can I stop my wayward thoughts in meditation? How does meditation affect my relationships with others? What do the books we are studying have to do with my everyday life, or even my meditation practice? As they explore these universal questions, I think you will be heartened and inspired by their reflections and responses.

In the process of developing the chapters of this book, students engaged in all aspects of the publication process, from initial composing, giving and receiving feedback, revising, proofreading, preparing the manuscript for print, and publishing it at lulu.com. It is really their book, the story of their experiences, challenges, doubts, and breakthroughs. Some of the students were deeply immersed in their own faith traditions— Judaism, Protestantism, Catholicism—others were skeptical or alienated from the traditions they had been raised in. In every case, however, they learned to look deeply into their own experience, to explore new ways of seeing and understanding, and to inquire into the way experience is conditioned in language. We hope you will enjoy their book. On the following pages you will find the original course description and the course texts.

RHE 330E. Non-Argumentative Rhetoric in Zen

Course Description

American rhetoric is strongly grounded in argument and persuasion, and infused with judgments of good and bad, right and wrong. This is true not only for public discourse in the media, academic discourse in schools, and professional writing and speaking, it is also true in everyday conversation. We are constantly trying to convince someone of our judgments, it seems, or that something or someone is good or bad, right or wrong—a restaurant, a movie, a car, a teacher. Everything is evaluated and every conversation is full of assertions of value. But what if there were a different, equally "real" way to talk about the world and each other? What if we believed that each person is quite capable of waking up to the reality around him or her, and responding appropriately, without being converted to some position or belief we share? What kind of language would we use, and how would we use it?

Zen training begins by kicking the props out of our customary ways of understanding and talking. It subverts value distinctions, challenges our habitual ways of expressing ourselves, and denies the superiority of rationalist, linear logic. It does not do this merely to "deconstruct" language, or to tear down all meaning. It has a radical project of waking us up out of the trance we create for ourselves and others through our habitual uses of language. This class will explore how contradiction, negation, story, surprise, gesture, and silence are used in Zen training as resources for awakening to reality, rather than as assertions or arguments about it. The cryptic pronouncements of Zen masters seem impenetrable. They appear to defy our western rhetorical traditions that depend on logic and formal reasoning as the key to building knowledge. Zen teachers complicate the issue by insisting that language is only "the finger pointing at the moon, not the moon itself." If you have ever tried to write about a meaningful experience, you will recognize the problematic relationship between language and reality. This course engages students in exploring the surprising uses of language and image to create meaning in Zen tradition and practice.

Students do not need any prior experience or knowledge of Zen rhetoric or practices. The first part of the class will provide background on Zen concepts, then we will consider the emergence of contemporary rhetoric of American Zen. Your own personal religious faith or spiritual practice will not be questioned, nor will it disadvantage you in this course. This class is not an introduction to Zen practice, nor a religious studies course, but rather an exploration of an alternative rhetoric, a different method of using language to construct meaning and shape relationships.

Course texts

Required

Steve Hagen, *Buddhism Plain and Simple*

Shunryu Suzuki, *Zen Mind, Beginner's Mind*

Joko Beck, *Everyday Zen*

Rick Hanson, *Buddha's Brain*

Dale S. Wright, *Philosophical Meditations on Zen Buddhism*

Optional Texts

Kosho Uchiyama, *Opening the Hand of Thought*

Walpole Rahula, *What the Buddha Taught*

Paul Reps, *Zen Flesh Zen Bones*

Stephen Batchelor, *Buddhism Without Beliefs*

Other Texts Recommended

Maurine Stuart, *Subtle Sound*

Steve Hagen, *How the World Can Be the Way It Is*

Joko Beck, *Nothing Special*

Cheri Huber, *There is Nothing Wrong with You*

Zen and Cooperation
Lindsay Pollock

Buddhism is not a philosophy I am very familiar with, but living in cooperative housing has made me more aligned with the idea of a collective being rather than focusing on the efforts of an individual. I feel that my actions are sometimes of little consequence for my house, and it has not particularly led to resentment for my peers, but it has given me an appreciation for the ability to "go with the flow." Before moving into my current house I had struggled with other roommates over bills, distribution of labor around the house, and inconsiderate noise. Moving in to the co-op did not eliminate those issues, actually, they practically doubled. What changed by moving in here was my tolerance for other people, and a better understanding of their situation. Sometimes at the co-op we live in filth, sometimes dinner is late, sometimes people do not do their labor, but the house still remains. I cannot clean this house for 100 people, or fill in for all of the labor missed, but I can help the new members to realize the impact of their actions. This idea seems very similar to the idea of Buddhism, to enable one to see rather than trying to change their behavior. A former trustee, the person in charge of the house, enlightened me to the fact that we cannot control the way people are, and the best we can do is pick people with proper motivation to move in. Some people leave this place without learning about cooperation, but most people say that they'll never be the same. I feel forever changed by trying Zen, because I will never forget the control I can have over my emotions or the esteem I derived from that empowerment.

Living with one hundred people has taught me a lot about humans, and how to cope with difficult, interpersonal conflict. Disputes often come from a misunderstanding about another person's viewpoint. We assume we know someone based on a crystallized version that we have created, and we fail to see the constant shift in their character. If we could habitually reiterate what someone else thought before reacting to what they had said, instead of trying to formulate our own argument first, maybe we could have less misunderstanding. This habit is really hard to break, because by our nature we seek to find information that confirms the beliefs we already have, instead of opening our minds to different interpretations. It seems that as soon as we have settled on a belief, we should realize that belief is flawed. By the very nature of settling we have become complacent with our experiences, and we will grow callous to ideas that conflict with our own. I am thankful for my lifestyle in a house amidst strong personalities because my ideas are often challenged by a worthy opponent, and that can lead to a better understanding of my belief, or perhaps a reshaping of my beliefs. In either case opposition is enlightening, and it is important to hear people before developing a rebuttal.

A lot of people move into the co-op expecting to change it completely, and make an impression. Although the thought seems productive it often ends in frustration because one person's will cannot drive the actions of a whole house. My problem is that I hold people to the same standard I hold myself, and when they fail to meet my expectations I feel that it strains my relationships. I find it very hard to give people third chances. I am hesitant to open up to them in the first place, and after a betrayal of trust the risk becomes too great. As much as I am aware of this pitfall in my relationships, I cannot seem to break the habit. This cycle is an example of the tendency to act without living in the moment. Preconceived notions of a person rule my interaction, and taint my perspective. I have shut out a lot of people who have changed and didn't deserve my dismissal because of my tendency to shield against possible pain. I know that changing my habit will take a lot of time, and I have chastised myself for it too often. Realizing that seeing this behavior is more important than correcting it is a big relief. If I could only realize that people are all struggling to overcome the accumulation of bad experiences it would be easier to see how they can do evil things, and despite those actions, still live as good people. With my family, I accept a lot of behavior that I would admonish in others. I give my family innumerable chances to correct themselves because I am invested in them. We cannot be invested in everyone, of course, but drawing conclusions from the behavior we see in people is flawed and unfair.

It's difficult for me to discern what it means to be awake, because my emotions complicate my capacity to make healthy decisions. I am often torn by my critical nature, because I feel like I put a barrier around myself to avoid getting hurt. This tendency doesn't help me cope with disappointment, and only functions to make the stakes higher when I am let down by someone. Zen has taught me to be less reliant on emotions as a guide for my reactions. Investing in emotions is dangerous because they drastically fluctuate. I used to have trouble walking away from arguments because I thought the emotion was an integral part of the problem. I never imagined how emotions detract from our ability to see, and have been more thoughtful of my state of mind before engaging in an argument since beginning meditation. I have often resorted to meditation in times of great frustration, and it has helped because I take my emotions out of the equation. I am most thoughtful in meditation because it is inaction, and setting time to think about issues without the pressure to act upon my thoughts allows me to make rational decisions.

Zen has helped me cope with interpersonal issues at my house. It's really hard to live so close to so many other people my age. Being so close-knit has severe downsides, and can lead to extreme emotional breakdowns and uncontrollable behavior. I was involved in a co-op relationship that caused a lot of turmoil for me. I was effected by the loss of him, and bombarded by the publicity of the event. He quickly moved on to other girls, and I was left to cope with the additional pain and betrayal from a fellow, female co-oper. I momentarily felt I had lost my mind, and found myself doing things that were uncharacteristic of me and I felt out of control of my situation. It was fortunate that I found Zen at this point in my life. I don't find myself entirely devoted to the idea of Zen, but meditation has been a useful tool for me to work though being so vulnerable and sad. When I am feeling out of my wits I have a resource to go to, but sometimes I forget how useful that tool is. I am somehow still attached to going with my emotions and have difficulty stopping in that moment to reflect in meditation. Meditation always helps, though, at least to put the issue in perspective. The problems still exist, but I do not feel at the will of my emotions. I cannot change him or the way that people act, but I can control myself. Feeling entitled to one part of my breakdown was really empowering and relieving.

The path I chose before Zen was to escape my problems and start over with new friends, in a new place, with a new companion. In my short college life I have disposed of three groups of friends and moved to avoid the problems that I have partially caused. I don't think Zen can help with relationships that are toxic, but I believe it is powerful for understanding our motivation and emotional barriers that in turn can help us understand the source of conflict and resolve contempt derived from the pain that we experience. Living in my co-op has forced me to deal with conflict head-on because I want to continue to be a part of this house. I have considered moving when things got hard, and my boyfriend had cheated on me with a fellow housemate. That incident happened shortly after I began this class, and meditation has relieved a lot of the suffering I felt because I had internalized the issue. Zen helped me see that it was not my fault, and made me resolve to work through the pain instead of dulling it. Enduring the pain was important for me, and helped me realize my own strength. Old members say that "If you can't live in the co-op you can live anywhere," but I believe a lot of people here cope through addiction and contempt. Both problems erode a person, but Zen supports maturity and helped me to become whole. After learning about Zen I decided I would not focus on what people had done to me, and released myself from their will. Who they are and what they do has little to do with me, just like many other unfortunate events, and it's real freedom to know that.

Previously, I did not look at my reaction to my troubles as a part of the issue, and I would try to focus on the outside circumstances that caused the problem. This logic is inherently flawed because I can only control my part in the problem. I sometimes catalog my history of hardships and bemoan the problems I have. By trying to escape our past, and avoid the pitfalls of life, we start ignoring reality. Although we believe we can alleviate suffering by avoiding life, we are actually "chain[ing ourselves] helplessly to uncertainty and fear" (Hagen 2). I liken the dullness of our perception to losing the sense of smell. I have an impaired sense of smell because of my allergies, but I am often thankful because of unpleasant odors. However, a complete loss of this sense would not only deprive me of the unpleasant and the wonderful smells, but also impair my ability to taste. Our inability to experience life outside of the good and bad does more than cripple our character, because it simultaneously inhibits our connection with our surroundings. We are missing out on more than we can perceive.

I think the notion of fleeting happiness is visible in the difficulty people have with recalling memories that are pleasant. Our deepest memories, the ones that shape our personalities and behavior, often make us cringe. The purpose of studying history, on a larger scale, is to learn to traverse the landscape of conflict and learn how to do it better. Yet even by studying history the ability to change an action and reform the pattern is still futile. Therefore, the reaction we have to the bad things in our past is to either forget them or try to change them. I struggle with regret from making foolish decisions, and wonder if I subconsciously made those choices to change my path. Zen meditation has enabled me to work through my choices from a perspective not riddled with emotions which make decisions harder. The mindset meditation puts me in is a useful tool for discerning where my emotions led me astray, and helps me eliminate the regret I felt toward my past. I think judging myself and feeling regret are two issues that Zen has enlightened me to. Bashing myself for poor choices is not productive, but I was taught that I should feel remorse for doing something wrong. Zen helped me see that it is more productive to try to see myself, and where I went wrong, instead of blaming myself for making a mistake.

There is still a tendency in American society to think that introspection is selfish. Psychologists are still considered an outlet for the weak willed. I believe dismissing our mind in favor of something potentially better is a disease ravaging our minds. At so many points in our lives, the inability to reconcile our ability to imagine with our ability to do, makes us discontent. I have seen it first-hand with the toddlers I babysit. The struggle to assert identity is so strong that it leads to tantrums and screaming when our will is denied. We grasp at identity to make transitioning easier, but that only makes the next step worse. Teenagers also suffer from a perceived loss of identity, but they haven't actually lost anything, because the person they thought they were was probably only the person that their parents taught them to be. I believe that each new phase of our lives only gets more complicated and soul crushing without the ability to see. When we over-correct our behavior to prevent bad things from repeating, we get even more lost. Although we believe that failing is the enemy, the attempts we blindly make to fix that failing is more profoundly detrimental because it causes us to stray farther from ourselves.

Sometimes we justify our behavior on the grounds that the ends justify the means of our actions. This justification seems utterly contrary to the principles of morality. Without the ability to see the result of our actions, how could we ever be certain the results could rectify our unsavory behavior? In fact, we can never know the morality of our desires, because they are rooted in our experience. Perhaps it is most dangerous to believe we are justified in our actions, and forget to question our intention. The morality of our choices is based on the intention we had in making them. It is obvious to any rhetoric major that changing our fundamental beliefs is near impossible, because these beliefs are so ingrained for a reason. By removing the confines of our experience we can access reality, but denying the influence of those experiences is also flawed. It is necessary to balance our impulse with thoughtfulness. We could get so caught up with what is right and what behavior is moral and good. The flaw in believing you know the path is the realization that we are all imperfect beings. For the same reason I rejected Christianity, I reject believing, and the notion that we can define some moral path. Studying rhetoric has taught me that the more certain someone seems saying that they are right, the more likely they are to be lying or ignorant. The people that are truly aware are more tentative to make claims without needing to reword their statements, or preface it with a qualifier (such as: I believe or it seems).

The Christian, American life is riddled with notions of belief. We are told to believe in ourselves and believe in God. This system takes so much power away from us as sentient beings, and rather than propelling us toward action, it traps us in uncertainty. Although I have never aligned myself with Christian beliefs, the idea of fate was still pervasive in my experience. I feel so out of control of my destiny. Sometimes it feels like bad things are happening to me, as if they are targeting me, which is utter nonsense if I consider the many difficulties the human experience presents. Then I start to believe that the way to reclaim control is by responding to the immediate problems. However, the issue is not some laundry list of trivial issues. Relieving any of the problems I can see will not get me any closer to happiness, on the contrary, I only become frustrated by the problems that replace the ones I have solved. Which relates to what Hagen said about choices. Our physiological needs become satisfied, and our desires begin to run rampant. "When Petty choices occupy the mind necessity is forgotten, and wanting and craving, picking and choosing take over" (Hagen 39), and we begin to lose touch with ourselves, because "we define what we want or don't want as something separate from us" (38)

Technology has ostracized us from each other, and from our own identity. All around the college campus there are people barely acknowledging a smile from a stranger because they are looking at their phone or listening to music. I had trouble meeting people in Austin before I moved into the co-op because people are wrapped up in their media. The beauty of the world around them is utterly unimportant and unnoticed because they want to create an identity that is more important than they are. Advancements in the longevity of our lives has only made it harder for us to experience reality and actually live. For a week I lost my I-pod, about a year ago. I saw the most incredible things, and noticed a lot of really funny things because I didn't have noise polluting my consciousness. The things our world has created is so beautiful, and the people around us so complex, how can we not be missing out on something when we shut it out. Sci-fi movies often warn of a complex, fabricated reality that exists because we chose to shut out the world for something better. Isn't that what we're doing already? Every addiction is the same, because it comes from a similar desire. We want to learn how to lessen the stress in our lives and cope with anxiety. Our habit for drinking, smoking, and eating too much becomes an addiction when it starts to make the stress in our lives much worse. I feel addicted to isolation, because it is what my nature tells me to do. Living with others, although soothing at times, is high stress for me. I chose to overcome my tendency to isolate myself by moving into a large house. It seems like the more uncomfortable I am about doing something, the more I grow from that experience.

I stopped watching television. Mindlessly tuning in to something I am hardly interested in to fill the silence started to seem utterly stupid after I moved into the co-op. Instead, when I am restless, I go outside and sit on the porch. Sometimes there are other people out there and sometimes I just appreciate the weather. People come and go, and we talk about a wide array of topics that sometimes get really personal or tense, but we are involved. Polite conversation is an unproductive discussion, because we are supposed to avoid topics that make others uncomfortable. When there isn't conflict, not only do we know less about the people we are interacting with, but we also forget to question ourselves. We deny this conflict in others, and in ourselves, because it is easier and less troubling than the alternative. The problem is that without conflict we can convince ourselves of anything and get lost in the lies. The chain of lies makes it harder to break, because we forget where the lie ends and the truth begins. Hitler's propaganda and subsequent regime illustrated that the most effective means to controlling people is to remove the dissenting opinion, and that is the way we can get caught up in a false reality. I think it is important to be critical of yourself, and to also have friends as a source of conflict. My sister and I are really close, and not because I call her to hear myself talk. I call my sister and go shopping for clothes with her because I know she will tell me her opinion honestly. It is surprisingly rare to find that quality in people, because social conventions have taught us that the middle road is the best one. We should reply with "Good" when someone asks "How are you?." The problem is that we are lying, and each lie is a detriment to seeing.

I became a vegetarian, because I thought it was important for people living comfortably to live sustainably. I come from a family that lives on meat and potatoes, so my idea of vegetarian cuisine was basically a combination of side dishes. I ate a lot of cheese pizza, macaroni and cheese, fruit snacks, and cereal. I did not really think it mattered what I ate, but had convictions about meat production. I was doing it all wrong, and I had simply traded one bad habit for another. My body was not a priority for me, and I took it for granted by mistreating it. When I moved into 21st Street Co-op the food was factored into my rent, and a plethora of fresh vegetables and fruit were available. There were other people living with me and cooking meals that ate vegetarian. I found a community and realized the importance of health, and the value of putting good things into my body.

Zen meditation has encouraged me to perpetuate that lesson and shown me the product of a well-maintained body. When I exercise and eat healthily my meditation is better and I am less prone to feel drowsy and lethargic. The effects of poor diet are subtle when we drown it out, but in complete silence I could not ignore the consequences.

I derive worth from external goal accomplishment, and fail to recognize a growth in my personality as proof of my self-worth. I feel that this issue arises from priorities in Western culture, and stands in the way of integrating Zen into my life. I sometimes compromise my integrity to accomplish my goals, and for a long time this was the issue with selecting a major. I thought it was important to have a prestigious major to show off to people from my hometown. However, I soon realized that striving for a goal I did not want was the reason I was unhappy and it was why I subconsciously sabotaged myself. I started doing things very uncharacteristic of myself—I would forget deadlines and slack on assignments to force myself into something else. It was really hard to get back on track, because I did not even know where to start to satisfy myself. I hadn't really thought about what I wanted, and I was wholly focused on pleasing my parents and getting that sense of accomplishment. I tried out several majors based solely on my hobbies: advertising, art, and English. Dabbling in my passions was so satisfying, and showed me the value of self-exploration. Taking a step back from the monotony of daily life and external influences made me free again. I am really glad I took the extra time and add a year to college so I could graduate with a major I believe in, and I think rhetoric hones my talents and is utterly satisfying and interesting to me.

I never found diamonds endearing because it's a generic trifle that has caused a lot of suffering. Reflecting on Zen made me realize that the motivation is the most important factor, and can legitimize our actions. Striving to become something else, because we are envious does not lead to a positive outcome. Measuring ourselves against another can only lead to dissatisfaction because we are not all equipped with the same tools, and we do not have the same drive. Wanting a diamond because it is a symbol of love and wealth is driven by the wrong reason. I can hardly think of a good reason to desire something so insignificant, but I definitely oppose the practice because it is what we are 'supposed to do.' It is sometimes hard to distinguish when our lives have become dictated and prescribed, because it happens so subtly. Our parents are the first influence we have, and it's hard to grow away from their example. The yearning we have is not something we were born with—it's a taught reaction. When we forget the source of our discontent we become slaves to its will.

I collected many stories about the house I live in for a project a had last year, and one of my favorite quotes was from a good friend of mine, Tiffyn. It was basically that "you can get really caught up in the flow of this place, and it all seems to happen so fast, but what you have to remember is that you can't change the way it works. This house is always changing, but no one person makes it happen. It will happen as it will, and you're just lucky enough to be a part of it." This piece of advice set my mind at ease, I stopped worrying about making this place better, because I could not possibly know what is best for the people here. I think my mind would be a lot more at ease if I could apply my perspective on my house to my life. Letting go of the control I thought I had feels really relieving because I never had the power anyway. Struggling to attain something out of my control compounded my problems and made the issues seem hopeless. The most important lesson I learned from Zen was that I should work on the areas I can, and try to recognize the places I am powerless.

Lindsay Pollock is a fifth-year student majoring in Rhetoric, and is an active officer at the 21st Street Cooperative House in Austin. She is interested in using her writing as a tool for positive change and for empowering the disadvantaged. She is also a second degree black belt in Tang Soo Do and an avid vegetarian.

Zen and Change
Zachary Schroeder

In preparing my chapter for this book I have decided to keep two different writing assignments, in more or less original form. The first of these was written less than two weeks into the study of Zen, and the second after a month of study. I feel this is the most accurate way to show snapshots of my mind at different states along its journey to understand Zen. Following these first two sections is an interpretation of the changes that have occurred. Because the class this was written for is under the Rhetoric department, this analysis is focused on how language use changed during meditation sessions and afterward. I encourage the reader to attempt to note any shifts in language use between the sections, and interpret them as a sign of the powerful effect of meditation and the study of Zen on language.

Less than two weeks into study

Like many young Americans, my first introduction to Zen was through my popular culture's representation and stereotypes of monks sitting still for hours in smoky, incense filled rooms, possibly doing Kung-fu battle after-wards, and then enjoying some fine green tea while composing nonsensical haikus; all of this occurring on some craggy mountaintop with wispy clouds gracing the rooftops. Soon after deciding to study *real* Zen, I found it was of course nothing of the sort (except maybe for the craggy mountaintops).

Before university study, a brief foray into Zen was brought about by reading Robert Pirsig's Zen and the Art of Motorcycle Maintenance during high school. Though to be fair, the author does preface the book by saying it really is not that much about Zen or motorcycle maintenance. That statement itself however is derived from the general inquiry of the book: Quality. Since reading, and re-reading the book, I have developed the same sort of intellectual affinity for a greater understanding of Quality as the author. This initial experience in attempting to broaden my apperception of such an obtuse and abstract concept, and to try to tie it into an equally abstract process as Zen, ultimately ended in becoming stuck against a wall and quitting (or so I thought) further inquiry in the subject. It did however cause me to decide to pursue rhetoric as a major in hopes of becoming more like the author/main character of the novel.

This decision ultimately led me back to Zen in a way that seems, as life often does, uncannily synchronistic. I was searching for upper-division classes for the first time, I found a course title: Non-Argumentative Rhetoric in Zen. There was no second thought, and I decided to plan the rest of my schedule around the course. Now, less than two full weeks into the course, my understanding of Zen is mostly in the practice of meditation. Though I had attempted meditation a few times in my life prior to the course, I never did so seriously, or with any sense that I was doing it "the *right* way." I have since determined that confidence is a key factor in getting results from a meditation session. If one begins a session thinking they will not get anything out of meditating, they are unfortunately likely to be right.

Fewer than two weeks in, I have begun to detect patterns and feel assured of speaking confidently on what I have found. First, the Zen meditation state is centrally connected with peace. That is to say, "inner-peace" appears to be the primary pursuit. On the surface this is seen simply physically. When doing meditation one is to become peaceful in movement; to be as still as possible. This peace of the body quickly, for me, translates into unconsciously deeper breathing, accompanied with an overall sensation of relaxation, with periodic releases of different muscle groups' tension as the session goes on. For some, the keeping still of the body is evidently more difficult, as I have observed in hearing the movements of classmates during group meditations. Fortunately, being a life-long computer freak is paying some dividends here, as long hours sitting still at a desk is apparently good training for controlling the body into stillness.

Continuing on the theme of peace, mentally, the effects of meditation have been very halcyon. I recognized the mental state of Zen as being purposefully open, observant, and non-judgmental. This mental space is then, for me, a perfect time to ask the *Big Questions* that are often passed off as unimportant in our modern, hectic lives. For me, the questions I find my mind continually returning to during a meditation session have been "What am *I?*", "Where does Quality reside? In the object? In the beholder? At the intersections of both?", and "What is my role in this universe?" At this point answers to these have not been forthcoming, but the peace of the Zen meditation state draws me back to them again, instilling a hopefulness that with prolonged effort, the answers will arrive.

Beyond the *Big Questions* inquiry, my initial meditations have been chiefly self-interested so far. To a point nearly of being categorically selfish, if this were any activity other than meditation. Regardless, what happens after settling into the meditation state for roughly five minutes is an increasing washing-out of vision, with a muted appreciation of color, details, etc. This appears to be the setting for the mental visualization stage, but I still remain ignorant of the phenomenon besides knowing it occurs repeatedly and that I have noticed it before in states of hyper-focus outside of meditation. Once this dimming has leveled off, I have often met a sub-personality of myself, generally appearing like as a small child's face. It is then possible to converse with this bit of myself, an experience that is increasingly giving myself a much greater appreciation for the complexity which I was previously unaware I had. This state is characterized by a much longer attention span for holding a single thought pattern, instead of distracting thoughts continually interrupting a mental conversation as they will.

Many classmates have been particularly interested in this phenomenon in particular. For those readers currently engaged in my suggestion of noting differences between language use, please consider this paragraph and the following one to be part of the writing done near the end of the course, rather than the beginning in which it is situated. My most vivid and lasting memory of such a dialogue, and one that precipitated change within my life, was a conversation I had with a sub-personality that usually manifested itself as the phrase, "I don't have the strength for *that*." It is important to note here that the easiest way I found to engage in a conversation of this nature is to be very aware of the voice of internal dialogue, to see if perhaps the voice sounds child-like or otherwise divergent from whatever is a "normal" voice for internal dialogue.

Once I recognized the diminutive tone of this phrase, with a bit of imagination I visualized a much younger version of myself as if it appeared to be sitting in front of me. Taking the approach of talking to a child, I first made it clear that I was interested in what it had to say, and that it was free to say anything it willed. I then posited the question of why it thought it did not have enough strength. The visualized early-self responded that it never had enough strength to run as far or as fast as Dad did. With some background knowledge of my father's decade spanning devotion to running at least once every day and his avid competition in marathons and other races, we have the reason for this hang-up. Hearing the words form immediately caused me to connect this early childhood misconception of physical strength as being fixed, to a long standing aversion to exercise. Once these connections were clear I took the initiative to begin un-training this misconception by having a dis-repaired bike fixed and committing myself to cycling weekly.

Returning now to the original writing as it appeared just weeks into the course: I have also noticed, that in meditation there is a greater capacity for mental focus and clarity that does not end once the meditation has ended. Instead the time after a meditation session is defined by a greater sense of well-being. This is truly a hard to describe sensation, but everything just seems to work better and go along smoother after a meditation session, for some hours afterward. Essentially, life no longer feels quite so burdensome or impossible to comprehend, a renewing of mental confidence and a restored gumption seems to take place.

Perhaps this serves as a positive note to wrap up my first encounter of Zen and meditation. Though I would still describe myself as mostly ignorant of Zen, it would appear to me that Zen is simply trying to be as observant as possible. Surely, the various sub-personalities I have been meeting existed before *I* noticed them, it was that I was simply not paying enough attention before, or considered the act of meeting them to be unimportant. Instead, what Zen is beginning to teach me is that nothing is as unimportant as it may first appear. Simply by paying more attention to whatever it is we are neglecting by keeping ourselves so busy, we stand to gain practical, useful, and fulfilling knowledge; learning how to create a *better* life with that knowledge. As distilled as possible, Zen's first lesson for me was that, I do not really know what I want or need, yet it does not have to remain that way.

One month into study

There has been much reading and meditation now a month into directed study of the subject of Zen Buddhism. Though practice has been enjoyable, no longer is it necessarily filled with the same invigorating enthusiasm as I came bounding into the study with. Zen has become not the complex, mysterious entity that I originally saw it to be. Instead, my study and time with Zen has made me realize the pervasive simplicity of what I have studied so far. The entirety of what is to be learned from Zen is mindfulness. To sit and think until that which-is-to-be-known, is known. This is hardly a condemnation or critique, rather praise for the ease that anyone should be able to approach Zen and understand why anyone writes about it. In the spirit of this simplicity, I have distilled what my focus has been in Zen this past month into three discrete categories of metacognition, meditation, and change for the sake of this particular section of the chapter. Each of these categories of course rests against the other, in the spirit of the interconnectedness Zen teaches us, but I will try to shortly examine each for the expansion of understanding and clarity.

Firstly my Zen study has been, what might be termed as, "self-focused." This beginning month represents my first successful endeavors in metacognition, initiating self-checks on the mind throughout the day, and especially during meditation sessions. Metacognition, as I use it here, means making statements about how I was thinking based on observing the thinking. Mainly this was done through a series of self-checks to make sure the thoughts I was having were not, even indirectly, going to cause unnecessary suffering for myself or others. The easiest example is recognizing that bad moods are often extended by thinking a series of negative thoughts in a cyclic loop. Once one is aware that thinking a certain phrase like "I am not smart enough to do that" sets off a cascade of other negative thoughts, it becomes naturally simple to self-correct. A replacement phrase is often in order. For this example, something inspiring like "Doing that will be difficult, but will make me smarter." is a more accurate representation of the facts at hand.

Early into the month, another example of metacognition was a repeated question posed to myself as, *What are my filters?* This was spurred by an in-class group meditation, after which another student began having a dialogue with the teacher on the subject of mental filters. In the teacher's explanation of how filtered the content of our stimulus are, how qualities are often immediately assigned based on preexisting suppositions, prejudices, family values, culture, and so on, I realized that this aspect of my nature really had not been examined. To this point I can say the most striking of the filters I discovered within myself was how condescending my behavior often was due to the filter of "intelligence" or in popular parlance, book-smarts. I am reminded of the Emo Phillips quote, "I used to think that the brain was the most wonderful organ in my body. Then I realized who was telling me this." My realization was one of how much relative value I was placing in my mental capacity, and even then, my mental capacity in the limited number of academic situations it had been used in. After meditating on this filter, I realized there is a remedy, I had to acknowledge an excess of pride beyond what I had accomplished. You might call that humility, but it was apparent very early on that I could not properly understand the first of the two concepts of the eightfold path, Right View and Right Intention, without initiating a change in cognition.

Initiating a change in cognition is not a task I was accustomed to before encountering Zen Buddhism. Once meditation began to be practiced, I did not have to search long for the answer to how and where one goes about changing thought patterns. First, it is imperative to see the thought patterns as they occur, in order to understand the thing which is to be changed, and the best place that I have encountered for internal observation has been my meditations. Here however, I have begun to have resistance. It seems the mind might be a trifle reluctant to change; returning to the Philips quote, I found my own mind thought it was already best how it existed. In meditation it would fire up questions, often very childishly, of *why do you want to change me, who got you this far already, do you even know what you are doing?* All of which were very reasonable, logical questions in one sense, but all also counter-productive to attempting positive change within myself. The shift was not abrupt in convincing the mind to drop its reluctance to change, and I can hardly say it is complete, or that the goal could even entirely ever be completed, but the point is, without meditation I would have been entirely unaware of my own mental filter of a stubbornness to change.

A secondary filter discovered in meditation brings me now to the larger, final, theme of the whole first month, *change*. During meditation I discovered how terribly sleepy I was, at nearly all times in the day. In class I was falling asleep by the end of nearly every meditation session, which led to the rather humorous focus of my meditations as simply repeating to myself "wake-up, wake-up, wake-up..." Once having grown tired of fighting to simply stay awake, and thus missing time to engage in meta-cognition, I began to search for the causes of my tired demeanor. The answer came in an entirely separate meditation on why I found it so hard to synchronize my schedule in order to hang out with new friends. I had forgotten how jam-packed my schedule was, now having had the same schedule, for 3 years of college: Two part-time jobs, an out of city commute, and a, thankfully, very involved family. I realized that at least two of the things were going to be, within the timeframe of this semester, largely unchangeable: my commute is tied to avoiding high rent in the city, and my family's involvement is actually a positive relationship that many are not so fortunate to have. I realized that the part-time jobs were a source of avoidable suffering. Studying could almost never be done during a weeknight as immediately after class I went to work until midnight at one of the jobs, ensuring that I would arrive home too tired to be in a state conductive to learning. Then I spend the entire weekend, the time when my peers were mostly resting and socializing, at the other job. So, by the start of the week I was already exhausted and had to fit the necessary assignments early in the mornings after waking up to a dreadful alarm. Once all of this was properly pieced together during meditation I initiated the steps toward eliminating one of the two jobs and getting the first college loan, which I had previously refused out of prideful individualism. Thus ensuring more time for sleep and schoolwork, and a more wakeful meditation, as was the original intent.

In summation of the first month, it had a leitmotif of difficulty. This is difficulty without any attachment to the assumption that difficulty is inherently bad, merely that my first month's meditations were spent finding points of difficulty in my own life. Where before I thought my mind to be a shining achievement of brilliance, whose radiance eclipsed any problem it was faced with (these are of course purposefully grandiose words to illustrate the hubris), I realized the hindrance of pride. In this same thought-line, I recognized the hindrance of any sort of mental filter, and the importance of awareness that can easily is achieved in meditation, of these filters as a source of difficulty in our lives. Finally, there is also the difficulty of simply living life in the same way from year to year, merely because you were able to live one way successfully one year, and how change to this life can be a way of ending a source of difficulty.

Two months into study

Having described now the effects and course of my first weeks getting accustomed to Zen, it is worth examining the relevancy to my studies as a rhetorician. It has been my observation that the changes that have occurred are attributed to language adjustment. The faculties already described as metacognition and strategy readjustment are simply rewordings of this core skill easily realized during meditation. A prime example of this occurred almost immediately upon beginning the meditation sessions: I began to notice reluctance to an apparent overuse of I-constructions, something I viewed as selfish. Though I did not have clear reasons initially for why this was an unnecessary addition to my internal dialogue, I made the decision to spend conscious effort in finding alternative constructions, when possible in the expanded mental room of meditation.

After experimenting in their replacement, I have come to some conclusions on why it is more accurate and mindful to make a simple change, such as saying "I am feeling hungry" or "I do not like this painting" to "There is hunger" and "This painting brings displeasure." First, when talking to one's self internally, there ought to be conscious knowledge of the fact that you are serving as both speaker and listener. When one is not conscious of the rhetorical situation of internal dialogue, then there is a barrier of abstraction and dissociation with one's thoughts, two conditions that I have found negative to Right Mindfulness. So by constantly inserting "I" into your internal phrases, you are actually abstracting yourself away from what you are experiencing; you have added an unnecessary pronoun when, if you were being mindful, you ought to know that you can only be speaking of "I's" when reacting internally to an experience. Using "I" when you talk to yourself is akin to thinking of a map as the territory it describes, keeping you from experiencing the full dimension of what is occurring.

Further language analysis also focused on the recognition of absolutist language. This is the recognition that I was a frequent user of phrases like "That *is* impossible," "He *always* acts like that" and other phrases that denied the constantly changing, relativistic world we live in. These phrases I found more resilient to change, and I suspect they are memetic in origin, likely culturally learned. The strategy I approached absolutist language with, was firstly to recognize when it appeared. This was often difficult due to how flippantly it appears in a thought-stream, especially when one considers the gravity such phrases carry. Having identified an instance of their use, I would take into account the situation, person, or emotion they were attached to, and decide if it was validated in use. In instances where it was not valid, alternative constructions that reflect the actual "shades of gray" reality were invented. Though no statistical survey was taken of how often they occurred, it would seem this strategy decreased their overall usage. The apparent cognitive benefit of this, is a much more approachable mindset towards problems, as the gumption-trapping drag word "impossible" ceases to be the first thing to come to mind when faced with a challenge.

In decreasing all types of undesirable or inaccurate language I quickly learned *not* to make any correction in a punishing or hostile manner. Early on in the course, it was easy and common to become frustrated at flaws and respond in a knee-jerk reaction. However, just as people do not like other people to treat them in a hostile manner, my mind did not respond positively if the tone of correction was harsh or condemning. In working on phrase/language readjustment the best path is a slow one. This slow path is free from criticizing yourself, but instead seeks to convince yourself in a logical manner that one usage is improper and that another is more accurate. This is a lesson that can extend beyond working on one's self, and is an effective way of avoiding disagreements with other people. Too often when convincing one another of various beliefs and facts we can rush to criticize and in so doing, do not develop in the mind of the other person, the necessary logical underpinnings necessary for understanding or even the willingness to care. While sudden realizations, light-bulb over the head moments, are highly stimulating, they are nearly impossible to induce by will. Understanding more often comes by degrees, and this natural path seems the easiest to emulate when attempting to teach one's self.

Using the same process of teaching myself, another large scale language readjustment took place with regard to the emotional processing portion of mind. The changes here were due to cross-discipline study in the psychology department, and the reading of *Buddha's Brain*, a scientific explanation of mind and the relation and benefit of Buddhist study on mind. When learning about the various neurotransmitters, specifically those used in the parasympathetic and sympathetic duality of the nervous system, I was presented with a more accurate way of wording experiences of emotion.

Whereas before I might describe talking before a large audience as making me nervous, in actuality this word "nervous" is characteristic of the complex activation of the sympathetic nervous system. The feelings I was associating with nervousness, when described in this scientific manner, are not as easy to become attached to as the culturally learned labeling system for emotional words. The "racing of the brain" when first standing before the large audience, is simply the first stage of the sympathetic system activating, characterized by a large release of the acetylcholine, a neurotransmitter that causes various types of cells to become energized. Following this, the adrenal glands are activated leading to the release of the transmitter epinephrine/adrenaline. This is the portion of the experience of nervousness that is subjectively most scary when not understood. Adrenaline activates the flight-or-fight center of the brain, and suddenly, though I may be standing in a well-lit room filled only with harmless intellectuals, my brain is in the same mode as if I were walking through the jungle and came upon a tiger. This flight-or-fight response is easy to recognize for the sweating of the hands, increased heart-rate, reddening of the face, tightening of the stomach, and shaking.

With a firm grasp on the *what* and *why* of a nervous experience, we invariably move to a remedy, as we can now see quite clearly in a scientific understanding, that the body's response does not fit the situation. We return now, back to the second half of the duality described earlier within the body between the parasympathetic and sympathetic systems. The relation of these systems is like a see-saw, and as one system becomes more active, the other system is deactivated. Knowing this, we can induce the body into activating the parasympathetic system to counter a nervous state. Here we return to the skills learned from Zen practice, in fact what most teach as the first skill for meditation, awareness of the breathing. It turns out, that with each breath in the sympathetic nervous system is activated to a slight degree, and with each breath out the parasympathetic is activated. Simply by elongating each breath out, and paying extra attention to the exhalation, we erode the sympathetic system's control over the body breath by breath.

Returning to understanding emotional responses under our term of language readjustment we are again confronted with a slow path. Attempting to not be overwhelmed by the sympathetic system is another process best learned by degrees. The most important skill is simply to be able to take a step back from the fright of the situation, and just be able to observe the reactions happening within the body. This alone will often mitigate the intensity of the flight-or-fight response in my findings. Using the terminology above, attempt to feel and describe all the changes occurring in the body. Once you have done this a few times, if you are anything like me, you will have far more freedom of thought and action in situations that induce the sympathetic system to activate, than you had before using the terminology society provides for emotions. At this point, being able to describe each step of the activation process as it occurred, I noticed the overall duration of the experience to diminish. If necessary or wanted one can begin the breathing exercise described earlier to hasten the return to the more comfortable control of the body by the parasympathetic system.

In many ways, this extended example of managing just one small agent of control for the body is the larger lesson I have taken from Zen as whole. The idea of the slow path, characterized by seeking to understand as much as possible before acting, is an effective strategy for dealing with the reality of our experience. This is why meditation is so key to Zen's teaching. In my understanding at least, meditation is a break from doing, and a time for understanding. Whether this is understanding different sub-personalities as I have described in the first section, or understanding reasons for suffering as covered in the second section, or understanding the effect of the language we use to talk to ourselves as I have covered here, the key point is that we are benefited by sitting down and thinking about a subject. It would seem that with a greater understanding comes a greater freedom, the longer we sit, the more freedom of choices appear before us.

In my case, I have woven these choices to be free day by day through the adjustment of my language. Perhaps this reflects the bias of my course of study, but the second large lesson I have taken from studying Zen has been the importance of the words we choose to use. We all are mostly aware of the powers of manipulation on ourselves by the outside agents of advertising, public relations, and politicians, yet it would appear to me that many, including myself, are lacking in understanding the manipulation our own words have on ourselves. If you speak internally as much as I do, then you are likely your own biggest source of media, and thus can cause large scale change through the small scale manipulation of your own language. Awareness of how not to cause frustration or argumentation within yourself and to have inner-peace can be achieved through the conscious effort of mindfulness.

My Path To Understanding and Accepting Zen
Tommy Tran

Introduction

What is Zen? Currently when I think of Zen, I associate it with little, bald, Asian men who wear orange robes. Obviously there is so much about Zen that I do not understand. Where do I even start? You have the Dalai Lama and Buddha; practiced in Tibet, India, Japan, China, Vietnam, and now Western countries. How are all these things connected? Are Buddhists the only ones who practice and study Zen? Do you have to be Buddhist to prescribe to and believe in the Zen teachings? Why do people practice Zen? How did it serve to enrich their lives?

Before we begin diving into my studies and emerging understanding of Zen Buddhism let me give you a brief background about myself to help you better understand my motivations into learning about Zen. My mother is Catholic and my father was raised Buddhist, although I do not think his family practiced regularly. Before my parents were married my father converted to Catholicism. My sisters and I were born and raised here in the United States, surrounded by my mother's side of the family who were all strict Catholics. My father had fought with the US in the South Vietnamese Air Force. During the evacuation of the South Vietnamese military in 1975, he completely lost contact with his family from 1975-2001. With that separation we lost the Buddhist influence of my father's side of the family. This class gave me the opportunity to better understand another aspect of my background and culture.

In 2002, on our first trip to Vietnam to reunite my father with his family I had the opportunity to visit Thien Mu Pagoda, where Thích Quảng Đức was based. Many do not recall the name but he is the Buddhist monk from the infamous photograph taken during the Vietnam War setting himself on fire in a busy Saigon intersection. I did not understand why he did this back then and still do not understand it to this day. For someone whose religion and philosophy is based on tranquility and understanding, to take such drastic action seems so out of place. It is really a mark of how extreme the situation was, that he believed this dramatic gesture was the only way to bring international attention to the plight of the people there. The self-immolation act was effective in drawing in the much-needed attention to the matter.

Upon further research, I found that the practice of self-immolation is tolerated by the Mahayana Buddhism as a form of protest. I must point out however that the act of harming oneself is prohibited in Buddhist teachings. This practice of self-immolation as a ritualistic act copied that of the Medicine King from the twenty-third chapter from the Lotus Sutra. In the Sutra, the Medicine King demonstrates his insight into the self-less nature of his body by ritualistically setting his body aflame, spreading the "light of the Dharma" for twelve hundred years. What am I getting myself into?

Beginning

It is the start of a new semester and I have don't have any big expectations for this class other than to walk away with a little bit of new knowledge. I am hoping to learn a new style of writing, understand rhetoric a little bit more, and learn a little bit about Zen itself.

What is Zen? Zen as defined by the Webster Dictionary is, "a Japanese sect of Mahayana Buddhism that aims at enlightenment by direct intuition through meditation." What does this mean? This definition does not really offer me anything besides the word "enlightenment." I do not think that a definition even begins to explain Zen. I think that the vastness that this word encompasses is too great to be written in a definition, but oddly enough though, in the book *Buddhism Plain and Simple*, Hagen sums it up perfectly in one word, awareness.

For us as students to understand Zen Buddhism, the course curriculum is laid out with various texts like: *Buddhism Plain and Simple* by Steve Hagen, *Zen Mind, Beginner's Mind* by Shunryu Suzuki, *Everyday Zen* by Charlotte Joko Beck, *Buddha's Brain* by Rick Hanson, Ph.D., and *Philosophical Meditations on Zen Buddhism* by Dale S. Wright. Along with the readings we are practicing meditation followed immediately by free writing, making observations of our learning in a learning record, weekly unquiz questions where we were able to ask our peers anything, and holding periodic group inquiry sessions with our professor, Margaret Syverson Ph. D., who also happens to be a Zen teacher. I was intrigued as to how all of this would work out and somewhat skeptical as to the result of it all.

Zen is a form of Buddhism with a focus on meditation. It is dedicated to spiritual awakening in search of truth. Meditation is meant to guide your thoughts to the here and now so that you can observe and acknowledge your thoughts and not be lost in them. This all made sense, but there was one problem... How does a person go about achieving this?

I am having a hard time wrapping my head around what is supposed to happen during meditation. I'm not really sure what this practice is about or meant to produce. What is its purpose? Where does the meditation lead you? How do you enter this state of mind, this awareness? I know that meditation is a part of Zen, but to what extent? People use meditation to enter a tranquil state to "look" at situations with a clear heart and mind. I wanted to achieve this. This level of being present and observing was so foreign to me. I rarely make the time to actually sit, observe, and reflect on much. I am always on the go or asleep.

In one of my free writing sessions following our class meditation at the beginning of the semester I reflected on my lack of knowledge with practicing meditation:

9/13/10: I really didn't have any thoughts again. I'm not sure if I'm zoning out or actually meditating at this point. I typically become tired when I zone out, but the sensation that I felt during our meditation is different. I don't really have any thoughts or any urges for movement. My limbs, head, and eyelids become heavy from my muscles relaxing. The muscles seem to let go of any tension holding the limbs in a particular position.

A month later I had progressed to understand that during meditation you are not supposed to suppress your thoughts rather sit and observe them. Here is one of my observations:

10/20/10: Today during meditation was the first time during a busy time that my mind didn't constantly spit out to-do lists. I noticed during one of my other meditations that when I was stressed about deadlines and burdened with other things to get done my mind would run rampant and want to create lists and prioritize the deadlines. I realized this and started to keep a daily to-do list and marked things off as I completed them. I only put on the list what I could feasibly accomplish in one day. By doing this I am able to put my mind more at ease to concentrate on the actual tasks that I need to accomplish. The worrying was extra stress that drained my body of energy keeping me from focusing. I realize that through observation it allows you to see a solution.

I still did not fully understand what meditation was but the progress had already begun to show meditation's effects and usefulness to me.

I continued to strive to understand what was to take place during meditation. I found the Suzuki's book helpful in my search to understand. To achieve enlightenment during zazen (meditation), Suzuki speaks of big mind and small mind. He states that the big mind experiences everything within itself. This resonated with me because often I see how I look at situations within the small confinement of the act but do not look at everything that encompasses the entire situation. I look at the situation as it pertains to me; this is what Suzuki refers to as the small mind. When I make decisions based on a small mind, I forget that their actions also affect others.

During the inquiry sessions we drove the discussion and

were able to ask Dr. Syverson anything that came to our mind. I began to realize that this class is very different from any other that I had taken. We had a variety of questions ranging from roommates, friends and family, to our own personal difficulties. It was interesting to me to hear all of these questions answered through Zen teachings.

I can already begin to see the things that Zen has to offer me, to better me as a person.

Middle

Do I have to be Buddhist to practice Zen? In the beginning, I thought you had to be Buddhist to practice Zen. That was my barrier to overcome before being able to grasp Zen fully. I am Catholic and Catholicism teaches that there is only one God and not to worship any other. I don't want to misrepresent myself as a highly religious Catholic. It is however the basis of my faith and moral structure. My father had converted to Catholicism from Buddhism. Why would I want to change? Needless to say, I had my doubts about practicing Zen, believing that it is a religion. I did not think there was room in my life for another religion.

Upon my professor's recommendation to look further into Zen and Catholicism I found that there are a handful of Catholic priests and monks who are also Zen masters and senseis. In a 2004 article, printed by the National Catholic Reporter, they announced that a Catholic monk named Kevin Hunt had been installed as a Zen Sensei, making him the first North American Catholic Monk to have achieved this. Hunt was quoted saying, "By coming to focus on the present moment through the practice of the techniques of Zen meditation, the Christian can become aware of God's immediate loving presence. This awareness is especially needed in the modern world, where the realities of divine grace are too often pushed to the margins of people's consciousness."

Although I was beginning to understand what Zen is and liked what I was learning, I wanted to see if there were others who were conflicted about practicing Zen, others like myself.

After some research, I came across a transcription of a talk that Yamada Roshi had given May 9, 1975. Yamada was instrumental in bringing Christians to the practice of Zen. In the transcription he stated, "I am often asked by Christians, especially Catholics, whether they can practice Zazen, and still preserve the beliefs of Christianity. To that question, I usually answer that Zen is not a religion, in the same sense that Christianity is a religion." He went on to explain that Zazen is what is at the core of all Buddhist sects. The core is the experience called satori or self-realization. The self-realization is an experienced fact; it did not matter whether you are Buddhist or Christian, we all experienced fact the same way. The barrier that I had about practicing Zen was beginning to crumble.

The combination of Christianity and Zen co-existing in my life was more probable now. Reading others' experiences and reasons for practicing Zen made more sense. I feel that a person's life is a culmination of bits and pieces of their experiences and life lessons.

After reading Buddhism Plain & Simple by Steve Hagen, I began to understand that Buddhism is more of a state of mind than a religion. In this book I was introduced to the Eightfold Path: Right View, Right Intention, Right Speech, Right Action, Right Livelihood, Right Effort, Right Mindfulness, and Right Concentration. I understood this path to lead you to enlightenment. I thought that enlightenment was like this light bulb that would go off once you understood Zen and that it would always be "on." That turned out to not be the case. Enlightenment, from what I now understand it is like the first time you tied your shoes by yourself; you figure it out, you see the truth, and you move on. Hagen sums up enlightenment in one word that I was able to fully understand it, awareness. How simple! To me it meant to be fully engaged in life and not live in a fog. It allows me to think clearly by de-cluttering my thoughts. It seems as though I am often wrapped up in the little things and miss the big picture. These little things over complicate a simple situation, or cause me to make rash decisions. I liked what I was reading and it seemed that the layers of Zen Buddhism were slowly beginning to unravel for me.

Based on my up bringing as a Catholic, I see Zen more like a philosophy or lifestyle, a sense of being, or a state of mind rather than a religion. Zen seems to lack some of the basis of a religion in a traditional sense; a god or central figure and answers to the human origin. I am open to the notion of Zen but not as a replacement for the basis of my religion. It is interesting to observe other religions and cultures as to better understand them and myself.

This combination of Zen philosophy and Catholicism began to make sense to me. As a Catholic, I am asked to believe in and subscribe to many things I have never seen out of pure belief and faith. To some degree, I do not have a problem with this, but some of this faith requires reinforcement. I believe that seeing the truth helps me understand better. It provides a sense of clarity.

My opinion of Zen is that the teachings try to achieve a state of mind and that it has more to offer than the teachings of Buddhism as a religion. Religion I feel serves as a model with rules and guidelines for me to mold my life to. It also serves to answer questions about the unknown. Questions like, "'Where did I come from?' 'What happens when I die?' and 'Where will I go when I die?'" Zen seems to deal with life in the present and leaves behind the unknown superfluous questions, tackling the present issues head on. I feel that with this state of mind, being awake, could only help enhance my life. It did not ask me to believe in anything, rather it worked to help me understand the world around me better.

Reflection

In Zen there is nothing to believe and everything to discover.

It is the end of the semester and looking back through my observations, free writing, unquiz questions, and notes for this class, Non-argumentative Rhetoric in Zen, has provided a time line of my progress in learning about Zen. I noticed that I spent a lot of time researching about Catholicism and Zen. Why was I doing all of this research?

Reflecting back on why I had done that, I began my research out of a sense of curiosity, but most of what I found were stories of people leaving the Christian faith for Zen Buddhism. I did not want Zen to topple over my Catholic faith; so, I began to build a wall. Eventually I found two articles that began to turn my fear into acceptance of Zen. The first article was about a Catholic priest who had found Zen to enhance his Catholic faith. The second article was a transcription of a talk Yamada Roshi had given, in this talk he addressed the issue of Christians practicing Zen. He stated that Zen is not a religion and that both Christianity and Zen strove to help individuals to become a normal person, a real person, and as far as possible, a perfect human being. Perfect! That was exactly what I was searching for. Finally, I could move past this barrier and determined that I was not going to let other people's experiences define mine. I tore down my wall and began to incorporate Zen teachings into my life. I realized there was too much good that comes from learning about Zen. Looking back I was scared that this new "thing" was going to change who I was. I realize that this fear was unwarranted. Zen was there for me to incorporate it into my life how I saw fit.

The language or rhetoric of Zen, beyond the spoken and written text, from what I understand provokes thought and question rather than provide an argument or a point of view. Questions never seem to be fully answered, but replaced by a more provoking question. This type of teaching in my opinion engages the mind and helps develop the intellect through inquiry. These inquiries broaden the mind like a tree. The tree grows, rooted by a system underneath the surface (my existing knowledge), but on the surface is one trunk (my question) with a sprawling network of branches (questions derived from the original inquiry). Soon inside my mind I have a forest of trees with deep roots into my core values, morals, and knowledge. All of this knowledge helps me think clearly and make sound judgment.

At this point my understanding of Zen Buddhism, besides enlightenment, is that it is concerned with truth. By learning to

observe myself with all that surrounds me, I began to understand not only situations but also how I reacted in them; this
was crucial. This recognition gave me insight into my rash decisions based purely on emotion. Instead of acting on emotion, I
observed how these situations made me feel and why I allowed
it to affect me in this way. By recognizing this I realized I could
begin to condition myself to not act irrationally on impulse,
but rather keep my cool to evaluate everything in its entirety
to make the best decision at that moment. With a clear mind
I could remove bias. Biases I believe are what Hagen refers to
as "leaning." When we lean, we take sides, losing some truth
along with it. The eightfold path assists me in achieving that
pure thought.

Faced with dilemmas daily I find myself asking, "'Is this
right or wrong?', 'How would I know if it is right?', 'Is this good
or bad?'" From the teachings of Zen, I realize my life is not
about right or wrong, good or bad, it is about being active in
the moment, taking in all of my surroundings and making the
best clear judgment at that moment. Suzuki addresses this
dilemma as duality. How can something be good, but bad at
the same time? Something that may be good for me could hurt
or damage something else outside of "you." He best describes
duality as a coin, it has two sides but it is one. I should not view
the coin as being heads or tails, but to see it as it is, a coin, that
is all that it is.

When I signed up to take this class, Non-argumentative
Rhetoric in Zen, I thought that I was going to get another
perspective or style of rhetoric. I could not have been further
from the truth. I have always tried to keep an open mind to new
experiences to better understand the world. The study of Zen
has begun to change how I view and approach my daily life for
the better. I have a better sense of why things happen and how
things end up the way that they do. I observe things beyond
what is in my little world. By changing my approach to situations, Zen has been able to make me a better person, a happier
person.

Being raised by my parents who are first generation immigrants, everything was new to my family here in the US: language, food, culture, morals, etc. My parents had always raised us to embrace other cultures including ours. Living here in the U.S. they began to understand the American way and culture, but worked to teach us our Vietnamese roots. Sometimes it was a challenge to get my parents to understand why my sisters and I wanted to do something. We found it difficult to understand why they would not allow us to spend the night with friends; it simply was not part of their Vietnamese culture, kids there never had sleepovers. As the years went by the rules did become more relaxed as my parents grew to understand the American culture. We always tried to understand where they were coming from when they said no, and why they did not want us to do certain things, although we did not always agree. My family constantly had to be open to new ideas. I think this openness gave me the framework to grasp the teachings of Zen a little easier.

This last year my older sister had a little girl, my parent's first grandchild. I am lucky and glad to be living so close to my older sister. Being that close in proximity it gave me the opportunity to spend countless hours playing with my niece and help my sister and brother in law out whenever my schedule allowed me. My niece is now thirteen months old. The other day my sister and I reflected back on what my niece had accomplished in one year: she learned to sleep through the night, how to eat, facial expressions, muscle control, how to crawl, walk, how to talk, who mom and dad are, etc. She put my year of college education to shame. I was able to see first-hand what Suzuki meant by "beginner's mind." My niece certainly had a beginner's mind, a blank slate without any biases, ready to absorb anything and everything around her. She learned by observing and then mimicking what she observed. By mimicking she was able to put into action what she observed and build a knowledge base. At one year old she is now able to link her understanding, observation, and experiences together.

In studying about Zen, I found much more than knowledge, I found a way to enhance myself as a member of a much larger community. This improved me will have the ability and understanding to make better decisions that I hope will benefit those around me because I know now that I am not alone in this world. What I do affects others and I want to be awake to try and make the best decision for that particular moment in time. I do not claim to understand Zen but I have been able to build a foundation because of the way this class has been structured and the text that it has provided me. I hope to continue to incorporate Zen into my life and learn more about Zen teachings. I think this is something that will continue to evolve throughout the rest of my life. As Dr. Syverson stated, "We can't read something and not be affected by it." These texts have affected me in a positive way.

Tommy Tran is a senior at The University of Texas at Austin. He is majoring in Rhetoric and Writing with a minor in Business receiving the Business Foundations certificate from the McCombs School of Business. He will be graduating in May 2011. Tommy is from Clear Lake, a suburb of Houston, Texas, but is an Austinite at heart.

Learning, Changing, and Living
Andres Aguirre

Initial Impressions of Zen

Upon arriving to this classroom, I had only a slight amount of previous knowledge on the subject of Zen Buddhism. Most of my previous encounters involved merely talking to others about it, or learning bits of information here and there from a random television program or movie screen. I was acquainted with the common stereotypes such as monks meditating in monasteries and their belief in reincarnation, but I did not fully understand the true nature of Zen Buddhism and the core beliefs in which it is rooted. Despite the many variations and beliefs that currently exist among Buddhists, I knew that Buddhism didn't perpetuate itself as a religion, but more as a state of being that advocates the practice of awareness and mindfulness. If one is able to meditate and free the consciousness, there exists a unifying force and state of mind that one can awaken to and become "enlightened." I knew that enlightened people were supposed to exemplify truth, knowledge, and peace, because they are freed from the mental constructs and assumptions that the modern day human takes for granted on a daily basis. I knew that Buddhists were in search of this state of enlightenment in order to be more attuned with life itself and to be alive in a more significant manner, but I could not understand exactly how, and the entire concept of enlightenment struck me as something very elusive and unattainable for the average twenty-one year old college student like myself.

In the beginning, I had trouble relating to the seemingly simplistic and paradoxical ideas I found within Zen. I couldn't really connect to the expressions and literary devices used in Hagen's and Suzuki's texts. Even their descriptions of the most basic Zen concepts seemed too vague and intangible when I first read them. I found myself questioning the authors and their words, wanting to relate them to something I could easily grasp or something I could classify as empirical and grounded in reality. What I did not realize was that by doing so I was shutting myself off to any real opportunities to change, and thus hindering my own development in understanding. Though I did not connect very strongly with these first couple of books initially, they were helpful in that they gave me a good taste of what was to come within the following weeks of the course.

It took a couple of weeks of reading and attending the class lectures just to broaden my understanding of the fundamental aspects of Zen and zazen practice. The course was carefully designed to be experiential and highly immersive. We had to participate in sitting meditation every class period, fully engage in the texts in order to reflect upon them, and ultimately apply them to our own lives in order to actually learn something about Zen. Zen Buddhism itself is all about being in the present moment, and this principle is what inevitably causes it to be an experiential and practical study. It is something that requires you to immerse yourself in new ideas and ways of understanding the world around you. This caused me to question many aspects about my life and understanding of it, quickly leading to some very intense and complex questions about my existence and my interpretations of it. Though this was confusing at first, it was thought provoking; and this broadened Zen perspective helped illuminate the importance of understanding the most fundamental principles of practice before trying to dive deep into any really complex Zen ideas. Thus, learning about the basics such as true awareness, right intentions, and correct posture during sitting meditation turned out to be a more useful approach for learning and developing as a student of Zen practice.

Obtaining this right posture was initially a source of frustration during the beginning weeks of the course. I felt that I could not meditate properly. I felt that there was some heightened mental state I had to reach, or some mode of thought that I had to make myself achieve in order to attain enlightenment. It was strange not knowing what to do, feel, or think during meditation. I kept thinking that enlightenment could not possibly be as simple and easy to obtain as sitting still. Yet once I began truly attempting it, I found out that sitting meditation is actually not as easy as I had thought. When you become still for a long enough period of time, you begin to notice many things about yourself and your reactions to your reality. I began observing a lot of the impulses I had to move around, or to focus on discomfort, or how my mind tends to wander. This in turn provided an interesting gateway for experience and understanding. In my case, it opened up a lot of possibilities for learning, and connecting these experiences to the books we were reading helped me see new factors about my own experience of reality. It proved to me how much my mind was already making judgments and assumptions without even realizing it. This intrigued me even more and gave me the drive to keep learning about the Zen philosophy and way of life, in order to understand its relevance and application to my personal life.

Once I entered this 'application' phase, I began engaging with the subject more wholeheartedly, and I began to see how every Zen concept we were discussing in class could be applied to my "real" and "empirical" life. Since the practice of Zen is a constant choice to be aware in your present reality, it is itself grounded in empirical evidence because you experience it as it happens. It is a philosophy that takes nothing for granted besides what is already there in the moment, and what you can constantly feel as reality. This constant awareness is the underlying concept of Zen Buddhist teachings, and thus, becoming aware and present became my main goal and focal point for future inquiry. Though later I would learn that in fact you shouldn't strive, or "lean," to achieve any goals from the Zen perspective, this idea now ingrained in my mind, allowed me to connect the previously obscure and elusive philosophical concepts to my practical everyday experience. This is what truly provided a channel for my development. From then on, I tried to use the immersive and experiential nature of Zen practice and Professor Syverson's course to expand my intake of the Zen Buddhist teachings I was to encounter therein.

Further Explorations

One of my main issues with Zen during the first half of the course was that I assumed there had to be a preexistent state of suffering and dissatisfaction in order for Buddhism to work. I had a hard time coming to terms with this idea and truly understanding what it means. I now understand that it is the nature of existence and life itself that makes this idea a fundamental aspect of Buddhism, yet I could not understand it when I first encountered it. After reading our first class textbooks and attending class for several weeks, I learned that in fact it is not problematic nor obscure, but sheer truth. By the act of living, we are also dying, and no human being can escape that fact. This is why the Buddha searched for an answer to the problem of the human condition - why must we all suffer and is there a way to escape it?

As it turns out, there is no escape from suffering. Every human being must go through "suffering" at some point in their life, even the enlightened. Yet, if you are able to reach that higher state of being, suffering simply ceases to be as important because you will see and perceive events only for what they are, and not whatever meaning you may assign to them within your head. The attachment to the ideas of good and bad will cease to be as apparent or useful as you approach the state of enlightenment. Perhaps this is what Zen Buddhists mean by finding the balance - realizing that not every event has a good or bad effect but that any circumstance may yield many of both, and that it is what you choose to see and act upon that matters. Perceiving a certain action or event as being negative will likely yield more negativity perpetuated in the form of thoughts and actions. So finding a clear, unbiased perception is essential to Zen Buddhists and their search for Truth. We know that one of the most basic rules of our universe is that everything changes and the world in which we live in is dynamic, as well as our beings, our minds, and our encounters and personalities. Consequently, we know that everything is "impermanent" and constantly fluctuating. In *Buddha's Brain*, Hanson defines it the following way;

"Consider the impermanence of the physical world, from the volatility of quantum particles to our Sun, which will some-day swell into a red giant and swallow the Earth. Or consider the turbulence of your nervous system; for example, regions in the prefrontal cortex that support consciousness are updated five to eight times a second (Cunningham and Zelazo 2007). This neurological instability underlies all states of mind. For example, every thought involves a momentary partitioning of streaming neural traffic into a coherent assembly of synapses that must soon disperse into fertile disorder to allow other thoughts to emerge (Atmanspacher and Graben 2007). Everything changes. That's the universal nature of outer reality and inner experience. Therefore, there's no end to disturbed equilibria as long as you live. But to help you survive, your brain keeps trying to stop the river, struggling to hold dynamic systems in place, to find fixed patterns in this variable world, and to construct permanent plans for changing conditions."

Events and occurrences in life are not necessarily "good" or "bad," they just are. And because of this fact, you have no choice and no control besides what you choose to do in response and how. Constructing these positive or negative meanings and assigning them to events is simply what your brain is hard-wired to do. This is a key premise of Zen - to understand that our attachment to the ideas of "good" and "bad" is actually a quite selfish assumption. If you stop believing the concept that every thing and event must have some determinate meaning or purpose, and see things only for what they are, when they are, then the truth will be much easier to find and much easier to carry forth through your actions while you live out your life from moment to moment. In order to help myself envision this idea, I like to compare it to an improvisational musician. The musician who improvises has no idea what he will play; and though it may or may not sound "good" at first, in the end it doesn't matter because as he strikes a note, he comes up with a new one in response in a timely fashion and continues the progression as it happens, which ultimately may or may not form a coherent musical piece. It would only make sense that through practice the musician could become better and better until he could come up with a perfectly harmonic melody and great progression every time and on the spot. Perhaps an enlightened person's experience in life is similar. As their mind is fully awake, they can see events only for what they already are and react to them in a timely manner, in a way that is accepting and truthful to whatever the given situation or adversity might be as it unfolds. Thus they are constantly perceiving and manifesting their own realities when they act out their lives at every moment.

This soon led me to another troublesome encounter. I began thinking that if the choice of being awake is momentary, exactly how small are these units of time? How fast is the brain in its cognitive and perceptive processes? Fortunately, *Buddha's Brain* answered a lot of these questions, and after reading the book, I was amazed at the capabilities of the human brain. The number of possible mental states that can exist in your brain at any moment, made capable by all the different neuron interaction combinations, is more than the number of atoms estimated to be in the universe. This simple fact baffled me. The possibilities are indeed endless. One idea commonly used in theoretical physics to explain and describe some complex concepts is the idea that time is not actually what we think it is. It is not a determinate passing of measured units that we have no control over, but more of a direction in four-dimensional space-time. In other words, it is more useful to visualize time as a semi-spatial dimension of direction that describes change through the other spatial dimensions, than as a vague measurement. This example, though seemingly unrelated, helps me understand and relate from a Zen perspective. If time is in fact not some uncontrollable measurement but rather something to be experienced on a broader existential scale, then we begin to let go of the thought that we have no influence over time and how we perceive it. After all, time is perceived in your mind and if you have awareness and mindfulness, your perception of time will be simple and clear. You begin to worry and stress much less about the things that are completely irrelevant in your current time frame – such as what you have to do, or what you should have done.

This brought me to one of the Zen concepts that most people have trouble with. How do you define the right intentions? If you are to not "lean" your mind towards anything in life besides the present moment, how are you supposed to get anything done? Isn't the practice of Zen and meditation also a conscious decision with the intention of reaching some ultimate goal? How can you become enlightened, if in fact, you are not supposed to be "trying"? To me at first this seemed impossible, and I still have trouble grasping this concept. We simply don't live in a world that can support this way of being. From birth we are taught and conditioned to know that we must try our best. We must work hard and plan ahead in order to be able to achieve our dreams and aspirations. How else can you accomplish your goals in life if you don't have the intention to attain something in the end? Is enlightenment, then, the only way to be fulfilled?

Hagen defines it in the following way in Buddhism Plain & Simple, "Right intention, the second aspect of the eightfold path, is what most distinguishes a Buddha from those of us who are not awake. Why? Because in the moment we are awake, for all practical purposes we're without intention. We could say that the intention of an awakened person is just simply to be awake. If we want to break the chain of suffering and confusion, our intention should only be to awaken. If our intention is partly to get something from being awake, however, this is already delusion. We don't get anything from being awake. If you're awake, you're just awake. And if you're awake, you'll act and

speak in a way that doesn't do injury to yourself or to others...
Thus right intention is simply the intention to come back to this
moment—to be present with no ideas of gaining whatsoever.
You cannot be here and hold a gaining idea at the same time.
Just becoming here and now is enough... The key is to have
wholesome intentions without being attached to their results."

Understanding Zen

So what is Zen Buddhism, and what have I learned? I think
it is safe to say that it involves true awareness. To me this is the
most accurate word to depict the purpose and intent behind
Zen Buddhist teachings. To be here living in the moment, now.
The enlightened mind is completely aware of its surroundings
and their effects on us as beings, and also completely aware
of our own mental biases and its externalized effects. To me,
this seems to be a very fitting term for enlightenment. If one
can be "aware" enough to notice these patterns of reality,
then it makes sense that the enlightened being would use this
knowledge to act in conjunction with life itself and to preserve
the flow of energies that we are and that surround us as living
beings on Earth.

Simply contemplating the most fundamental Zen concepts
of impermanence, dependent origination, and no self, was
enough to make me understand the Zen perspective on life. We
are all impermanent and dependent, in every sense. There is a
fluid continuity of experience between us, and there is a necessary interdependence between each of our realities. Everything
is contingent upon something else, making everything empty,
or lacking "self-nature." That's not to say that we do not each
have our own "self," but that your "self" came to be through
many other factors beyond you.

This constantly captivating idea of Zen thought is the notion
of "dependent origination." This concept still blows my mind in
terms of relating to distant time periods as well as my own. The
simple fact that nothing is completely and originally produced
is something very profound to consider. Everything depends
on numerous other factors in order to come to existence. At any

time, you cannot escape the many influences that you currently have and have had in the past. These include interactions, ideas, experiences, objects, people, and anything else that may even come to your mind, tangible or not. This combined experience of reality and time is what causes you to be what you are now. So nothing is completely original, because it all came to be due to factors beyond itself.

In a class lecture, we discussed the method of textuality in Huang Po's time period, and how the Huang Po we have come to know today is in fact the product of a long lineage of transmission and evolution. The ideas we know today about Huang Po "originated dependent" upon many factors. There were innumerable monks that had added to and edited the manuscripts throughout their circulation from monastery to monastery. Then they had to be interpreted and translated into other languages like English, inevitably undergoing manipulation and evolution, and then read and understood by us in the present. Huang Po's words and thoughts themselves were also undeniably influenced and shaped by other texts and ideas.

This raises many questions to credibility and authenticity in terms of our modern way of thinking, but we concluded that this long line of transmission only proves that the important and worthy teachings of Zen were transmitted and disseminated. Through time, the editing and evolving process of the text was inevitable - such as it is with anything else. We may in fact not know the original words of Huang Po or what he was even like, but we can be sure that through the extensive legacy of Zen followers he created, his true Zen philosophy is still transmitted and is available for anyone seeking to find it. Wright explains with greater detail in the following passage.

"One fruitful way to understand the status of these texts entails calling upon the seminal Buddhist concept of 'dependent origination.' As Buddhists in many eras have known, this idea is useful to explain how it is that things are impermanent, and how they come to be the particular things that they are. According to this traditional Buddhist theory, all things, including texts, are always changing because they depend, at the moment of their origin and at all times, on other things which are themselves changing. All things come to be exactly what they are at any given moment not because it is their own inherent nature to do so, but because other things influence them, shape them, and make them what they are... If we work hard, however, to understand the "lack of true self" that we discover in these texts through the Buddhist concept of "dependent origination," we will be able to get over our disappointment about the status of these texts and discover something extremely important about the process of transmission."

In our modern thinking, we constantly seek a determinate, defined origin. This is not the case in Zen thinking though. Once you understand dependent origination, you see that nothing has a definite origin, creator, or "true self." This notion is in sharp contrast with many of our currently established ways of determining authorship. We commonly acknowledge and give credit to a single person for creating any work, whether it is a text, or any work of art or human self-expression. Yet, when we realize, they cannot possibly be the absolute originators of their creations, because their creation was brought about by many other factors beyond the creator. Even the creator's actions as well as thoughts, which enticed him to create the work in the first place and allowed him to execute it, inevitably originated due to many other influences and life experiences. Though having this thought sometimes makes me see my own writing and works of art as trivial and unimportant, it actually also serves to help me realize how truly unique my perspective is. No one else can share the same "dependent origination." So in this sense, you are original and this is your true, unique "self." Each of us has an extremely complex and incomparable set of influences and experiences that constantly shape the person we each are. But it is important to note that we did not choose for this to happen, nor was it the inherent nature of the world to create the situation that we live in now. The inherent nature of the world is change through impermanence. This never ending cycle of dependence and transience is what allowed me to understand what the term "emptiness" means for Zen Buddhists.

The following paragraph from Wright's book helped me truly grasp this idea.

"The concept "emptiness" derives from, and eventually encompasses, the key elements in Buddhist contemplative practice: impermanence, dependent origination, and no self. For something to be "empty" means that, because the entity "originates dependent" upon other entities, and is transformed in accordance with changes in these "external" conditions, the entity therefore lacks "own-being" or "self-nature." The thing is not self-determining; on its own it would have never come to be what it is. Its existence and its character are attributable to the multiple factors that condition its origin and subsequent transformations. Coming into existence, changing over time, and passing out of existence, empowered by conditions beyond itself, the "empty" thing lacks any trace of "aseity" or permanence. This "lack," furthermore, this negative dimension at the very heart of the thing which the concept "emptiness" highlights, is the "nature" or "essence" of all things without exception. When Buddhists contemplate anything - an entity, a situation, or an idea - this "dependence," "instability," or "void" within it directs the mediator beyond the thing itself to its determining conditions, other things, situations, and ideas which similarly point beyond themselves to others, ad infinitum. Empty things are what they are contextually; their being is relational. Understanding anything, therefore, requires explication of context, as we know very well."

So every situation we experience and thing we do is dependent upon everything else, and we cannot possibly be the absolute originator of anything. I can see an interesting parallel specifically within the world of music. The same patterns of communal authorship can be seen throughout many phases of musical culture in several time periods. The first stages of human music, like the textual transmission of Huang Po, involved a large community of participants working together, or learning and transmitting the song to other places and communities. Throughout almost any given time period we can notice the common songs, hymns, or chants that have no definite creator but that nevertheless have a strong influence on the culture for a long period of time. It was not until the renaissance that composers identified their musical works as entirely their own. But even then, we can note many plurally authored musical works appearing in later periods of time. One great example of this is the rise of blues music in the United States. The roots and absolute origination of many of the seminal songs of the genre are hard to pinpoint. Many of the classic blues ballads still heard today go so far back to a place so unknown to many, that their authors are still not clearly defined. Deciphering the origination of such blues songs entails going back to the end of the 19th century and analyzing every factor that may have influenced this music to come about. In doing so you would find the many complex factors and intricate networks of influences that created this specific surge in musical self-expression.

Even today, with our sophisticated and advanced technologies, we cannot escape this fact. A return to the more communal form of authorship is certainly noticeable, especially within the world of electronic music and commercial pop music, though the shift in recognition is much more apparent in the former. The recent explosion in remix culture has illuminated the fact that music cannot be original. Most artists today using computers to produce works of music are continually sampling other sounds, songs, singers, and musicians alike. These are extremely apparent, direct sources of influence. Within electronic music, numerous producers sample indiscreetly as a form of art, causing them to hide their identity through the use of a pseudonym or pen name for the fear of legal repercussions of copyright infringement. In a sense, the return to the selfless authorship is established, but for the most part we still maintain a perspective of determinate authorship within our culture.

It all ties back into our society's ideals of recognition and status. Different people feel they should be socially rewarded or recognized for the good things they may do in life. And unfortunately this is what inspires many people to carry out their actions in life, whatever they may be. Such is the case with the commercial pop artist that creates new hits for recognition and more money, as well as with the student that only gets A's but in the process learns nothing. To their possible dismay, reward and status are not measurements of success. If you are first successful as a person by being good to others, being aware, present, inspired by life, learning, loving, and changing, then you will undoubtedly be recognized by others, which then may or may not bring the fame, status, or money.

I know many people that believe status brings success, when in fact it's the other way around. Success brings status; but it is simply impossible to succeed and eventually attain that merit unless you are doing what you are doing in a whole-hearted manner, without any preconceived notions of reward and the like. You do it because it is your innermost desire to do it, and you expect nothing from it. "The key is to have whole-some intentions without being attached to their results." Either way though, if you are doing something you love, the recognition is so secondary and unimportant compared to what you are doing. People that get caught up in those illusions of fame and grandiosity simply become delusional and dysfunctional humans, not knowing what to focus on - it's like being worried and stressed because you set a deadline for some goal you want to achieve, but you don't know what it is that you want to accomplish, or why. The act itself is what makes you happy; you don't need to be rewarded in order to feel good about yourself or what you have done. Being recognized and achieving a high social status can only be byproducts of what you intend to do with yourself and your time on Earth. These can never be the true reasons, and if they are then you have already failed your mission.

Thus, these ideas of right intention, right resolve, and inspiration are what keep pushing me to learn from Zen even after this class comes to an end. You can apply this concept to literally everything in your life at any scale, and it can definitely help you become a better person by illuminating the most important aspects of life to you. The main takeaway I have is that life itself is relatively short and fleeting - so don't let anything other than being alive be your goal for existence, and do so in a truly wholehearted manner. Yet in order to carry this out and be alive correctly, you must be aware.

As I'm writing this I can think of a million different ways in which I am violating the previous thought. I know every decision I have made in the past is not line with this, and I know I will make several more decisions this week that will contradict what I just said. I smoke and drink frequently. Sometimes I don't put in all my earnest effort into what I do. I'm not always nice and compassionate. I get irritated with myself and others. Sometimes I don't make an effort at all, but at least I'm aware of it now.

I realize that everything I learned at the beginning of the course could have been flat out wrong or misinterpreted. Even what I believe now about Zen and how it can bring me closer to living a more meaningful life is changing, and is momentary. It does not matter though, as long as I have the correct inspiration and effort. In some sense, I can get closer to attaining this happiness by knowing that I'm learning and changing at every second, and that I'm aware of it. And if change and self-transformation is not the point of this course, attending university, and living life itself, then I do not know what is. As Professor Syverson said, "You can't stop life from happening to you, but you can always be the person you want to be."

Andres Aguirre is a fourth-year Rhetoric & Writing and Advertising double major. He was born and raised in the border city of Reynosa, Tamaulipas in Mexico, though his family moved to McAllen, Texas when he was about ten years old. He is currently very interested in what the study of rhetoric and writing can bring to the many other aspects of his life such as music production, general social interactions, and advertising if he has to. He is thankful for the numerous revelations he has had while taking rhetoric courses at UT, for these have allowed him to see past what initially meets the eye, and served as a guide to correct expression.

May you have all the success that I lack

Chloe Chiang

Introduction

I left the first day of class thinking, what have I gotten myself into? Professor Syverson begins class with 15 minutes of meditation followed by five minutes of free writing. In the beginning I caught myself falling asleep, or else rapid trains of thought would clutter my head. I would try to organize the rest of the day or week, decide what I should make for dinner, what work out I should do, and sometimes I would play back the week and all that happened. I was assigned five books to read over the course of the semester. There were no book reports, book checks or quizzes over the readings. So I guess it would have been easy to not do the readings. But I found myself really getting into the books and wanting to practice Zen outside of class. I started adding quotes that I liked from the readings to my Facebook, talked about the teachings to friends and applied those teachings to my life outside of the class. This course is unconventional and yet I think I have learned more in this class than any other I have taken at the University of Texas. My business classes require a textbook, tests and memorization. In rhetoric, long drawn out research papers with five paragraphs and a thesis statement are the norm. This class has allowed me to write and think freely and to embrace my curiosity. The most influential thing I will take from this class is my ability to communicate with myself. I have all these preconceived notions and ideas about myself. I am only 22 years old so most of what I know about myself has come from what other people have told me. I have this mentality that I am this mentally strong person and nothing and no one can break me. Sticks, stones nor words could hurt me. People tell me that I am brave, strong, and confident, and that I have this "badassness" about me. I don't care what other people think. In reality, I don't think I am any of those things, but I pretend to be because that's what I have been associated to. Perhaps when I was younger and in high school I was that way. Over the past few years, and especially this year as a senior in college, everything is changing. There are so many emotions and confusion about what I should do with my life, who I am, who I want to be. How I will be successful? Does GPA really matter? Should I really be working this many hours? My thoughts are so different now than they were a few years ago. I care about different things, I have different goals and I don't know if I should hold on to who I was because that's what I know, or explore this new person with these new ideas. Strangely, studying Zen has been incredibly therapeutic and has helped me think through this craziness. Writing down my thoughts, observations and acknowledging my emotions has allowed me to be a more calm and patient person. Before I go into my experiences with Zen, the beginning, middle and end, I want to explain how Zen has impacted my life.

From lecture and the documentary of Joko Beck, it appeared many people were interested in Zen because of a tragedy they had experienced. For me, I hate to feel weak, so I try and control my emotions by pushing them back. I push all painful experiences and memories to the back of my brain so that I never think about them. When I was a freshman in college my dad was diagnosed with terminal cancer, with only eight weeks to live. I never experienced hurt like that before. I am not the kind of person that would turn to drugs or alcohol or bad behavior. Instead I pushed it all back and pretended to be unaffected by it. Meditation and Zen gave me the tools to move those memories from the back of my brain to the forefront of my mind. With a

lot of practice and patience I believe that I will be able to acknowledge those feelings and for the first time allow myself to
be aware of them. I have slowly started to do this. Awareness is
a key concept in Zen. In Zen, I don't have to analyze why I think
what I do or figure out an answer to all my questions. Simply
being aware of the thought or feeling is enough. Wow! That is so
simple and yet extremely difficult. Here is my path as it played
out from the beginning, middle and end of the semester. These
sections were written throughout the semester. The reader will
be able to see my progress and development over the span of
about fifteen weeks.

The Beginning of the semester

(Everything is new and exciting. I am enjoying learning the
basic concepts so far).

Buddhism is a new concept to me. I haven't studied anything quite like it. I started going to church a couple months
ago because my boyfriend wanted me to understand his faith
and why it is important to him. Growing up, I had a negative
view of Christianity. I thought many of the people who went
to church were hypocrites. Drinking, smoking, lying, cheating,
stealing etc were un-Christian like things to do, and yet they all
went to church on Sunday hung over. How can you practice a
religion and not live by it? Praying and believing in something
that I can't feel, touch or see makes Christianity and other religions difficult for me to follow. I guess what I really want is to
be in control of my beliefs. Zen Buddhism is a way of life. There
is no creation story, disciples or saints and there is no God or
bible that tells you the "correct" way to live your life. There is
no heaven or hell- there is no afterlife. Buddhism teaches the
present; how to live in the now and see things as they are, not
what you interpret them to be or what you want them to be.
I think Zen is a great way for me to understand myself better
because it challenges me to simply see rather than analyze. So
far everything I have learned is fuzzy. These are concepts that
are almost contradictory to what I have been raised to think.
For example, Professor Syverson said, "In Zen, there is noth-

ing to believe and everything to discover." I first thought, this is a nice quote, a good concept. I nodded my head along with the rest of the class like we had all finally understood what we have been trying to grasp so far. However, once I had time to think about it and even now as I am writing this, I realize I don't understand this at all. There is nothing to believe? What if I want to have faith in something that I haven't yet discovered? I have dreams of becoming a millionaire, am I practicing Zen wrong? Do Buddhists dream about things they haven't discovered and believe them? I have so many questions and I don't know if I will find the answers. This is becoming a little frustrating because I enjoy everything I am learning, but when I apply it to my life it doesn't fit. One of our class assignments is to write down our observations. I realized that I began to answer my own questions through this assignment. September 9th I wrote,

"I am attempting to apply some Zen techniques to my relationship with my boyfriend. I tried not to analyze or argue, but just listen and watch. I wanted to see his point of view without thinking of mine. I tried to completely forget my opinion for a little bit. In the end I still disagreed with him but at least I had kept an open mind and understood his side. I struggle with seeing the "truth" because what I think is true and what he thinks is true is different. I like to think that I am right in the argument, but perhaps neither of us is right and that's what truth is. In that aspect I agree that seeing isn't believing, because if you see it, then there is no need to believe. [I can 'see' that both of us are right and neither of us are right, thus the need to believe each other's side of the story isn't the point].

Truth isn't about being right. It is about seeing, being present and living in reality. Hagen says, "If we don't see exactly what the problem is, we're going to perpetuate it." This teaching has helped me with arguments not only between my boyfriend and I, but also with myself. The internal arguments I have with myself, such as, should I work or study for my test, isn't a problem of which is more important. It is problem of time management. Zen teachings are about getting down to the basics and acting on them.

The first book I read was Hagen's *Buddhism Plain and Simple*. The concept that life is fleeting is one of my favorite teachings of Zen. Hagen says in order to be fully alive we must be fully present. "To understand that life is fleeting, you must understand that you are already complete, worthy and whole. Finally, you must see that you are your own refuge, your own sanctuary, your own salvation." These are powerful words for me because I find real comfort in them. When I read something like this, it empowers me to take control of my life and appreciate the present moment. I often try to make reality into something that it isn't. "We try to rearrange and manipulate the world so that dogs will never bite, accidents will never happen and the people we care about never die." This is the truth that I, and many people, find hard to swallow. One day we will be faced with death, our parents and friends too. Hagen uses an example of a flower to express this view. Flowers will die even though they are beautiful and wish them to live longer than they do. Weeds will flourish even though they are ugly and wish they didn't grow. A rose with its beautiful petals, vibrant colors and silky texture, smells fresh and makes me happy. But within a few days the color turns brown, the smell fades, the texture becomes rigid and rough and they end up in the trash. I could buy a fake rose made of plastic- one that never dies, but also never lives. Hagen asks, "But is a plastic rose what we want?" No, we want a real rose because it does die. "We want it because it's fleeting, because it fades. It's this very quality that makes it precious. This is what we want, what each of us is, a living thing that dies."

Zen teaches you to accept responsibility for your life, your words and your actions. I love this concept because it gives me control and power over me. The only person who can receive the credit and blame is me. If I chose to give this authority away or allow someone else to tell me what to do, how to live my life, or make my decisions then I am choosing to give up that power- no one can take it from me. The ability to wake up and be aware lies within me. What does being awake really mean? What does enlightenment consist of and how do I know if I am enlightened? How do you free your mind? I didn't realize how hard it is to be "aware." However, I found that Zen has actually helped me to approach my problems in a different way. Buddhism doesn't help me solve problems; rather it gives me a new perspective on the issue. When I meditate and practice Zen I recognize my emotions and what bothers me. Two of my observations sum up this experience.

"Lately I have been really irritated. I don't know what it is regarding or

why this is, but I observe myself many times throughout the day feeling annoyed and not knowing why. It can be something I see of Facebook, a stranger's mannerisms, something some one said or did- it just irritates me and I can't concentrate. I observe it coming on, lingering and going away. I observe myself getting frustrated because I'm irritated without a good reason."

"I am still irritated- a whole week. I know that I am supposed to be aware of the feelings and emotions, but I want to know why I feel so overwhelmed and irritated. I caught myself making excuses and making up reasons why I feel this way. Basically, it was the fault of anyone but mine. Then, I get mad at myself for not being happy and appreciative. I have so much going on I feel like I need to be productive every minute of the day. I started meditating twice a day in order to calm myself down. Hopefully that will help!"

What I did was listen to myself. I had to take authority over what I was feeling. I couldn't get rid of it or escape it, so I just acknowledged it. The irritation and anxiety went away and it wasn't because of some outside force, but because of my own ability to see what triggered those emotions and to stay away from them.

The Middle of the semester

(This is where I begin to ask more specific and detailed questions. I have experienced more frustration now than I did before).

One thing that I have improved on is posture. I can relate posture to my experience is gymnastics. "When we have our body and mind in order, everything else will exist in the right place, in the right way" (Suzuki 27). I really like this philosophy because it is something I actually relate to and understand! In gymnastics, your mind and body have to be on the same wavelength. There needs to be communication and agreement between the two. For example, when doing a back handspring on the balance beam the mind has to tell the body where to go. If the hand is not in the right place then you can fall and get hurt. Sometimes when you are mentally exhausted, the body has to work twice as hard or rely on muscle memory. The same goes for the body. When the body is weak and tired the mind has to work twice as hard to make the body do what it does not want to. Thus, it is hard to change something outside ourselves if we are not in order. This order and intention is really hard to obtain!

I like a lot of the stories about Buddha. I didn't realize that Buddha was from India. I associated Buddha and Buddhism with China. I also thought Buddha was a God. The fact that Buddha is a not some mystical being makes his teachings much more real to me. Buddha was a teacher, an intelligent man sought out for his knowledge and advice. The advice he gave the farmer is found in Hagen's *Buddhism Plain and Simple*. It was so simple, yet it had so much meaning. The story goes like this; A farmer traveled a long ways to find the Buddha and ask him for advice. The farmer says he likes farming, but sometimes his crops don't grow. He loves his wife, but sometimes she nags him too much. He has good kids, but sometimes they don't respect him. The Buddha listens to his story and says he can't help him.

"Everyone has problems," the Buddha said, "in fact every-one has eighty three problems, and there is nothing you can do about it."

The angry farmer shouts, "What good is your teaching?"

The Buddha replies, "Well maybe it will help you with the eighty fourth problem."

"What's the eighty fourth problem?" the farmer responded.

"You want to not have any problems," said Buddha.

I started thinking about my "problems." I realized I don't really have any. The problems I think I have aren't actually problems because something good comes from them too. What would a world be like without any problems? I can't even think of how it would be. As much as I complain about my responsibilities and busy schedule, I wouldn't have it any other way. The point is, everyone has problems and without them we wouldn't be able to enjoy life. I think what Buddha is teaching the farmer is to appreciate what he has. Every flower has weeds, for every death there is a rebirth, for every tear there is a laugh and when one problem is solved another problem with come up. That's just life. That is reality. Deal with it. According to *Buddha's Brain*, the mind can train the brain to remember positive experiences over negative ones. Without forcing myself to think positively, I can take an issue or negative thought and reframe it into something positive. It doesn't mean to manipulate the situation- it means to be aware of the thought and the emotions it brings up. Then find a way to make it a positive experience. For example, I fought with my best friend because she lost my black dress. Is that really a problem? The first step for me was to see the problem and be aware of it. This wasn't physically hurting me. I wouldn't say that it was emotionally or mentally damaging. I guess I could say I was disappointed that I trusted my friend to take care of my belongings. But in reality, it's only a material thing. The problem is the dress is lost. However, I have a good friend. It's better to have a good friend to share material things with than to only have material things. It is better to have the friend than the dress.

As the semester goes on, I have become frustrated with some of the topics in Zen. Suzuki says, "Nothing is special. If you continue this simple practice every day, you will obtain some wonderful power. Before you attain it, it is something wonderful, but after you attain it, it is nothing special." I hated this concept at first. I thought the purpose of the journey was to get you to the goal or wherever you were going. I see now that the journey is the most exciting part. The joy is in the journey. I know that once I overcome a challenge or accomplish my goal then I set new ones. This has been the case throughout my whole life, but namely in gymnastics. Once I mastered a skill,

I would move on to the next one. I remember the long days in the gym and the body aches and the blood, sweat and tears it took me to accomplish that goal. But once I got it, I was already moving on to the next one. It's not that I don't remember the feeling of accomplishment or the act of doing the skill, because I do. However, I look back on the hard work it took and the character it built more so than the goal. As long as you aspire, there is little to no disappointment. The disappointment comes from expectation. However, I have high expectations for myself. I want a lot of things for myself. But, I have tried to reorganize by hopes and dreams into aspirations. I am trying to see that my dreams are not something that is expected. They are something to aspire to. I may never achieve my goals, but I will continue to aspire to them.

Suzuki says, "Always be a beginner." Steve Jobs said in his Stanford commencement speech, "The heaviness of being successful was replaced by the lightness of being a beginner again." He said this in regards to being fired from Apple computers. He went on to start Next and Pixar, two successful companies. Jobs' speech helped me understand Suzuki's idea of being a beginner. At first I thought being a beginner was bad- it is better to be an expert. People respect and hire you for jobs when you have experience. However, a beginner's mind there is more possibilities. The mind is more open, while an expert's mind is narrow. The beginner's mind is passionate, not limited and boundless.

Suzuki also says, "You should be grateful for the weeds you have in your mind, because eventually they will enrich your practice." I, like everyone else, have opinions and ideas based on experiences in my past. I cannot discount them or forget about them, nor do I want to. These experiences and memories make me who I am. Throughout my study of Zen I have felt like I have to let go of all that in order to be conscious of the present and for my practice of Zen to be purer. Now I understand that I should be grateful for these "weeds" because they "enrich my practice" of Zen. Of course, an overflow of weeds can cause a lack of nourishment. So how do I apply my experiences to my every day Zen practice without forcing it? This question along with many others is still unanswered.

The End of the semester

(I have grown in my Zen practice over the semester. I have started to understand the concepts that frustrated me in the beginning. I have applied many of them to my life outside of the classroom).

"You can't always get what you want, but you can always be who you want." At this point in the semester I have reached a new level of my Zen practice. I want to call this phase some-thing- I think it needs a particular label because it is probably the most eye opening experience in the course thus far. It is a selfless phase. I can't always get the things I want- a new pair of shoes, the job, the relationship, or even the maintenance guy to come fix my air conditioner. But I can discover the self, I can control my thoughts and I can break down boundaries. Zen practice has shown me a different way to see things. I have a wider perspective than I did before this course. Professor Syverson drew a small circle on the white board with a stick figure in the middle. I am in that small circle. She drew "matter" outside of the circle and then erased the circle so that the figure and matter were the only things on the white board. I realized that I live in a small container that has boundaries. The con-tainer keeps a lot of things out. This is a limited way to live life because all it does in confine and limit me. I need to challenge myself to put myself in some different situations like talking to a group of strangers or making conversation with someone on the bus. I could learn to play soccer and try new cuisine. Here is an observation I made on October 12th:

"I understand the container analogy as being open-minded to different

opportunities, people and things. It really is about being aware of my surroundings and not passing judgment, but rather just seeing things as they are. When professor Syverson said stop imagining some ideal person you want to be, I realized that is exactly what I am doing. I am trying to be the ideal student, real estate agent, girlfriend, friend and actually the ideal me-whatever that may be. This thinking makes my container smaller because I can't see anything outside this ideal realm. But now I realize there is no ideal anybody. I think it is good to challenge myself and continue to be the best I can be, but that doesn't mean I have to manipulate the situation or things I see to make myself who I think I should be."

This widening container is something I am still working on. I have already noticed a small change. I feel different. It is hard to explain or give a specific example. But I feel happier because I am more open to people's opinions and ideas. I know it sounds horrible, but I use to get irritated with people who didn't agree with me or weren't tolerant of my opinions. I tried to convince them I was right. Now, if I don't agree with someone, I am less inclined to be outwardly disapproving. I say something like, "well, I never saw it that way before. That is interesting." Although I still like to be right, I don't feel the urge to prove someone wrong. To continue with the container analogy, I see myself as the center of the circle. Me being in control and everything revolving around me. From the very beginning of my childhood I was told by my parents, teachers and coaches that I was special and different. Since then I have always felt the need to live up to being different. I have dated guys who I felt special with. I did sports that were different like gymnastics. I made it a point to be the center of attention because that's what I thought it meant to be special. It came to quite a shock when I realized the world didn't revolve around my needs and wants. The world kept spinning. I learned that by losing my dad- the one person that who I felt I inherited by "different" personality from. He was always the life of the party. After fourteen years, I quit gymnastics. I was forced to quit because of my dad's illness. I was lost for a long time because I had only been known as the girl who did flips. I used gymnastics to describe who I was, and without it I was just a normal girl who went to school and work. Who am I now without my dad and without gymnastics? I felt unimportant. Worst of all I was bitter and jealous of anyone who I felt threatened by their success. If someone was smarter or more athletic I would challenge myself to be better than them in some way. All the competitive energy went to proving to my own self that I was still different and unique. A couple years later and reading *Buddha's Brain* helped me conceptualize those feelings. I understand now that those thoughts are purposeless and exhausting. Hanson says you don't need to be special. He offers some advice at the end of *Buddha's Brain* that challenged everything I have been taught to believe as a child and all that I have struggled with trying to maintain. He said, "Believing that you need to be special in order to deserve love and support sets a really high bar that takes much effort and strain to clear... and it sets you up for self-criticism and feelings of inadequacy and worthlessness if you don't get the recognition you crave." I am trying to hold back from quoting this whole passage, but it is something that I have read over and over again. Reading this made me realize how much stress I have put on myself trying to prove to everyone that I am special. I was never able to put into words what I felt until I read this. Hanson suggests saying things like "may I be loved without being special. May I contribute without being special? I give up being important. I renounce seeking approval." I do feel some peace in this surrender, but it will take a long time to redirect 22 years of this train of thought.

I had so much jealousy that I couldn't be happy for even my best friends. I earned a scholarship to college for gymnastics. This was my lifelong dream to do division one athletics. I was training and living the dream in Orange County, California. Because I quit in order to come home to be with my family, I had so much resentment pushed back that I couldn't be happy for anyone, not even myself. When something good happened, like when I made the UT cheer squad, I couldn't be happy for myself because I wasn't doing gymnastics. I wouldn't have the same respect I had in my other sport. I got so down on myself when I wasn't perfect and I was envious of people who had what I wanted. I became self-centered and selfish. I was possessive of people's attention. Hanson used the analogy of a knotted fist. "When you open the hand to give, there's no more fist-no more self." I have kept so much of my "self" to myself that my hand hadn't really released from a fist. On my white board by my desk I wrote this phrase to remind myself every day "to free myself from the clutches of envy, send compassion and loving-kindness to the people I envy." I obviously have a love for quotes- I find the inspiration to be comforting. So far, I have not found a quote that has influenced me as much as this one; "may you have all the success that I lack." I don't know why this has affected me so much, but it has me wanting to know more about Zen. I say that to myself whenever I feel threatened. It has been helpful so far.

The semester is coming to an end and I still feel like I have so much to learn. I am grateful that professor Syverson has offered this course. As a senior, I appreciate courses like this because it is so refreshing to want to learn. Studying Zen is something I will continue to practice.

Chloe Chiang is a senior rhetoric and business degree student at UT. She has had a passion for writing ever since her first grade teacher gave her a journal. She enjoys working as a Realtor in Austin and plans to continue that career after she graduates in December of 2011.

Walking the Razor's Edge

Harrison F. Bequette

Understanding

Initially, the "non-argumentative" part of our course title grabbed my attention. Someday after my undergraduate studies, I hope to be accepted into law school and I quite certainly may never have a chance to learn to use rhetoric in a non-argumentative way without a course like this. I also took two philosophy classes in the spring of last year, "Yoga: philosophy and practice" and "Vedanta," each of which truly piqued my interests in meditation and one's dharma. Professor Stephen Phillips, who taught both courses, engaged my mind to think in non-ordinary ways. I mean non-ordinary in a new and stimulating sense, which revitalized my contemplation of the surrounding world and my existence within it. As a philosophy major, I have always been interested in studying the diverse systems of thoughts and ideas which the whole of mankind has contemplated throughout history. It is my hopes that by increasing my knowledge of different rhetorical systems, like non-argumentative Zen rhetoric, and by generally improving my own personal rhetoric, I will learn to convey the knowledge I absorb in an interesting, adaptable, and concise manner.

I will have completed my minor in rhetoric after successfully passing the two rhetoric courses I am enrolled in this semester, and because of my recently elevated interests, I have even been thinking about making rhetoric my second major. In my other rhetoric course, my teacher Ms. Ferreira-Buckley quoted Aristotle in saying, "Rhetoric is the discovery of every available means of persuasion." Although this is only one man's definition (one man I am almost certain was not privilege to study Zen), it appears contradictory to have a class called non-argumentative rhetoric. Upon further investigation it is not such a paradox, but initially it seemed almost counter-intuitive that one could use rhetoric in a non-argumentative or non-persuasive manner.

Consideration of this question was at the forefront of my mind in the early part of my studies in this course. After reading Suzuki's *Zen Mind, Beginner's Mind* and the Non-oppositional Disagreement handout on the web, it seemed clearer how rhetoric and non-argumentative rhetoric can co-exist. The metaphors the book offers are quite persuasive without being overly argumentative. One of my favorites is, "Weeds will flourish, though we hate them and wish them gone; flowers will fall, though we love them and long for them to remain." The truth expressed here needs no argumentative structure, rather, it points towards a realization that can be universally understood. It is a straight forward fact that lacks any judgment, making it extremely persuasive. Each one of the texts assigned in this course increased my urge to understand and wield this type of rhetoric. I began to see that non-argumentative rhetoric works effectively, at least for me personally, because it often lacks judgment and maintains an impression of curiosity or openness towards other ideas.

Alongside of improving my various studies, I began to realize how Zen concepts could be quite beneficial to my actual life and the way I choose to live in a daily sense. When I was in high school, I read a book called A New Earth: Awakening Your Life's Purpose by Eckhart Tolle. If you are unfamiliar with the book, he focuses on internal awareness and fully understanding inner-peace. He deemphasizes the diversity of world religions, and does an amazing job of identifying certain core concepts which are common to all religion, especially ideas found in eastern religions which are comparable to western religious ideas. A synopsis is unnecessary, but this book basically started my interest into the study of Zen.

Though I use the word study, it was more like the first time I began to contemplate the world in a new and unique way. I began to resist the urge to let my emotions rule my life, good or bad, and I also began to appreciate good things more. Not good things in a subjective sense like an "A+" on a test or getting a new car, but more objectively good; Good things like appreciating my existence more fully, finding joy in nature, and inspiring others to find true joy in their existence. I would often escape from the noise of my house and go to the neighborhood park, where I sat in stillness and attempted to be utterly and entirely aware of myself, a practice I was introduced to by Tolle's book. Ironically, despite many hardships I experienced during this period, it was truly a very peaceful time in my life.

I mention this because once I was accepted into college I seemed to lose touch with this peace, though, of course I know now that inner-peace does not just run away. If anything I ran away from inner-peace. It was almost like I became so busy that I had no more time for peace. However, I feel like my studies in this course have revitalized my contemplation and reminded me how to become more aware of myself in totality.

The awareness I have become more attuned to allows me to separate my thoughts and my mental reaction from my actual Self. Our class's weekly observations, for example, conditioned me into examining my judgments and my actual observations separately. And separating those two things is an extremely peaceful experience for me. Now, I will catch my mental judgments with an "oh wait" moment in my head which is a pleasant reminder that I had forgotten until now. It reminds me to stay humble, and not be attached to my judgments. If someone who has hurt me in the past enters the room, an ex-best friend for instance, I might be inclined to immediately make a defensive judgment. Something such as: "She is always so rude, I simply cannot stand to be around her." But by making this type of judgment, I am attaching to my past emotional pain and limiting myself from present possibilities, which are endless. The author's of *Buddha's Brain* refer to these types of judgments or reactions as "second darts." "Inescapable physical or mental discomfort is the 'first dart' of existence... First darts are unpleasant to be sure. But then we add our reaction to them. These reactions are second darts – the ones we throw ourselves."

I think we can all agree life inevitably comes with discomforts, both mental and physical. But I think we can also agree that we are not these reactions themselves, only the facilitators of these reactions. These reactions are dynamic and changing; they are also a product of our minds. Not only does clinging to these types of 'second dart reactions' create more angst for me personally, I also began to see that the more I cling, the less open I am to other people. If I automatically make a judgment about someone based on the past, I have not even given him or her a chance to be rude or friendly in the present.

Before I actually began studying Zen, I would often have similar trains of thought during the midst of unsatisfying situations. I've always considered myself one to look on the brighter sides of a situation; to find the silver lining in even the darkest clouds. After whatever dissatisfying situation had concluded, I sat and thought to myself something like, "Well at least I am still alive." Or, "At least, I have one more day to smell a flower or even just open my eyes to the sunlight once more." That might seem corny to some, but I have always found those thoughts extremely comfortable, even after particularly problematic situations.

After my inquiring into Zen this semester, I recognize that the inner-peace those thoughts brought me came from my conscious or unconscious attempt to separate my actual Self from the problem itself. In a heated moment like during a clash with my parents, it might feel like my world is coming to an absolute close. If I can calm myself, step back and realize that this is just one instance in a larger picture of my relationship with my parents, I might also realize some of the heated comments I had been making were just a product of my anger. In this state of present awareness, I can tone down the personal "heat" I am bringing to the discussion, and also more holistically understand the heated comments my parents are making. By separating myself from my reaction in this manner, I am more aptly able to respond to negative situations in a positive manner. And that itself is the third noble truth: "Whatever is subject to arising is also subject to ceasing. Thus since dukkha arises, it is also subject to cessation. The containment of thirst transforms its energy so that it can be useful: nirodha." Wielding this positive energy makes what one might interpret to be a negative situation less internally chaotic, and brings about clarity of the mind which invokes peace.

Realizing the human condition as dukkha and understanding the fleeting nature of joy and sorrow in the world is a tad daunting. As daunting as it is, personally, it is the most concise and true understanding of the world available. A life characterized by "thirst, craving, desire, wanting," or samudaya, is a life which seems initially destined to be choke-full of misery. The pain of those "second-darts" which we throw at ourselves is truly real. But I find peace within the realization that I am a pure, aware consciousness and not a "thirst" or a "craving." Although thirst and craving might be a natural characteristic of human life as a reaction to identification with reality, they are not a natural characteristic of my Self, nor are they characteristics which I must identify myself with. In fact, it is identifying my Self with these cravings which brings me the most internal conflict. When I say, "I am so angry this happened!" I have made my first mistake. I might feel angry, but I am certainly not the emotion of anger in my entirety. It is important for me to identify this feeling of anger, but this anger is fleeting and not my natural Self. Suzuki perfectly elaborates this aspect of Zen at the end of his chapter on Right Practice:

"When you are sitting in the middle of your own problem, which is more real to you: your problem or you yourself? The awareness that you are here, right now, is the ultimate fact. This is the point you will realize by zazen practice. In continuous practice under a succession of agreeable and disagreeable situations, you will realize the marrow of Zen and acquire its true strength. (pg 40)"

I am not my problem, or my samudaya. Rather, in my zazen practice, I begin to realize I am only here and aware: "the ultimate fact." It is this realization that allows a calmness and peace to arise within me. It is also, for me personally at least, the most complete explanation of my Self in relation to reality and my reactions to reality.

Practice

I began to find that the difference between Buddhism and other "–isms" is its natural and intuitive nature (although Hagen's book states that Buddhism isn't really an "-ism" anyway). At least for me personally, the four noble truths of Buddhism just seem inherently like the correct, most appropriate response to reality and the world around us. The world is hectic and full of ups and downs. It is beneficial for me to transform the negative energy or cravings that I have to change reality, and accept or transform those feelings into something different, something positive (nirodha). Buddhism is not asking me to adhere to a strict doctrine of beliefs, rather, it is asking me to accept facts about reality and how best to live in this reality according to my true nature. My initial grasp of this idea was as follows: Inevitably, there are negative things in the world, but my reactions to those things do not have to influence my Self in a negative way.

Although Zen's natural and intuitive nature is intellectually pleasing, I first struggled with the practical application of these ideas. How does one know the appropriate response in any situation? How can I treat others in such a way that I do the most good for both me and them? How can I be truly aware of myself in the midst of a day-to-day life filled with emotional responses and mental afflictions? I think that type of clarity in awareness was easier when I was younger, because I had fewer responsibilities, worries, and "first-darts." I also think as I grew older, I began to unconsciously add more "second-darts" or attach my Self with the negative reactions in my mind.

In a world of constant hustle and bustle, it is sometimes hard for me to still my mind and contemplate my actions or

thoughts with clarity. Although I certainly maintain that awareness at times, at the beginning of the course I wondered if there
was some sort of key to enlightenment that would allow me to
maintain it all times. I deeply respect that complete clarity and
yearn for it. The "Zen in a Nutshell" handout we received in
class was full of ideas that I can implement in my day-to-day
life which might help this process, although, I now believe true
peace can only be achieved by implementing all of the ideas
found in Zen, not any one singularly. Of course there isn't one
key, so I decided perhaps more meditation and self examination
was necessary to figure out my exact path towards peace.

As a mentioned above, in the beginning of the course I was
extremely eager to figure out which of these "keys to enlightenment" would fit best for me and allow me to maintain inner
peace at more constant intervals. Contrarily, after reading
Suzuki, I realized that perhaps my understanding of the practical
application of Zen was skewed in a dualistic manner. My urge to
find these spiritual "keys" presupposes an idea that someday
a "door" will open and I will be enlightened in constant peace.
With the keys, I will be good; without them, I will be bad. But this
idea itself is not the right understanding. Suzuki says, "What
we call 'I' is just a swinging door which moves when we inhale
and when we exhale." He goes on to say further, "You and I are
just swinging doors. This kind of understanding is necessary.
This should not even be called understanding; it is actually the
true experience of life through Zen and practice. (pg. 29)" As a
swinging door, I need no "keys."

Rather, practicing zazen allows me to live like a swinging
door, and purify myself through my focus on breathe and
posture during meditation. During this practice of meditation,
I become less inclined to identify myself with my surroundings
and more inclined to identify myself with my true nature: the
principles found in the eight-fold path. I recognize my surroundings as dukkha, but am not forced to identify myself with that
idea. I can acknowledge things as they are, whether they are
pleasing or displeasing, thereby accepting and abiding the
waves of life.

In the beginning, it seems almost too simple to find some ethereal peace through merely sitting still and quietly. Living a life of constant movement and thought has conditioned me to avoid the natural peace found in the stillness of both mind and body. Surprisingly, zazen is initially complicated, despite its apparent simplicity. But as the saying goes, "practice makes perfect." And I found that to be somewhat true after I began practicing for fifteen minutes daily. Of course, my practice is not perfected by any means, but my effort is genuine and my stillness is more easily attained.

"Before you determine to do it, you have difficulty, but once you start to do it, you have none. Your effort appeases your inmost desire... Just to be sincere and make our full effort in each moment is enough. There is no Nirvana outside our practice. (pg.47)" Suzuki reminds us that peace is found in, not through, this real effort to connect with our innermost desires. There is no theological degree in enlightenment that grants permanent peace. It is a livelihood of constant and sincere practice that cultivates this peace. In that regard, our class meditation, as well as my own personal meditation at home, has helped me realize more about my true nature which I can continue to incorporate in my day-to-day life.

Practice has taught me about patterns or habits that I might not have been able to understand without stillness; patterns that are hard to notice in the clamor of college life, but more easily understood in the quietness and solidarity of zazen. For example, I often have an urge for everyone to like me and sometimes, in order to gain approval, I will do things that I shouldn't. Practice allows me to see these types of habits and understand them holistically, which is calming and serene.

The peace I find is not ethereal, it is rather simple, and comes when I attune my actions to my innermost desires. I become aware of these desires through practice: "When your effort becomes pure, your body and mind become pure. (pg. 37)" As my mind becomes more pure, and my effort remains constant, I begin to see where I find true happiness in my life.

I came to realize right practice must coexist with right understanding of Zen in order to see the benefits it brings into a person's life. Personally, I struggle more with the practical aspects than I do with attempting to understand the underlying concepts. The concepts seem like inherent truths to me, especially the four noble truths and the eight-fold path of Buddhism. But Zen practice requires a sincere and committed effort which is not as simple as just mental intuition. It requires dedication to right practice which is often hard for someone entangled in business and personal attachment to the surrounding world.

Especially as a college student, it seems oddly unorthodox to practice zazen daily. I often feel extremely entrenched in my social activities and sometimes distracted by pettier things than the sincerity of practice. But as Suzuki reminds me, with this dedication comes simplicity. Just taking fifteen minutes out of my day to practice zazen is beneficial, whether it seems magical or not. "If you continue this simple practice every day, you will obtain some wonderful power. Before you attain it, it is something wonderful, but after you attain it, it is nothing special. (Pg 46)" Living in such a way that I am always attuned to my innermost desires is something wonderful, but it is also the correct way to live. It is nothing special, in the sense that it is most natural.

Sincerity and the Razor's Edge

Personally, perhaps the most fundamentally challenging aspect of Zen was understanding how I can apply this wonderful art into my day-to-day life. Initially living in such a manner seemed so unearthly, almost out place in the common world. I remember thinking to myself, "Well it sure would be easier to practice zazen regularly and be at peace, if I just lived in a Zen monastery for the rest of my life..." Sure, the concepts seem wonderfully intuitive and the practice, although hard at first, begins to flow more easily with time. But what about outside of zazen? What about outside of our classroom walls?

I began to wonder how I could take these things I have learned about myself and apply them in the most successful manner outside of the classroom. In essence, I wanted to be an enlightened person in this busy world; one of the few calmly aware in a turbulent sea of oblivious people.

In retrospect, that goal seems pompous and when I read it now it certainly sounds that way. I am not afraid to admit that my early intentions might certainly have been misinformed, but as our class progressed I began to see the beauty that Zen awareness and clarity can bring to a person's life, especially in the heat of day to day activities. I began to notice that just as zazen is dependent on sincere effort, so too is living a life of Zen. The effort need be almost more sincere because of the utter commotion of modern life, unlike the stillness found in zazen practice. For example, when I sit in zazen, it is easy for me to understand a past instance of unnecessary disdain. But when I am face to face with a person I feel I cannot respect, I must make a genuine effort to act in a respectful and appropriate manner, although I certainly might have an urge not to respond this way. Zazen becomes a guide for my actions in trying times like these when sincerity is crucial.

Joko Beck's *Everyday Zen* framed my understanding of practicing outside of our class in a more correct manner. "The problem with talking about 'enlightenment' is that our talk tends to create a picture of what it is- yet enlightenment is not a picture, but the shattering of all our pictures. And a shattered life isn't what we are hoping for (pg. 173)." Originally, I imagined enlightenment in this way; a perfect picture of peace, my life in a constant state of bliss. But Joko is quick to throw this picture out the window. Rather, the enlightened person lives on the "razor's edge," a rather eerie sounding notion at first glance.

The first step in walking the "razor's edge" is realizing we are upset, whether it be anger, jealousy, bitterness, or irritated. Certainly, a contemplative life is easier when life is going well from our perspective, but it is this inevitable discomfort that life brings which makes Zen harder. It clouds the clarity of our awareness and that is why practice is essential, in order to help us recognize ourselves more fully outside of practice. In that regard, life becomes a practice. Joko calls for us to embrace this "razor's edge":

"When we do zazen and begin to know our minds and our reactions, we begin to be aware that yes, we are upset. That's the first step, but it's not the razor's edge. We're still separate, but now we know it. How do we bring our separated life together? To walk the razor's edge is to do that... when we are experiencing nonverbally we are walking the razor's edge- we are the present moment (pg. 157)."

Walking the razor's edge calls for us to accept and understand these feelings of pain. It is against our nature to embrace pain, but separating ourselves from this natural discomfort only furthers the problem. Accepting these feelings and becoming immersed in the present moment of life is to be enlightened. "The paradox: only in walking the razor's edge, in experiencing the fear directly, can we know what it is to have no fear. (pg. 158)"

The eeriness of the "razor's edge" is pleasing after further understanding of the concept arises, because it is actually something that can be achieved, unlike some unrealistic perfect picture of peace. There is no person, or at least any that I know of, that has a life completely devoid of discomfort, sorrow, or pain. It is simply a natural condition of our connection with reality. If you did not know sorrow, you could not know happiness. It is our attempt to run away and detach ourselves from a sad or unpleasant situation that creates the most sorrow.

As I begin to understand this "edge" in relationship to my own personal life, I can take the awareness I find during zazen and incorporate it into my day to day activities. Of course, I am not perfect by any means. But my effort is sincere, and along with that sincerity comes a certain degree of clarity in my awareness. When I am stuck in situations that trigger anger or discomfort, I can identify those reactions more readily. I find joy in identifying things which might have bothered me in the past, and I encourage myself to remain connected and present.

For example, seeing an ex-girlfriend at a local bar truly bothered me in the past. I used to think "this is my space, my time, and you are seriously encroaching upon it." It bothered me immensely! But after deep contemplation, I can understand the pain I experience and embrace it. I can bring that understanding with me when I go places, and when I am triggered to be angry or hurt I remember not to separate myself from the present. I walk the edge and try to keep a smile on my face. The more I smile, the better I feel, knowing that I will not allow my pain to rule my Self.

In that regard, my practice becomes my life. Yongey Mingyur Rinpoche describes his version of walking the razor's edge in a similar matter: "Ultimately, happiness comes down to choosing between the discomfort of becoming aware of your mental afflictions and the discomfort of being ruled by them." Zen has shed a light on a truer, more real depiction of happiness. While that quotation might seem depressing to some, to me it is extremely gratifying. Understanding that I am not my mental afflictions, nor do I have to be controlled by them is an extremely liberating notion.

Just like Zen, the teachers I experienced this semester are extremely upfront. When I say teachers, I mean not only our professor Ms. Syverson, but also Joko Beck (whom we watched a documentary on called Nothing Special and all the other authors of the texts assigned. This upfront nature was not always what I expected or wanted to hear, but it was tremendously gratifying. My teachers did not beg me to believe something; rather, they called me to experiment for myself. This experimental nature of Zen is intellectually appealing, and unique in many ways. Enlightenment is not found in any book. Rather, our teachers pushed us to understand these concepts through transmission and experimentation. In the end, we can only see the truth for ourselves, though are teachers can guide us in the right direction. This is why I began to understand how sincere practice is so essential to progress when understanding Zen.

Surprisingly, Zen has truly taken a tight hold of my curiosity. Our course was beautifully constructed towards exploring this study in the best way possible. The meditation at the beginning of each class, the website that allows group comments and interaction, and the guidance of an experienced teacher brings the benefits of the study of Zen outside the classroom.

In other words, it becomes more of a class for living life to the fullest, rather than a class for achieving a certain grade. At the beginning of our semester, achieving a certain grade seemed almost easier than living life in accordance with my Zen studies. In fact, my grade in the course was at the forefront of my concern. Certainly, grades are important, but I know that with a continued and sincere effort in my zazen practice, living a life of Zen will be far more simple and beneficial than any grade. I only wish that everyone was lucky enough to experience the spiritually thrilling nature of Zen.

Harrison F. Bequette moved to Austin from Houston, Texas to study at the University of Texas. As a third year philosophy and rhetoric major, he plans to attend law school after his undergraduate graduation in 2012. Thus far, his collegiate experience has provided him with direction for his future and helped him understand his potential both academically and personally. Although his main focus is education, he is also interested in music, sports, and social networking.

On Your Mark, Get Set, Go
Jenny Anderson

I have learned two very important lessons from growing up with three older brothers: one, avoid at all costs being checked into the Smack Down Hotel, and two, when in doubt, run. Or perhaps it was Forrest Gump who taught me that. Nevertheless, one thing I do know for certain is that I've been given a gift: the ability and the passion to run. Even as a young girl, I used to tell my parents I had this craving and so they had no other choice but to take me to the wide-open park at the end of our street and let me run free. It had to have been quite amusing for them to watch this little girl leap out of the car and dart across the grassy field in just seconds, as if she hadn't seen the light of day in years. Running is just as much my outlet now as it was then. It's that temporary release from the tugging commitment, responsibility and obligation that I crave. It's the fleeting liberation from the unrealistically high expectations I set for myself that I crave. It's the ease in which I can so effortlessly slip into my most natural self that I crave.

I played soccer and ran track and field in high school. My favorite race was the 400 meter dash because my strong competitive spirit would kick into gear on the last reach—this is also one of the hardest races to run because it's a long sprint, and the timing on each curve has to piece together perfectly. The race was as physically draining as our grueling practices every single day, but nothing in comparison to my first practice of meditation. That fifteen minute visit alone inside my mind, in absolute stillness and silence, was one of the most mentally exhausting and challenging practices I've done—and it undeniably trumps the race. The two practices are very similar in that they both require commitment and practice every day. I didn't just decide to take up track one day and expect to run a sixty second 400 meter dash, nor did I expect to master meditation and attain enlightenment on the first day of class—although in my mind I had imagined mediation to be less challenging and more relaxing. In track and field I have to practice with my body; in Zen Buddhism, with my mind.

I must admit that my experience in this class has triggered and addressed many of the same uncertain and anxiously excited feelings that used to flicker in the pit of my stomach just moments before the starting gun would sound at a track and field event. The thoughts and feelings I've experienced during the three command start of a race parallel with my experiences from the beginning of this course, through the middle and to the end.

Runners take your mark...

I eagerly make my way over to the far outside lane, relieved at the misconception that in this lane I have a head start over the other runners.

It's September 8, 2010 and I am three class discussions, two fifteen minute periods of silence and one of five books into my study of Zen Buddhism. Walking into this class, I thought I was already ahead of the game with some insight into the practice from a book I read last summer by Elizabeth Gilbert called Eat Pray Love—but it didn't take long for me to realize that this book covered only the surface of an infinite ocean of inquiry and discovery. In Zen Buddhism, it's not the answer to the question that matters; it's about the question itself. Dr. Syverson once said, "In Zen, there is nothing to believe and everything to discover." But I'd be lying if I told you that I understood this on the first day.

In the beginning, I found Zen to be so straightforwardly simple that it was difficult. What I mean by that is the concepts are so basic that it is hard to accept them for what they are; it is almost impossible not to attach any unwritten meaning or perplexing interpretations to them. Our goal in the classroom is to broaden the understanding of our own minds and to free our curiosity that is otherwise limited and trapped behind the bars of a typical classroom. So if I know anything at all, it's that inquiry and an open mind will be the path to success in this course—which is funny because it was mostly curiosity that landed me here in the first place.

After reading only a few pages into the memoir of Gilbert's search for self-discovery through Italy, India and Indonesia, I was addicted. During my freshman year of college I studied abroad in Italy, so I could share her love and passion for the slow-paced Italian lifestyle and culture. But it wasn't until I read Gilbert's honest account of her experience with meditation in the Indian Ashram that I developed a curiosity for Zen Buddhism. Gilbert's experience was by no means a walk in the park, as she cleverly transcribed the ongoing battle between herself and her mind during meditation. I found myself completely captivated with her experiences, albeit her difficult and sometimes impossible attempts to sit still and not wrestle with the constant flow of thoughts. Or perhaps it was because of these struggles that I was drawn to her story. It is no wonder that I jumped at the opportunity to take a class called Non-argumentative Rhetoric in Zen—my curiosity can only simmer on the back burner for so long.

I do some quick last minute leg stretches and walk backwards into the starting blocks, my mind in a slight panic as I try to control the sudden rush of worries and what-if's: what if I false start; what if I trip and fall; what if I come in last place?

What I love most about the class so far is that it's an open curriculum—the class discussions stem from our own questions and inquiries; it will take whichever course we lead. When we are all comfortable in our seats, the meditation period begins with a bell that chimes—and I don't mean the kind of alarming bell that rings and immediately jerks you back to the reality of being stuck in a classroom, or jump starts your run to class so you can make it just before the professor closes the door. No, it's more of a smooth, comforting tone that calmly brings our attention into focus. The blinds are kept opened, the lights turned off—taking me back to one of my high school English classes; our teacher always used natural lighting in the classroom, as opposed to the headache-inducing, fluorescent lights—allowing our eyes and our minds and our bodies to simply relax. But, just because the setting is one of relaxation, doesn't mean that fifteen minutes of sitting in complete stillness and silence is simple, or even relaxing. Suddenly, my mind was as busy as it was in the starting blocks. For starters, what are you supposed to think of in order to keep yourself from thinking anything at all? How do you even begin to clear your mind of everyday thoughts, and then keep it clear for fifteen minutes? As soon as I could find a calm spot and settle in, questions would abruptly interrupt and charge my mind. What am I going to do after I graduate? Should I live here or there? When is the electric bill due? What time am I working tomorrow? My thoughts were wildly darting around as if I had just released 100 little bouncing balls from captivity—and the harder I tried to contain them, the more out of control they got.

It has become easier with in-class and outside of class practices as we've been learning new techniques and ways to practice mindful meditation. Only on the first day did I think meditation was supposed to be peaceful relaxation with a silent mind. On the contrary, we aren't necessarily supposed to void our mind of all thoughts but instead pay closer attention to them. In other words, I shouldn't be trying to neglect the negative thoughts or memories that keep pushing their way to the forefront of my mind. Instead, I'm supposed to be more aware of them in order to understand their meaning and let my mind rest. After all, they are there for a reason—they're trying to tell me something. It's just like when you ignore a problem in your life. The problem never really goes away; it just becomes buried within you, gradually growing stronger and stronger until the tiniest irritation sets it off. And often, that is when our anger is misplaced and directed at something or someone that doesn't have anything to do with the true problem itself. In my case, I tend to be a non-confrontational person and far too often I try to ignore the problems that cross my path, hoping they'll go away before I have to face them. They never do—and just as neglected, negative thoughts scream louder, all ignored problems grow stronger.

As far as my understanding of Zen Buddhism at this early point in the semester, awareness is the most important concept I have taken away from our class discussions and readings. In *Buddhism Plain and Simple,* teacher and ordained Zen priest Steven Hagen writes, "The point of Buddhism is to just see. That's all." The only way we will ever truly know ourselves, or anything else, is to experience it solely for ourselves. As I continued reading, I came across a Buddhist teaching that I love—and being the avid quote collector that I am, I've seen it once or twice before. Gautama, otherwise known as the Buddha, teaches this:

Don't believe me because you see me as your teacher. Don't believe me because others do. And don't believe anything because you've read it in a book, either. Don't put your faith in reports, or tradition, or hearsay, or the authority of religious leaders or texts. Don't rely on mere logic, or inference, or appearances, or speculation... Know for yourselves that certain things are unwholesome and wrong. And when you do, then give them up. And when you know for yourselves that certain things are wholesome and good, then accept them and follow them.

This class has inspired me to try and experience everything for myself, exactly as it is. I often worry too much about what other people think, and many times I am too quick to believe what other people tell me without listening to my own intuition. I find that when this happens, I often look back and wish I had been more questioning than accepting, realizing that what is right for one person will not always be right for everyone else, but I am the only person who knows what is right for me.

Awareness is the starting point for not only my understanding of Zen, but for my own mind. Up to this point in my life, I've never taken the time to dig deeper into my thoughts—to go beyond their manifestations and into their creation and significance. I have learned that the purpose of Zen Buddhism is to be enlightened, and to be enlightened is to be awake. While I haven't figured out exactly what that means yet, I know that with inquiry and practice, I'm headed down the right path.

Get set...

I settle into my starting position with my strongest foot in the front block and my fingers pressed hard against the starting line. I close my eyes and imagine every ounce of nervous anxiety transforming into positive energy.

I'm on the second starting command and halfway through the semester. Even though I am still a beginner Zen student, I've noticed a slight transition from my initial amateurish fascination with Zen Buddhism to a deeper, more informed curiosity of it.

When a runner accelerates out of the starting blocks, the most force is usually generated by the strongest foot, thus the runner's strongest foot should be placed in the front block. My coach used to line us up in practice with our backs toward him, and without telling us when, he would push each of us forward. Whichever foot we instinctively landed on would be the foot that we place in the front starting block. Most of the time I would psyche myself out when setting up my starting blocks and forget which foot goes where. I'd frantically keep switching my feet around because nothing would feel right. But, normally, my right foot felt most natural to land on. My left hand feels most natural to write with. My right arm feels most natural to carry trays of drinks at work with. My left foot and my right foot both feel natural to kick a soccer ball with. My left arm feels most natural to throw with. This is the easiest way for me to understand Buddha nature—to be as I am without being conscious of it—but it vanishes the moment I question it. Each and every one of us has Buddha nature. Everything from flowers to trees to rivers has Buddha nature; everything is Buddha nature. According to Shunryu Suzuki, author of *Zen Mind, Beginner's Mind*, "Buddha nature is our own original nature; we have it before we practice zazen and before we acknowledge it in terms of consciousness… If you want to understand it, you cannot understand it. When you give up trying to understand it, true understanding is always there." Do you see what I mean about it being so simple that it's difficult? It took many days of frustration for me to make any sense of this because it seems like nothing but one contradiction after another. From the beginning, my main goal, aside from mastering meditation— or even just getting through meditation, has been to attain enlightenment. Much of this can be accredited to Gilbert's attempt at describing the indescribable euphoric state of being "pulled through the wormhole of the Absolute" where she comes to understand "the workings of the universe." I mean, who wouldn't want to experience that? But I've gradually come to realize that this goal itself has been my setback all along. I've found that the more I learn about Zen, the more eager I become to attain enlightenment—and if there is anything you shouldn't be doing in Zen practice, it's that. Buddhism is not about trying to attain a goal, or anything else for that matter. My goal of reaching enlightenment will always hinder my ability to do so, so instead I try to maintain a youthful curiosity with no particular outcome to reach. Have you ever gone for a drive for no other reason than to just drive? I love the feeling of jumping in the car with no definite direction or destination in mind. I never know what I'll find along the way, but I don't have any expectations either. Thus, I can see the things I pass by for what they are, and not for what I expect them to be.

I have to finish in first place. I have to finish in first place. I have to finish in first place.

In one of our class discussions, Dr. Syverson brought up a very interesting point that keeps coming back to me. As students, it is so instilled in us that the goal of school is to achieve high grades. So we go to class, we take notes, we study and memorize the lesson for the mid-term, and once it's over, we disregard everything and shift our focus to the final. If the earned grade is low, we're upset, but not because we don't understand what was being taught; rather, we are upset because of the low grade itself. Now I'm not trying to downplay the importance of hard work and high marks. But, let me ask you this: are you even interested in what you're learning? Of course every college student knows that sometimes taking classes of no personal interest is inevitable, it's just part of the package if you want a degree. But here Dr. Syverson made another interesting point: If you maintain an open and curious mind, almost everything will be of interest to you. The problem is, we aren't actually learning the information because we are interested, we are pseudo-learning it for a good grade. My problem with school is that my laundry-list of goals has ultimately shriveled down to a narrow focus on the goal of the grade. Instead of taking the time to thoroughly learn the material and develop a genuine interest, I cram in and memorize as much as possible the night before a test. Many of the classes I've taken have served no value to me other than to fulfill a requirement, and unfortunately I've passed through them in a trance. If I could go back and change one thing, I wish I would have maintained an open mind throughout each and every one of my classes because I'm sure I could have found some real interest in topics that have slipped in one ear and out the other.

In other cases, Dr. Syverson explained that we should practice learning our triggers. Find out what triggers your appeal to something. In other words, find out what you like, and then simply pursue it. It's funny because every time I'm out shopping with my Mom, I always point out clothes with stripes. It never fails. "Oh I love this shirt," I'll say, and she'll laugh. I didn't realize for the longest time that it was the stripes that triggered my attraction to the item; I just knew that I liked the shirt itself (or the scarf, or the jacket, or the bag). It was never the stripes that first came to mind, although now it's very clear they were in fact triggering my attraction. On the other hand, I've also discovered there are certain negative triggers that irritate me and elicit an emotional response before I even realize what is truly upsetting me. I go about my days at such a hurried pace, and when something does not happen right the first time, instead of taking the time to think it through and try again more patiently, I instantaneously feel frustrated and defeated. By being both still and aware, I have been able to identify my triggers, thus allowing me to recognize when in fact I am being triggered— and just by being able to recognize this, I can step back and see exactly when I am creating unnecessary dissatisfaction for myself. What practicing Zen Buddhism has taught me is to be aware of my personal triggers, both positive and negative, in order to fully experience and understand the root of my merriment and misery.

My legs feel weak and my heart is beating uncontrollably— but my mind, my mind is calm.

Moving through the semester, I've seen a slight improvement in my ability to calm my mind during mediation. I can't jump into a clear mind at first, but by acknowledging each thought as it passes, I can slowly calm it down. Surprisingly, my thoughts need more attention than I ever would have guessed. One technique Dr. Syverson suggested for our meditation practice is to think to myself, "Okay, I'm having a thought" after every single thought. Try it. I realize it may seem strange to recognize your thoughts in this way—even creepy— but quite literally it makes you think about what you're thinking, and personally it settles down the active beehive of thoughts that resides in my mind. It's one thing to have a thought, but it's completely different to acknowledge and be aware of it. By following this technique, I have been able to learn personal thought patterns and recognize when these patterns occur in other situations in my life. For example, when I feel stressed out about something in particular, anxious thoughts repeat in my mind, moving in a swift but constant circle until I reach a breaking point. Because I've never attempted to understand what each thought was trying to tell me, it's like they freeze on repeat, growing louder and more demanding. I've learned how to listen to them, thus enabling me to recognize when I am repeating the same anxious thought—and now that I'm aware of this pattern that arises in stressful situations, I can control it before it controls me.

Somewhere along the line, I came across a paradox in Zen Buddhism that halted my understanding and ability to move forward. Going back to the beginning of this section, I quoted Suzuki's take on understanding Buddha nature, "When you give up trying to understand it, true understanding is always there." If I read and studied this hard enough I could usually make sense of it, yet somehow I always found myself coming back to it, perplexed. The statement conflicts with my practical way of thinking. I'm a Christian, but in the back of my mind I can't help but unfold doubt. I struggle with religion because it forces me to abandon my logical reasoning for faith, and I have a hard time grasping things I can't make sense of, or see for myself. And most of the time, I do remain true to my faith, but just as I keep coming back to that statement, I keep coming back to religion. As I understand it, the whole point of Zen Buddhism is to be aware of everything. So when we ask a question, sometimes the response is simply, "Good question. Be curious about that." But my problem is this: if we are trying to arouse this infinite sense of curiosity, how come we shouldn't try to understand Buddha nature? The moment we even attempt to understand it, our understanding vanishes. If I'm curious about it, it means that I want to understand it, but if I try to understand it, I simply never will. I was lost as to how I could simultaneously let go of trying to understand this concept while still maintaining a curiosity of it. It's like an infinite sense of wonder without ever receiving an answer.

But, as I said before, Zen Buddhism has nothing to do with the answer, and everything to do with the question. Japanese Zen master Dogen Zenji once said, "To study the [Buddha] Way is to study the self. To study the self is to forget the self. To forget the self is to be enlightened by all things of the universe." The ability to fully grasp this concept and master it is, to me, the ultimate goal in attaining inner peace and restfulness, i.e. being totally comfortable with who I am, where I am and where I am going.

Go!

I've done everything I can to prepare up to this point. All I can do now is be fully in this moment and run this race—nothing more and nothing less.

As I near the end of the semester, I've noticed yet another transition in my mind: I'm realizing, slowly but surely, that I have full control of my thoughts and happiness. My realization of this idea has come largely from the fourth book we were assigned, called *Buddha's Brain* by Rick Hanson and Richard Mendius. This book provided us with a completely different take on Buddhism: the relationship between science and contemplative practice and meditation. It teaches readers about the scientific workings of our minds, and how we can shape our own brains to create happier and more fulfilling lives. I found it very helpful for my understanding because of its tangibility and practicality. Furthermore, it provides us with a different outlook that allows us to connect and compare our own understandings from the first three books with the science from *Buddha's Brain*.

This book teaches us that we can use our thoughts to change our brains, and I find comfort in knowing that we have control over this. There are many things outside of our control, but we can choose our thoughts and the ways in which we deal with the cards that we're dealt. In all honesty, one of the main reasons I liked this book so much is because it closely relates with my life at this point, and it has taught me that I don't have to let unfortunate circumstances get the best of me. This past summer, my boyfriend and I broke up after two years. It was a very difficult time and even knowing I'm young and have my whole life ahead of me didn't make the situation any easier or less hurtful. I'd like to think that I'm a strong and independent young woman, but sometimes it feels impossible not to let weakness triumph my strength.

In Chapter 4 of *Buddha's Brain*, called "Taking in the Good," Hanson and Mendius explain that our experiences sculpt our brains, thus shaping our minds. While "some of the results can be explicitly recalled: This is what I did last summer; that is how I felt when I was in love... most of the shaping of your mind remains forever unconscious." This is our implicit memory, which includes our "expectations, models of relationships, emotional tendencies, and general outlook... it establishes the interior landscape of your mind." While The Wise Effort section of Buddhism's Noble Eightfold Path, which paraphrased from *Buddha's Brain*, says "you should create, preserve, and increase beneficial implicit memories, and prevent, eliminate, or decrease harmful ones," our brains are unfortunately wired with a negativity bias that preferentially registers and recalls negative experiences more so than the positive ones. The way I see it, I have to work harder to foster the positive experiences in my life in order for them to permanently live within me. As if life isn't already unfair enough, right?

There is a silver lining. The first step to fixing a problem or changing a bad a habit is to first be made aware of it. So, the advantage to learning the negativity bias is the understanding that we can change it by using our minds to change our brains. In other words, we can train our minds to recollect positive experiences over the negative ones—and this book offers everyday practices to help do so. One way to gradually replace negative implicit memories with positive ones is to consciously bring the positive aspects of the experience to the front of your mind while simultaneously placing the negative aspects in the back. Here's an excerpt for you to think about from *Buddha's Brain*: "Imagine that the positive contents of your awareness are sinking down into old wounds, soothing chafed and bruised places like a warm golden salve, filing up hollows, slowly replacing negative feelings and beliefs with positive ones." I paused when I came across this passage, re-read it, and then closed my eyes and visualized it. The rich imagery expressed in that sentence immediately brought a calming sense of security to my mind, as I mindfully replaced the emptiness in my heart with the love of my friends and family.

The first question on a take-home quiz from Dy. Syverson asked us, "What would make this course the most profoundly transformational, challenging, and enjoyable experience of your life?" The most important part of my answer to that question was, "I will take out from this course everything that I put into it"—and on a deeper level, this extends far beyond the classroom. With anything I do, I have to put in effort in order to see adequate results, and so I've always carried on thinking the harder I work the greater results I will see and the happier I will become. But here is where I've noticed the most significant shift in my understanding of Zen Buddhism in relation to my own life: my focus now isn't necessarily to push myself to my utmost ability in order to achieve perfect results. Alternatively, my focus has shifted to a desire to be genuinely present and awake in every passing moment. I want to be awake to each lesson that my professors teach me and to every word of wisdom and advice that is passed down to me. I want to be awake to any difficulty and every accomplishment that my friends and family reveal to me. I want to be awake to everything I do, every noise I hear, scent I smell and flavor I taste. I want to be awake to every image I see and object I touch, because only with this enlightenment will I experience the ever-changing world around me. If I can ever reach this level of enlightenment, then I will have achieved something far greater than I ever set out to accomplish. I have been made aware of a whole new approach to life, and although the class has come to an end, my race has only just begun.

Jenny Anderson is a senior Rhetoric and Writing major, with a minor in Communications. After graduation, she plans to pursue a career in Public Relations. Jenny was born and raised in Vancouver, Canada, but has lived in Texas for eleven years now. She has a strong passion for travel and is always open to trying different things and meeting new people.

My Journey of Understanding Zen

Valerie Stockton

The First Noble Truth

To begin my learning and to get a good idea of the basics of Zen, I decided to focus on the Four Noble Truths. They seemed to be the cornerstones of the philosophy. I read that the first of the Noble Truths is that "human life is characterized by dissatisfaction." (Hagen, *Buddhism Plain and Simple*) This struck me as very fatalistic. I had heard that one of the most prominent critiques of Zen philosophy is its fatalistic attitude. Do humans really spend their wholes lives dissatisfied? I've had my fair share of disappointments, who hasn't? But I do not believe that my life is characterized by my disappointments. This word "dissatisfaction" struck me as inappropriate for the true meaning behind this first Noble Truth. Reading further into Hagen's book I discovered that he too believes that dissatisfaction is not entirely accurate. The term that the Buddha first ascribed to this noble truth, dukkha, is not one that is easily translated. Hagen says it is analogous to the idea of a "wheel out of kilter." This I could understand. It is not that our lives are fraught with dissatisfaction and disappointment. It is more that our lives are not smooth sailing, something is out of alignment.

Professor Syverson helped me understand this with greater clarity by explaining that the first noble truth more accurately means that "no human life can be lived without encountering any suffering." This does not sound as fatalistic as I first felt about Zen. This sounds more like common sense. Life will undoubtedly encounter dissatisfaction or suffering because we are not in control of what happens. We can only control how we respond in life.

I came from an existentialist point of view when I began this course. The previous year, I took a class on existentialist philosophy and I found it to be truly profound. Camus' ideas of Absurdism are what I found most inspiring. As he explains in "The Myth of Sisyphus," absurdity is a confrontation with man's desire for significance and meaning, and the meaning-lessness of the universe. This is the idea that came to mind when I read about the first Noble Truth. So instead of saying that life is characterized by dissatisfaction, I would say that it is characterized by absurdity. We don't always get what we want. We sometimes experience pain. We cannot ignore pain or hope that it will go away, because it won't. These are the ideas of both Zen and existentialism. I find it oddly comforting to believe that life is absurd. It is not supposed to make sense. But that in itself is how life does make sense to me. I expect absurdity. I expect life to be out of kilter. This may then sound like it negates the absurdity, which I suppose it does. I believe that may be what Camus meant for us to do by embracing the absurdity. If we learn to expect the unexpected, it is no longer unexpected. Life is vast and complicated and the universe is completely beyond my control. So how could it be possible for everyone's expecta-tions and desires to be fulfilled all of the time? I am not going to be satisfied 100 percent of the time. No one is. It wouldn't make sense.

The Second Noble Truth

Zen and Absurdism seemed to have different explanations about why life is absurd or out of kilter. I tried at first to deter-mine which I prefer or how I might marry the two ideas. Camus believes that we are faced with absurdity when we try to define ourselves, our life, in a meaningless world. This simply means that there are no absolutes. According to Zen philosophy and the Second Noble Truth, our lives are out of kilter because we have wants and cravings. We crave and cling to transient things to ignore our real problem of confusion.

After spending more time in class and hearing responses from Professor Syverson and other students, I believe I may have misunderstood this idea. Professor Syverson explained that the situation is actually the other way around from the way I just explained it. The craving and desires come up with encountering suffering and dissatisfaction. I first believed that suffering came from wanting. So knowing that they come up together, I now understand thirst to be what we develop in our search to alleviate the suffering. It is a way of avoiding what really makes us suffer. If I am sad because my boyfriend just broke up with me I may want another boyfriend so I won't be sad about the break up. I focus my attention on finding another guy. I decide that having another boyfriend will make me happy again. This craving and thirst will not take away my suffering. It is just how I distract myself from my sadness. If I were instead to allow myself to be sad about the break up I would be able to overcome it. When faced with suffering, we need to allow ourselves to feel the suffering. We need to look at it and look at ourselves. What is making us suffer? Why do we feel this way? What do I want to do about it? By asking ourselves these questions and by noticing the real issue we can effectively overcome the suffering. Distracting ourselves with cravings will only prolong it.

I understand what Camus means by his explanation of Absurdism. When we try to define ourselves by absolutes it means that what applies to us always applies to us as well as everyone else. This is impossible. We are changing, the world around us is changing, and therefore the way we live must change. We are all different so the way we live is not going to work for everyone else. But if we try to force such an absolute, absurdity rears its ugly head. Trying to force absolutes is what leads to hatred, fighting, and war. However, Zen teachers believe that when we forget about or ignore the here and now, the real situation, we will never be able to attain satisfaction. We ignore our real situation by wanting things that we think will make us happy and by clinging to the goods times, trying to make them come back. I do believe that objects are not what will make us truly happy. We might think they will but it is only fleeting happiness.

Every Christmas or birthday I used to try to come up with the gifts that would make me happy for the rest of the year. What can my family give me that will take away my unhappiness? It never worked. I realized that there is no object that will make be forever happy. But is it wrong to want things? I have desires for trivial things and they make me happy. I know it is fleeting happiness but it is fun. Even in those temporary moments I am happy and having fun. Is it wrong to want things for those few moments of happiness? I recognize that I cannot control when these moments occur just as I cannot control when bad moments occur. These are the worries that I first encountered when I began learning about Zen teachings.

I see now that these worries are misguided. Zen teachers are not asking us to forgo all happiness and desires. My first impression of Zen was that of a self-sacrificing practice. It seemed to me like followers were expected to abide by strict rules of discipline. Meditation was supposed to be uncomfortable. My initial interpretation of Zen teachings was that emotions were wrong, especially happiness. My initial misinterpretation of the first noble truth greatly contributed to further confusion. When I initially thought that it was saying that human life is characterized by suffering, I took that to mean that if there is happiness that it was fleeting and irrelevant. I thought in mediation we were supposed to focus on the suffering. This misguided idea really turned me off of Zen. However, after discussions in class and notes from Professor Syverson I see now that I greatly misunderstood. There is suffering in life, that is unavoidable, but human life is not characterized by it. Zen teachers are not trying to teach us not to feel. We are supposed to feel things. It is good to feel things. We are supposed to allow emotion and observe it to understand it. Zen teachings mean for us to not fight against our emotions, especially during times of suffering. We also need not feel ashamed for or disregard our happiness.

Happiness is just as unavoidable as suffering. The only difference is that we tend to cling to the happiness and reject the suffering. This is what Zen teaches against. We should not cling to anything. Nor should we reject anything we feel.

Once in class, someone asked Professor Syverson about Cognitive Behavioral Therapy, (CBT). She seemed to think it quite ineffective. The idea behind CBT is that we have an unhealthy thought that needs to be replaced with a new thought. Professor Syverson believes this is unhealthy and unhelpful. In few cases does this solve the real problem. The more energy you put into trying to get rid of the negative thoughts, the stronger they grow. My belief now is that meditation could be much more effective for me and for others who have found CBT to be unhelpful. Meditation requires us to look at the thought instead of ignore it or replace it. If we can see the unhealthy thought, observe it for a while, think about it, and feel about it, we can come to understand it better. Once we understand it, we will know why it is there. We can then embrace it as a part of ourselves. We can then also decide how we want to handle the unhealthy thought. Once we've had to chance to look at it we may see that the thought, we see that it is not unhealthy but that our emotional reaction was inappropriate.

This is what I feel is the most important and significant lesson I have learned from Zen teachings. I should accept my thoughts and the way I am. I have a story for each thought that adds to the larger story that is me. Each thought and event in my life is a part of me and I should not try to change or replace them. So desires and happiness are ok and accepted by Zen practice. They are seen for what they are. If they become a source of suffering, we can recognize how that suffering came about. What Zen tries to teach us are the skills to find how best to handle our thoughts and desires.

It is ok to want and enjoy things. What is important is to not place unnecessary significance and importance on these desires. I can be happy without getting the things I want and getting the things I want will not take away my suffering. As long as I am aware of this, I will have a healthy approach to wanting things.

According to Camus, recognizing that I can't control or make sense of the way things are is my encounter with the absurd. According to Zen philosophy, realizing the importance of the here and now and real situation is seeing. So once we have reached these steps we can work on combating our dissatisfaction or out of kilter feelings. But how?

The Third Noble Truth

I understand the existentialist answer to this question. From my class on Existentialism, I learned of two options for when we have encountered the absurd. Suicide is the acceptance that life has no meaning so is not worth living. This is the wrong choice to make according to the existentialists. This is not living fully engaged. It is not living at all. What Camus believes one should do is accept and embrace the absurd condition. To live without absolutes give us freedom to define our lives subjectively and not objectively.

The third of the Noble Truths of Zen philosophy says that cessation of the out of kilter life is possible. What I did not understand at the beginning of this class was the Zen way of achieving this. What I have figured out with the help of Professor Syverson is that I need only to pay attention to what is going on. If I observe the moment for what it is I will not feel so out of kilter. I will discover how to live with the out of kilter way, thus negating its effect.

Hagen's book mentions "less desire" and "forgetting the self." After reading this, I understood forgetting the self. I do not live alone. I live in a world with and endless number of other living creatures. My actions and decisions should be tailored to take them into account. I should do things to help the world and its inhabitants. What I did not understand was less desire. Desire is a good driving force as long as it is not the only driving force and as long as we know that not all desires will be fulfilled. So what is the healthy Zen way of having less desire?

As I have mentioned, Zen practice does not teach us to get rid of desire. The phrase "less desire" is a misnomer and misleading. Zen teachings allow for desire as long as we recognize it for what it is and do not let ourselves be consumed by it.

The Fourth Noble Truth

The fourth Noble Truth is an eight-fold path to bringing about the cessation of suffering, of the out of kilter life. Does this mean that suffering and pain actually go away? I have always believed that pain is an inevitable part of life that we must experience to learn. I now understand this to be the first Noble Truth. I hope by the end of this course to find greater clarity about the fourth Noble Truth and the eight-fold path.

I feel as though I did not gain greater clarity of understanding about the fourth Noble truth, specifically. I am still unfamiliar with the eight-fold path. However, even though I do not understand the specific terms included in this fourth Noble Truth, I believe that the understanding I've gained of Zen practice in general will help me appreciate the eight-fold path when I read more on it in the future.

Meditation

The greatest struggle I have had with Zen philosophy is with meditation. Every class we start with 15 minutes of silent, still meditation. We are supposed to relax and observe our thoughts. However, when I sit in silence I can't relax. My mind races and I get overwhelmed by everything that is running through my head. It is too much all at once. My body begins to feel tense. Questions and worries keep popping into my head. What is work going to be like today? Am I doing a good job at my other job? Will I have time to do my homework tonight? What am I going to write about for my English paper? Why do I have this song stuck in my head? Am I swaying to the music? Do I look as uncomfortable as I feel? My jaw feels tight. My eyes can no longer remain still. I found myself searching the room to see if anyone has noticed my turmoil. Of course they have not because it is all in my head. It is foolish to be worried about what the other people in the room might have noticed or thought. Most of my worries are foolish and irrational or it is just foolish to be worrying about them all at once. I actually have rational responses to most of my worries. Work is probably going to be slow but if it's busy I can handle it. If I wasn't doing a good job at my other job they would've told me. If I don't get to my homework tonight I still have tomorrow. I have over a month to write my English paper. I will think of something to write about but I don't need to solve that problem right now. If this song is stuck in my head I must at least subconsciously enjoy it so I should go download it this evening. Who cares if I'm swaying? Everyone else is meditating so they probably won't notice and why should I care if they do?

What I didn't understand at the beginning of my practice is that meditation is not about relaxing. It is simply about noticing, observing the present moment. So that is exactly what I was doing. I noticed how I felt physically. I noticed what thoughts were in my head. What I was doing wrong was clinging to the idea of relaxing. I had it stuck in my head that that was what I supposed to be doing, so I tried to force it when it didn't happen naturally. This ended up only creating stress and tension and ultimately exhausting me.

When I am already worked up and agitated there is nothing I can do to calm myself. At least that is how I have felt in the past. What I craved was a distraction. But this would do me no good. What I needed something to bring me back to the moment, the here and now. This is what Zen philosophy says we are supposed to be focused on. By doing this I can see that my worries and emotions are constructed in my mind and I can control how I feel. I can choose to not feel stressed or tense. I can choose to be calm.

I think that I was not able to relax during silent meditation because there is nothing going on in the room when we meditate. There is nothing for me to ignore. This doesn't really make sense when I try to explain it. I just notice that if I am watching a movie or TV I have a much easier time of "zoning out" and not focusing on anything around me, including whatever it was that I was watching. "Zoning out" is not the appropriate phrase. That is a trance which is unhealthy. At the time, that was the best way I knew how to describe what I was going through. I see now that it is more that I can become emotionally detached from my thoughts. This isn't entirely accurate either because I do feel emotion; they are just usually positive ones. I can observe what I am thinking without turning them into anxiety inducing worries. By paying attention in this way, I have greater control of how I choose to act on these thoughts. It works the same way when there is loud music playing. When I drive I always play music and it is usually quite loud. This is when I find myself relaxing and letting go of anything stressful. I can think about all the different things I have to do without getting overwhelmed. I'm sure there is some explanation for this. I just don't know what that is. I am trying to find a way to make the meditation we do in class produce the same relaxation but as of now, I have been unsuccessful.

My Life, Zen Teachings, and My Work at The House of Torment

Recently I was hired as an actor at the haunted house in Austin, The House of Torment. One night, I was working in my scene. It was really slow so there were big gaps between each group. My room was very dark with strobe lights and loud blaring music. I usually paced around the room, practicing my scary walk. A girl from the next room came over and asked me what I was thinking about while I did all that. I told her I was practicing what would look creepy. As I continued pacing I noticed that I wasn't really focused on anything at all. I was not planning ahead all of my commitments, I was not regretting anything dumb I might have done earlier. I was simply there, observing all that was going on around me. Any thoughts that I did have, were not angry or sad or anxious. They really were just thoughts.

What I seem to have discovered is that my mind always needs a distraction from my worries for me to be calm. I think that is why I keep myself so busy. I work at a shoe store. I also work at a haunted house. I am a full time student. I am a student teacher. I volunteer at the Austin Wildlife Rescue Center. I work in the nursery at my church. I am on the vestry with my church.

I am almost constantly doing one of these activities and as long as that is so I am calm. But as soon as I have a break and free time that I should be able to enjoy, my mind falls apart. People who hear voices wear headphones to drown them out with loud music. I think my worries act as my voices in my head and I ignore them by distracting myself with activity. However, all this activity adds to my worries. I never get that chance to unwind and relax so when that time does present itself, I don't know how to use it.

My hope was that Zen philosophy would help me to relax. I have tried to visualize breathing as Suzuki describes it in his book, *Zen Mind, Beginner's Mind*. I try to visualize myself as a swinging door that connects the outer world and my inner world. We are not separate. We are one. The world is not out to get me because I am the world. This is an interesting mantra to take but it has yet to be useful when I am in the midst of an anxiety overload.

I tend to have difficulty falling asleep. This usually leads to extreme frustration and anger. One night I was trying to sleep and I couldn't seem to ignore the sound of my dad watching TV downstairs and the light from downstairs coming into my room. I was getting angrier and angrier so I tried focusing on something else. I tried to focus on breathing and to calm my mind as described in our books. It didn't work, but I think that it is something to continue practicing. I am not very good about relaxing an already agitated mind. I need help to do this. My hope has been that as I learn more about Zen practice I will find ways to successfully calm my agitated mind.

My dad and I were talking once and he told me about his method for dealing with overwhelming stress. When he is feeling overwhelmed he stops what he is doing and pretends that he is a tourist. He looks around wherever he is as if he is seeing it for the first time and it is all there for him, like in a hotel room. He says this helps him focus on and experience the here and now without feeling the stress.

When I began working at the House of Torment over the Halloween season, I was really nervous on my drive there. My heart would beat quickly and my stomach tightened. I kept worrying about what I might do wrong or whether or not the managers liked what I was doing. After a while working there, my feeling of nervousness became excitement. The physical sensations were still the same and my thoughts were still the same. I wanted to make sure I didn't make any mistakes and I wanted to impress my managers. My emotional response to these thoughts and sensations was the only thing that had changed. I was no longer feeling sad or scared about not doing a good job. I was happy and proud to be working there.

This seems to be exactly what Zen philosophy is teaching us to notice. My understanding is that we are to be in the moment and observe that moment. What I have been taught is that if we take a fresh look at what is around us and only what is around us then the Truth will become clear. Our actions will become clear. We will see what to do, or what not to do. There is no right or wrong. There is only what the moment has provided for us. Truly seeing the reality of the here and now means that we will do something that by our traditional standards of right and wrong will be the right choice. We cannot cause harm to ourselves or others unless we are ignoring the true reality of the moment. Seeing the moment means that we will see harm our actions will do. So we will not take that course. This is what I have taken from the Zen teachings.

I find it comforting to think that there is no right choice or a wrong choice. Not in the sense of good or evil but in the sense of what I should do or should not do. So when I am feeling stressed out about what to do next or what to do in the future, it is potentially comforting to know that there is no wrong decision. When that moment presents itself, I will observe the facticity of it and makes my decision then. Once made, new moments with new decision will present themselves. Life is not a "choose your own adventure book." I don't make a decision and then run out of options. There will always be more moments and more decisions to make.

When I was hired at House of Torment, I needed to be up there almost every evening for training. After one day of training a few of us were talking with one of the managers who has been doing this for a while. He told us that he used to be a field engineer for some company. It was steady job with a reliable paycheck, but he was miserably bored. It was unsatisfying. So he quit and he now works full time with House of Torment. He took a pay cut and works irregular hours and shifts but he is happy and satisfied.

I believe he had a moment where he was faced with a decision. At that moment he was unhappy with his life. His steady job was helpful for the future and ensuring security but he was not satisfied. So he quit and found a job that he loves. Many would look at this and say that he made the wrong decision. But according to Zen philosophy there is no wrong. He made a decision about what to do and what not to do anymore. He is happy now. He is not causing harm to himself or anyone else. So for him, this was the right decision. He is now living in the moment and enjoying it. This choice is one I admire and I would love to have the courage to do that. I do wonder though about Zen philosophy and planning for the future. Is it not harmful to always be in the moment? I think my misunderstanding here is that when we plan for the future we are living in the future. We are living for the future in the present moment. What I need to be careful about is clinging to the plans I make. I can make plans and this will set out a direction that my life will take, but things change. I must be willing to change too. I should not use my plan as an exact set of instructions for my life but more as a guide.

Concluding Thoughts

My worries and anxiety tend to have a lot to do with the future and decisions I will have to make one day. I am rarely living in the moment unless distracted by some activity that is very demanding of me. At those times, I have no choice but to live in the moment. I want to find a way to live in the here and now by choice. I want to find a way to calm my worries about the future. I believe that finding a way to successfully meditate will help me to do so. But I am concerned about pulling too far away from thoughts of the future. How does Zen account for this? I have learned that by properly living in the moment I can still plan for the future. There are decisions I can make and things I can do now that will set a course for me for the future. I should choose to focus on the present and the decisions at hand. Doing a good job now will help take care of the future. I have very little control over what is going to happen and more control over the here and now. So I should work on that and by making the best decisions for me in the present, an appropriate future will unfold. I still have so much to learn and I am finding so many more question as I continue learning. But I am enjoying what I discover along the way. I hope that I will soon find answers to some of these questions so that I can find away to be calm and in the moment.

Valerie Stockton is a third year student at the University of Texas at Austin. She is doubling majoring in English and Rhetoric and Writing with a minor in Mathematics. She hopes to be a writer of short stories and novels but would also enjoy writing for a magazine or newspaper. Valerie has spent most of her life in Texas with only a brief time spent in Massachusetts while her dad finished his masters in Theology at Harvard University. Valerie would love to follow in her father's footsteps and study at Harvard for her graduate degree.

Zen and its Correlates

Aaron Walther

Part 1: An Impersonal First Glance

> The first image he told me about was of three children on a
> road in Iceland in 1965. He said that, for him, it was the image
> of happiness, and that he had tried a number of times to link it
> to other images; but it had never worked. He wrote me, 'One
> day I'll have to put it all alone at the beginning of a film with a
> long piece of black liter. If they don't see happiness in the film,
> at least they'll see the black.'
> Sunless, 1983

This quote possesses a certain staying power that I cannot put
my finger on, but I believe that it reflects Zen well. I have heard a
number of times now that contradiction and haikus play a part in
Zen rhetoric, but these two factors alone could not suffice. Thus
far, my impression of this rhetorical form is something of the
following sort: it is evocative and non-argumentative. A large
part of me wishes to fight against the validity of the inexplicably
evocative. The world that I know is causal, graspable by the
human intellect; and yet a large part of me also thinks that this
is the proper mode to accept. It argues more effectively than
do any syllogisms, for I think that the most effective rhetorical
strategy makes the audience feel as though they have arrived at

a conclusion by their own volition.

I have read a number of essays by philosopher Alan Watts, which seem to relate to Zen practice. The idea of inseparability plays a large part in a call for non-violence; for if all is fundamentally one, then if I choose to shoot somebody, I'm really choosing to shoot myself! If I decide to blow a hole in the earth, then I'm really deciding to blow a hole in myself! Have we not all emerged from the dust of this earth? The issue of identity, according to Watts, is further problematized by the ways in which we use our everyday language. When I say, "My head hurts," it is as if I were implying that my head were something separate from myself, that I own my head as if it were my property. It's not my head that hurts; it's me! The same applies for "my hands," "my feet," and so on. We're so linguistically predisposed to think in this way that it's impossible to get around it. Perhaps these are sentiments shared by Zen thinkers.

Buddhism, Plain and Simple by Steve Hagen certainly struck me as interesting. The buddha-dharma, or "the teaching of the awakened," seems to primarily be a way of dealing with existential anguish, or the pain of trying to find meaning from a world in which no meaning is given. Meditation, as a means of observing the path one treads upon, seems like it could yields nothing but positive results at first glance, given a healthily functioning mind. The little experience I have had of it so far has led to recognition of the personal absurdities[1] present in my life, and if I continue I feel as though I might be able to get a firmer handle on these. In attempting to ameliorate this existential anguish we are all born with, though, whether meditation is the correct course of action is unclear. The Zen methodology seems to prescribe the solution of being present, but is this solution really ideal? Is it not the case that Zen teaches the acceptance of meaninglessness as inevitable? For now, at least, I think that there are different and more effective ways to remedy it.

Why not make your own meaning in the world? Manifesting

---

1.   Albert Camus coined this term, referring to situations in which one realizes the absurdity of life. This could be the fact that we get up every day and do the same things only to realize years later that we've lost who we once felt we were.

the importance in my life has generally led to positive results that could correlate with Zen. To this, I think that the Zen responder might say something of the following sort: "When applying one's own meaning to the world, the search to actualize this meaning will inevitably yield defeat and therefore suffering. When one's eyes are fixed on the future they are not situated in the present." If my understanding is correct, then this Zen outlook on life confuses me. How can we not have expectations? "The sweet ain't as sweet unless you tasted the bitter in life," a wise man once told me.

"Right intention," as described by Hagen, seems to give rise to a stagnant life, a life in which the path is directed by the world you live in and not yourself. If you have a mind that doesn't lean in the least, then will you not be a slave to your own compulsions and environment? If you don't have any intention in the things that you do, then you might as well be a walking automaton. Part of this human experience I have come to know is looking into the future and picking a proper path upon which you at least attempt to tread. This leads me to the question, "What does a Zen thinker suppose in the realm of free will?" Perhaps he would say something to the extent of, "there is no subject of which a will can belong," but that muddles my understanding even further. How is it the case that the self does not exist?

I am curious to delve further into the Zen frame of mind. It possesses a certain mystique that I wish to embrace, at least for a little while. It's interesting to contrast the study of Zen with my concurrent study of philosophical metaphysics, as the two are so diametrically opposed. Whereas the one is content with a dynamic reality, the other wishes to pinpoint the what, how, why, wherein, what-have-you of everything. As far as this goes, I certainly belong to the former school of thought. Life is just what it is; it is thus, as Hagen often describes it.

Part 2: A Personal Revelation Regarding Form

The previous section was written as not a student of Zen practice, but rather as an outsider looking into the supposed tenets it espoused. Having sat through multiple hours of inquiry, meditation, and personal interpretation of Zen Buddhism, I now align Zen more congruently with my lifestyle than I did at the beginning of this search. Oddly enough, the perception of this alignment emerges mostly from the Zen teaching that I previously contended most with. I have been living my life with "right intention" without realizing it.

Before delving into a discussion of right intention, I must point out that I may have been disingenuous by leaving out the extent of my interactions with meditation before this search. For a while, I merely tried off and on to get into the meditative mindset, but the preponderance of methods available online simply overwhelmed me. This past winter, though, I found a series of audio recordings specifically designed to ease the mind into a meditative state by way of brain-wave entrainment. I religiously listened to various thirty minute recordings daily for six months straight, and during that time some major shifts in my life occurred. I began to live more in accordance with right intention during this time.

Living a life of right intention is the difference between being guided by aspiration rather than expectation. As Joko Beck puts it in *Everyday Zen*, "Aspiration, in the context of practice, is nothing but our own true nature seeking to realize and express itself." Additionally, Hagen has this to say, "...right intention is simply the intention to come back to this moment, to just be present with no ideas of gaining whatsoever." These quotes together clarify the idea of right intention for me. It's about letting our curiosity guide us on our life's path without worrying where the path will take us, discovering our own true nature as we go along.

In the fall preceding that period of stimulated meditation I began working for the Texas Travesty, the official humor publication of the University of Texas. I had little success in the publication due to a combination of personal health issues and an attitude that can be summarized as, "Well, I can go work on the current issue, but that won't really get me anywhere in the long run. I had better do homework instead." Although I was genuinely interested in getting an article of mine published,

I didn't feel that the organization had any real-world worth. Something clicked inside of me, though, during the winter of that year. I began to see the publication as not a means to some end, but rather as an outlet for expressing myself and developing what I thought might be my true nature.

At the same time, I began to consider seriously pursuing a career in acting. I had helped some friends of mine in the film department out on some video projects beforehand with the same attitude as the one I had approached with the Travesty. Suddenly, though, I saw the opportunity not to make a career but to develop myself in a craft that I legitimately enjoyed. The aspiration to discover my true nature continued to manifest.

I followed down these two paths with passionate rigor throughout the spring and into the summer. I laughed to myself occasionally at the thought of actually doing what I was, but continued down them regardless, satisfied to grow in these paths I used to think of as fruitless and without merit. Much to my surprise, the two paths converged when I was promoted to Media Editor of the Travesty. The job of creating regular online sketch comedy videos for the Travesty created a very exciting challenge for me, but I had to make an unfortunate choice at this time.

I was following respective paths of writing and acting; and, although they happened to converge, they still had their different directions. Over the summer I had gotten an acting agent and a writing job for a local music review site. I had to choose between attending a renowned local acting workshop that my agent frequently attended and weekly Travesty staff meetings. My agent called me a "dumbass" for even considering to drop out of the workshop because of the potential I showed, and a good friend of mine told me that I needed to do "what was best for my future." I toiled internally for two weeks, wondering what the "right" decision was and what I "should" do.

If I wanted to take the route that most likely would lead to success, then I would have stayed in the acting workshop; but that didn't satisfy my curiosity in the same way that holding full creative control over the production of comedy did. I chose to fully devote my time to the Travesty's position, led by an aspiration to discover my true nature as opposed to an expectation to become successful by conventional means. As far as I can tell, this is right intention. Had I been governed by ideas of gaining, I certainly would have not gone in this direction.

I am inclined to think that my meditative time during this period has catalyzed these events, at least in part. I espouse this more confidently now that I am formally learning what it is to truly meditate; it is not to sit and actively vanquish thought but rather to truly live in the moment, nothing more. I have likewise come to see the importance of both meditating under the guidance of a teacher and reading texts like those assigned for this class. Whereas before I learned that meditation helps me live life more authentically, now I have learned why this is the case, which invigorates my affinity for practice all the more. For example, I see that having right intention alone did not produce the decision I went with. In order to see the opportunity for what it really was I had to adopt "right view," another one of the aspects of the eightfold path.

Hagen presents an interesting photograph of a cow on pg. 28 of *Buddhism Plain and Simple* that's manipulated in such a way that some people have a very difficult time seeing the image for what it really is. Personally, I still don't fully see the image, but seeing the image is not the point. It is rather a representation of the complex, dynamic reality that sits in front of us all, requiring real personal reflection and perpetual presence in the moment to actively engage in. As Hagen puts it on page 69, "Right view omits nothing, holds up nothing in particular. Instead, it points directly to actual experience in each moment. The only way we can be free in each moment is to become what the moment is."

I could not have arrived at my decision had I maintained the static view of reality that I had a year prior. If I had looked at where I am now from the perspectival lens through which I viewed reality then, I would have seen nothing more than how I viewed Hagen's picture, as a blob of incoherent ink; but, through constant evaluation of my true aspirations, I began to see that

that this "ink blob" was really a coherent picture of reality that I could situate myself in.

The problem I have with keeping an eye open for the dynamism of reality is that I cannot help but slip into a lifestyle defined by habits, as they seem to be a necessary component of the human condition. If I had to make a conscious decision to, say, scratch my nose whenever it itched, then that would certainly lead to a very tedious and mentally draining life. Instead, most of the time I am not even aware of the itch until I find myself reaching up to scratch it. Although they have their place, the mere idea of habits conflicts with the idea of living in the moment. I now see that the more I let habits define my life, the less perceptive I am to the present and the true opportunities available to me at any given moment. The life that I used to know was defined by school, wherein if I would get a job if I did well, which in turn depended on maintaining a high GPA and adding to my résumé positions of leadership, creating an employable image of myself.

I chose to interpret the world through static paradigms in which a set number of decipherable categories sit. It's easy to interpret the world statically; once we have made judgments about enough things we feel like we have effectively "figured out" the world. But the world is not some static object for us to "figure out." It changes daily, just like we change daily. David Hume's picture of the non-persistent self makes a lot of sense to this end and fits in well with the Zen picture of no-self. If I were introduced to myself when I was twelve, the twelve-year-old me would be horrified. He probably wouldn't even recognize me because of the fact that we're two vastly different people with two vastly different pictures of the world. If I trace it back even just a year, I would certainly startle the me of the past greatly because of the large differences which emerged between then and now. I think that Zen thought starts with seeing these inconsistencies and extends them to conclude that there is no self at all.

Notions of self aside, I initially misinterpreted living in the moment as living a life of excess and abandonment with no concern for the future. I now see clearly that this is not the case, factoring in "right action," yet another element in the eightfold path. Right action basically is that which does not harm yourself or others, something that leading a life of excess and abandonment would seem to lead to. Planning for the future and having an idea of gaining are naturally two separate concepts. It's the difference between buying groceries for the week and expecting a promotion. We can't exactly do "nothing" either, for would that not do us harm? To live is in and of itself an active process, so I have come to the conclusion that the only option we have is to do that which doesn't harm ourselves or others to the best of our abilities.[2] Our manifold ability to do harm to those around us, though, makes this task quite difficult.

Complex social organisms have engendered the capacity to extend the length of childhood and have massively increased the cognitive capacity in our species as a whole, as Rick Hanson and Richard Mendius point out in *Buddha's Brain*. A social organism creates the need for social interaction, and social interaction creates the need to be present with one another, actively listening and addressing the needs of others. Many times I find myself in a conversation with someone with my mind somewhere else entirely. I have the tendency to filter conversation through my own wants and desires and rarely just listen to what the other person has to say in lieu of a complexly subversive modus operandi.[3] I've learned in this class that the only way I can know how not to harm others is by actively listening to them and attempting to understand where it is that they come from. Just like with the way we view reality, Zen study has taught me that approaching social interaction with an idea of gaining in mind (other than gaining a genuine relationship) disingenuously promotes your own goals to what will become a closed-off listener.

2.   While there are eight distinct aspects of the eightfold path, I think that they all stem from the foundational tenet of "being present."
3.   Even when I don't think that I have a subversive goal in mind, if I dig deeper into my attitude I see that there is rarely an instance in which my attention is completely devoted to understanding the other person.

This aspect of Zen, formally called "right speech,"[4] has helped me immensely in many aspects of my life, most pointedly in the realms of improvisational comedy and acting. Improvisational comedy is interesting, as it's based around the idea of co-creating a reality in which no parties have any idea of at the outset. Affirmation is the only steadfast rule here. Let's say that you walk on stage with a person to start off a scene, and the first sentence out of the other person's mouth is, "It's really cold up here on the moon." It would be inappropriate to deny that you two are actually on the moon because of a different idea that you had for the scene, and it would go nowhere if everyone fought for their own static view of the scene. Instead, the structure of improvisation is based around the concept of "yes, and."

In the situation above, the proper way to treat an initiating line like that is something like, "Yes, it is cold up here, and we're going to have to decide who gets the only space blanket tonight." This both affirms the reality that your scene partner has given you and adds some additional information for him or her to play with. More importantly, the scene has become about a relational conflict between two people, and the fact that it takes place on the moon is merely incidental. I have found that I cannot "yes, and" somebody if I am not in the moment, listening to the information that they gift me. A consequence of this "yes, and" rule is that there is never anything wrong said on the stage. If after the scene your scene partner says "you should have said this," then they don't get it! The scene is always as it is, just as life is always as it is. There is no "should"; there is only "thus."

Although something like this seems easy, most improvisers have a hard time with it at some point. When I have a specific initiating line in my mind, many times I'll sit on the side of the stage and play the scene out in my head. When the time comes to go on stage and play the scene out, my scene partner will invariably take the scene in a direction I did not expect, throw-

4. Hagen says that an important aspect of "right speech" is "right listening."

ing me through a loop. Sometimes I won't even get to say the
initiating line I was thinking of! The scene suffers, then, because
it did not go as I expected. Even if I am "yes, and-ing" in a scene,
I have the tendency to stay in my head as opposed to submit-
ting myself completely to the scene. My attitude here is one
of, "What's the funniest thing to do from here?" as opposed
to just being present in the scene and organically reacting to
whatever happens. I have been taught and fully believe that the
latter option is the one to aim for, and Zen practice has helped
me thoroughly with that.

These ideas apply for acting as well. The worst thing that
can happen to an actor is for somebody to catch him acting,
and every actor's biggest problem is his or her tendency to not
"be present" in a scene. If I can just do that, then I will have
succeeded beyond reasonable expectation. Real, genuine interaction among people in a scene has resonated much more with
an audience than any kind of contrived emotion. Meditation has
helped me with this, improvising, and everyday social interaction as a whole, for when I am in the moment with someone
then I am likely fostering a genuine connection with that person.
There is nothing stronger than really connecting with someone
and seeing the world through their perspectival lens.[5]

A key aspect of right speech that has resonated with me is
never viewing other people as means to my own end. They are,
like me, other people trying to find their own paths through life
they can follow, and to treat them as ends to my own means
has never ended well. Factoring in the idea of inseparability and
no-self, I see that other people are not ultimately even other
people. They are as I am, as you are, as everybody is. I had a
very odd experience with this while meditating once but will
save that for later and first talk some more about what meditation has come to mean for me.

If I wanted to truly pursue a life of practice, should I just drop
everything and go to a Zen monastery to dedicate a couple of

5. Connection in acting/improvising is not necessarily the same
as connection in everyday social interaction. If the scene calls for a
conflict, then you won't be connected in the same sense as everyday
connection. Conflict arises out of perspectival disparities.

years to regimented meditation? Well, Suzuki-Roshi makes a point about why this is the wrong idea. Zazen is not about dropping everything in our lives to dedicate ourselves to practice. It's about being present in our lives while they are going on instead of just going through these habits and regularities until we one day find ourselves to be old, thinking, "How is it that I ended up here?" This is the point of meditation, as I understand it now. Joko Beck and Suzuki Roshi both say that it never ends, either, but rather perennially de-conditions us from our lives defined by habits and narcissism, allowing us to be free and connected with the present.

Alan Watts makes a helpful analogy in one of his lectures, pointing out that we tend to live our lives as though we were running a race, rushing toward the finish line as if there were something special waiting for us there. Well, there is something waiting for us there, but it's not particularly special or fulfilling. It's death. I think that death is a ridiculous thing to rush towards, but I do it all the time. When I wanted to get my first article in the Travesty published, I thought that I would be happy once I achieved that goal. Once it happened, the feeling was great, but it left shortly after. Then I thought that I would be happy once I achieved this, or did that... My point is that my own gaining appetite can never be sated, so I am now trying to throw off the entire "I'll be happy when x" paradigm in lieu of a more desirable alternative.

Life, according to Watts, is more like a symphony. It's quite a silly idea to rush through a symphony just to get to that last note as if it were the only important one in the entire organization. The ultimate note has no meaning whatsoever outside of the context of all those that precede it and give it meaning. Going through our lives savoring each note, chord, crescendo, and beat of our life-symphonies seems to me to be the most fulfilling way to live; for, if we do live in this way, then each new note gives every note that precedes it a new meaning, a new relevance, which will undoubtedly change again when a new series of notes plays. Adopting this perspective, my life becomes a masterful piece of art wherein the past, the present, and the future are all changing. Through meditation I have come to appreciate this more.

Having meditated for a few months now, I feel that I have a firmer grasp on what it is. The phenomena that occur during the times I meditate can be very strange. For example, I sometimes have slight ocular hallucinations, typically predicated in two objects of the same structure or type that appear to be beckoning one another; I once saw that two lime wedges in my water bottle appeared to be dancing with the other. Sometimes my body attunes to a metronomic sound in the room by swaying naturally along with the beat, which is always a very pleasant experience. I am always caught by surprise when these things happen, though, as their points of origin are never my intention.

For the most part, meditation has not gotten any easier, as Joko Beck points out is true for all. There are times when I find it easy to sit, but more often than not I find it particularly difficult. In the sixth grade I was diagnosed with Attention Deficit Hyperactivity Disorder and have always had trouble sitting still, so this comes not as a surprise. I think that if I continue to practice meditation, though, I might be able to abandon the medication that I've been dependent on for years and finally gain the ability to regulate my own life. While it's true that meditation has not gotten much easier, I have noticed the resonant effects it has on my daily life. I am able to stay focused longer in many different contexts, like schoolwork, conversation, and performances.

Another interesting aspect of meditating has been viewing my arising thoughts during these periods. It's easy to get captivated by the thoughts of the day, but Joko Beck points out that this is not what meditation is about. Instead, I try to try to take a bird's-eye-view of the traffic of my thoughts as much as possible, to use one of her analogies. A helpful tactic I have learned to cultivate through the guidance of Peg Syverson is the method of addressing a problematic thought by tracing it back to its causal origin. This originating thought is always much easier to deal with than the pattern it created. I tend to treat problems like I treat a lost item, a common tendency I am sure. When I misplace something, I aimlessly wander about in hopes that somehow I'll magically come across it. I look over and over again in the same five places, each time yielding the same result. Until I enact a systematic search, mindful of what I was doing when I lost it, I just repeat this same process. So it goes with problematic thought patterns.

While this will successfully bring me back into the present moment at times, mostly it does not work; although, as it has been the most helpful tool to this end, I will continue to use it. Sometimes I just need to sit for longer periods of time in order to fully engage in the moment, allowing the thoughts to leave on their own accord. I have certainly found that the longer I sit, the easier it is for me to stay in the moment. Fifteen minutes is typically enough to get me to a place where I can say that I am there, and it feels like after that point I am really meditating. Now is the appropriate time to bring up that odd experience I had while meditating mentioned earlier, which has been my most memorable experience with my practice. First, some context is necessary.

In class one Monday, we talked some about suffering and how it is a part of human nature. Judging by the way the conversation went, I concluded that I must have become an emotional monster over the course of my collegiate years, a notion that genuinely troubled me. What do I mean by that? The shooting that occurred on our campus in October left me completely unaffected, other than having the thought, "Well, this really messes up my schedule." This is not an isolated case. Any thought of loss at all leaves me completely unaffected unless it affects the way in which I live my life. It's not that I'm unable to connect with people; I am very deft at intellectually empathizing with people or comforting them when they are in pain. I understand quite well what emotional pain is but have virtually ceased to experience it myself.

How did this situation emerge? What I imagine started this was a break-up with my girlfriend of two years, an event which all who have experienced losing their first love will know is quite devastating. I handled it poorly, and ended up closing myself off in a general sense. My spiritual life, which was strong, considering I was on the path to attend Concordia Lutheran Seminary in my post-collegiate years, has extinguished due to constant re-evaluations of the logic behind dogmatic religious schemas and a perpetual application of Occam's Razor to my faith.[6] Add in a similar trend with friendships and I have become a completely emotionally walled-off person, which made the following experience very noteworthy.

I decided to try sitting for thirty minutes in the cross-legged position as opposed to the fifteen I usually spend. I noticed my eyes were watering about eighteen to twenty minutes in, which I would have attributed to allergies were I not inside. A single tear then dropped down my left cheek. I thought to myself, "What could possibly be the cause of this? It is clearly a tear, but my mind is away from sad things." After a couple minutes of exploration, my mind landed on the memory of insects I had killed while reading outside for no other reason than their presence around my person. At this point, I could not help but openly cry. It couldn't have been more than ten seconds of sobbing before my alarm went off. I had not cried like that in years.

While I don't want to add undue significance to this, I do know that I suddenly felt more connected with those bugs than I had ever felt with anything before. I remember distinctly feeling as though I were killing myself, and while I have believed the notion that I and the earth are technically one for a while now, it had never affected me emotionally like this. Afterwards, the feeling of unity departed, leaving but a trace, invigorating my practice. Whether or not it was an actual breakthrough is not important to me; it felt like a breakthrough. I felt emotional pain for the first time since I can remember, and it completely arose on its own.

I've really valued this time spent studying the practice of Zen Buddhism, and I certainly plan on continuing practice into the future. The idea that has resonated with me the most is the idea that reality is always as it is. I used to continually dig myself into holes by saying, "things should be this way," but reality always

---

6.   Why posit the existence of a God when everything can be explained by way of mechanistic, physical operations?

just is. I can now find solace by simply situating myself in the present and enjoying the ride. My writing process has grown to great extents during this time, as I have been opened up to the idea of utilizing personal narratives in an essay. Before this chapter, I had a great fear of using the first person voice in a collegiate environment, but now that trepidation no longer exists. The stylistic disparity between the first and second part of this chapter astounds me, for the temporal difference between when they were written amounts to no more than a couple of months. Most of all, though, I walk away from this class with a much fuller and richer appreciation of "living in the moment" and "excluding nothing. These sentiments I will certainly keep with me forever.

Works Cited

Watts, Alan. Nature, Man and Woman. New York City: The Noonday Press Inc., 1963. Print.

Watts, Alan. "Music and Life." Lecture.

Marker, Chris, Dir. Sunless. Dir. Chris Marker." Argos Films: 1983, Film.

Aaron Walther is a senior philosophy major at the University of Texas at Austin. His philosophical areas of focus are in existentialism and the problem of free will. Comedian at heart, he is a part of local Austin improvisational troupes City High and DJ Danger Dad. He is also the Media Editor for the Texas Travesty. After college, Aaron plans to secure a job in the entertainment industry in some form.

Zazen: Life's Ocean

Sean Harkins

Coming to the Shore

I don't know much at all about the practice of Zen, but I've always thought of individual self-exploration as something of importance. Although I've never studied Zen specifically, I often reflect on my own actions and attitudes within my daily life. I find the study of social interaction absolutely fascinating. Perhaps applying the sort of meticulous observation to one's own self in the way that sociology or psychology requires one to look critically at the actions of others, can help a person find happiness. Certainly the goal of Zen seems to be to improve one's life. Again, I don't know much at this point, but I certainly hope my studies of Zen will help me improve my own existence. I hope to find productive ways to relieve the daily stress I feel, and proactively improve the relationships around me.

Especially when discussing rhetorical arguments, the practice of Zen focuses on observing and understanding. As someone mentioned in class, it seems so weird to treat a 'problem' as something of individual occurrence. Something that I see as a problem might not be considered a problem by any one else. This view of the world is not necessarily totally foreign, but applying it on such a singular level is new to me. But Zen also comes across as the study of one's self, not just the study of one's effects on others. To really learn about yourself, to understand why you feel the way you do, is extremely important. By practicing the techniques I learn as I progress, I aspire to become a happier, more productive person. On a day-to-day level, it would be wonderful if I could relieve some of the stress I feel and the anxiety that often gets in the way of positive action. This is not to say that stress is not natural or even possible to completely erase, for all stress is felt for a reason. But that's exactly what I find so interesting about practicing Zen; attempting to understand where the stress comes from and the relationship one has with his/her own struggles can be a great individual influence in the right direction.

I honestly thought that Zen was a technique of the Buddhist religion. I suppose it is affiliated with the Buddhist religion but I don't think one has to be a Buddhist to practice Zen. In fact, it almost seems like anyone can practice the virtues of Zen. I wonder if it can strengthen or support the belief systems of other cultures? It is after all based on curiosity and seems to support the good moral nature of most other religions in the world. Still, I'm not sure if true Zen masters believe in reincarnation. I personally don't, but I'm confident that it won't affect my learning. Quite honestly I don't know anything about Buddhism, beside the belief in reincarnation but I'm pretty clueless about that particular belief as well.

What unexpected benefits will I reap from my studies? There will probably be skills that I cannot predict that will become useful to me later. I have negative tendencies; can Zazen help to 'fix' them? I wonder if there are any bad effects that Zen has ever brought people. The whole point is to better oneself and those surrounding but I'd like to know in particular how Zen students react to violence. Whether this violence is by an individual, or on a widespread scale, it will be so intriguing to understand how Zen teaches people to deal with some of the more harsh situations in life. We've discussed passiveness, and the difference between being peaceful and letting someone walk all over you. But this doesn't seem as simple as the 'free love' hippie movement (not that it was all that easy but it certainly didn't last long). No, Zen teaches methods that have lasted for a long, long time. Unfortunately I'm not too familiar with the history of Zen but I hope to become so, soon. I can't wait to apply what I learn in my everyday life. I sincerely hope the studies make a difference. I wonder if Zen masters believe they have achieved true happiness? Perhaps they understand that there will always be sadness in life, and that happiness comes from understanding the relationships within this life and navigating them effectively. But how can someone who's felt extreme grief, suffered a terrible loss, or been through a traumatic experience them selves expect to find peace? I'm not sure if the practice is that psychological, but if not it would seem only skin deep.

Though we haven't dove into the deep particulars, I do enjoy the practice of meditating. I have never meditated before and now find it quite healing (I especially enjoy having time to meditate after a long school day). It'll be fun to find out exactly what chemicals are at work in the brain when we remain perfectly quiet and absolutely still (this is in anticipation of our class reading of *Buddha's Brain*). From what my fellow students have discussed, it sounds like meditating is a very individual act, one that is unique to each person. While my mind often runs wild because I do not have to focus on any one thing in particular, other students have mentioned that their thoughts wander to whatever events happened that day. If one is feeling sad, stressed, or angry about a particular event, meditation seems to allow careful analysis of one's personal experience. This reflection might not bring the happiest of thoughts, but it is important to think about subjects and events that are not exactly the most positive because life if full of both aspects.

Besides exploring deeper in myself, I aspire to better understand the world surrounding me. Where we as a race have come from, and where we are going. How has the world changed? And most importantly, how can I have a positive impact on the direction of my own life and those around me? I'm no Zen master, and I'm certain I won't be one by the end of this year. I am excited though; excited to expand my boundaries, learn in ways I've never learned before, and open up a world of possibility for my own view about the world and life.

Getting My Feet Wet

As I continue my study of Zen I'm finding that the practical application of Zen practices is not always very easy. Many times I find myself striving to act or react in a specific way that I designate appropriate to the study of Zen. However, as I read further into *Zen Mind, Beginner's Mind* I find myself often confused by many of the observations Suzuki puts forth. But after reading a few of the observations of my peers and even some from previous semesters, I think I might be finding a new prospective way to understand Suzuki's teachings. Although his diction is often confusing, after several reads it always comes off sounding like somewhat of a riddle to me. Though riddles seem confusing, they often have very simple answers based on information given, or known, but overlooked. I constantly find myself looking for answers within Zen, sort-of like a 'how to do' instruction book or something. But there's no 'Life for Dummies' book out there, and even if there were it surely wouldn't be relevant to individual people.

So I have to ask myself how these Buddhist practices are applicable in my own life. In some cases I feel like I can directly apply the practice of Zen to events in my life fairly easily. For instance, I felt suddenly annoyed and angry when I came home to a sink full of dirty dishes and food that was left on the counter in the kitchen after I had cleaned it the day before. Rather than yelling at my roommates for being slobs, I cleaned up and calmly asked my roommates to please use a paper plate if they weren't going to put their dishes in the wash after they used them. Thankfully, my roommates are pretty decent guys so since then they have cleaned up after themselves rather nicely. I have to admit, though, that in that moment, when I came home to the filthy kitchen, I felt immediately angry. I was pissed off and wanted to take it out- express this feeling I had externally. Thankfully I was able to control myself and endure the momentary suffering I felt so that ultimately it would not be prolonged. But what if my roommates hadn't taken my request to heart?

What if they continued disrespecting our shared space? I know I can't change their actions, but I'm not sure I would know how to react in a positive manner that would be applicable to Zen teachings.

Perhaps I'm striving too hard to try to form my actions in accordance with what we're learning. I know understanding is key, but it's just so difficult for me to understand without wanting to do something about it. Suzuki's analogy about the waterfall equated to life and all things within it makes sense, but what doesn't make sense is what I'm supposed to do with this understanding. How am I supposed to react when things just are the way they are? Suzuki writes that all life begins, just as a river is one before it crosses the cliff. When the river crosses the cliff, each droplet of water is separated. In this same way each individual thing, being, animal, plant, human- whatever, becomes its own. When the waterfall crashes to the ground, the individual droplets become part of the whole river again and continue moving downstream. Life is a continuous cycle, we all become one in death. When I start to think about the world this way it depresses me to be perfectly honest. This notion seems to imply to me that everything is connected. I suppose it's unsettling because there are certain aspects of the world- maybe perhaps just of humanity alone- that I do not wish to be connected with.

When I ponder about universal, infinite connection in this way I think about the negative, destructive forces in the world; the violence, the sorrow, and death, and how these are elements are embodied within myself. I might have many friends, but my constant self doubt about my morality, dignity and worth are constant shadows in my psyche. The grass always seems to be greener- somehow. But then again, maybe my yearning to fix things in my life when they don't seem to be going perfectly well is actually natural. I think this could be a common occurrence for everyone, Zen students or not. As I've learned through Rick Hanson's teachings In *Buddha's Brain*, it is only natural for us as humans to remember more vividly bad or traumatic memories of our past. It is part of a "flight or fight" response that we've developed as a race very early on to avoid being eaten by saber tooth tigers or some animal of the like. The problem is, that in this day and age when there are no giant cats out to get us (unless you're Steve Erwin exploring the African landscape or something) so this idea of remembering the bad events in our lives is sometimes poisonous. It's difficult not to worry about the future. It was interesting to learn about the chemical functions that take place when I feel anxiety. A "feeling tone" produced by our individual amygdala within the brain. So right now, as I write these very words, I'm thinking about the two other assignments I have due this week. I can feel the chemical effects of amygdala- I'm thinking about the future; worrying. All of these thoughts are unnecessary. Yes, I'm going to have to work hard this week to complete my schoolwork, but thinking about not doing well on my assignments won't help anything. I am able to recognize my anxiety as just an apprehensive nervousness. And let me be truthful, some assignments I just do not want to do; but I have to. I know that I have to for my own betterment. But rather than looking at the situation from a perspective that toils with anxiety, I'm beginning to recognize the importance of being mindful of the good that my action is doing, even if it doesn't feel good. The stress, or anxiety, I am feeling is my own perception of it. I say "perceived stress" because, again, the stress that we all feel about anything, whatever it may be, comes from the fear of failure. We've all failed at something sometime in our lives and the goal of the stress is to prevent such an occurrence from happening again. So as I feel this now, I'm trying to remember my sitting. Sitting is suffering. Though it may not always be comfortable, it keeps one in the moment- thinking only about the present; what's beneficial now, in anticipation of the future or for the present moment.

For me, the most difficult aspect of practicing Zazen is to recognize that such stress is a product of my own doing. Remaining here, in the moment, is essential to recognizing where such anxiety comes from and then using it for my, or for that matter anyone else's, advantage. Practicing Zazen has begun to show changes in my everyday mindset. Let me explain, I am no Zen master and certainly can't retain the qualities of Zen training every moment of everyday. However, when I have a large paper assigned or a test date posted, I attempt to use my "feeling tone" to define the amount of work that needs to be done. I write out a list of assignments in order of importance and address the most pertinent (the ones due first) as I work my way down the list. Making a list like this has really started helping me tackle one thing at a time and apply my focus more concisely. It's not that I've never used or a planner (they're essential to survive in college) but it just helps me to sort-of go a little further and make a to-do list this way. I suppose it's because it helps me check my individual progress, especially for big writing assignments that have far away due dates but require a lot of work. So by putting forth a plan of action, I don't get as easily overwhelmed by my perceived stress.

This doesn't seem so hard, or at least it didn't to me once I sort-of figured it out. But, frankly, it can be. As students, workers, and professionals, we are all faced with stressful tasks all day long and most of the time all at once. That means that I'm probably not going to always be able to make a nice little highlighted schedule of when certain work will be done. Life is surprising. Hey, sometimes I think I just have to roll with the punches, in which case it may be hard to remain focused. But that's just the point. See, like many of my fellow students (and countless numbers of adults who may or may not be familiar with Zazen) whether we wanted to admit it or not, Zazen will not make our lives better. It's not just some formula. So when life throws a curveball it's normally very, very difficult for me to step back and say, "Well I'm going to remain very calm and figure what is the most important procedure for me to go through with right now, in the present" because there might be several pressing issues in my life that all need immediate attention. I might feel down one week for making a few mistakes at my job at the optometrist office, while having to work really hard to prepare for a rhetorical analysis and a test. What if I'm not able to see my friends as much because of all this responsibility? I might feel guilty for missing out on my youth.

As a Zazen student, I'm beginning to realize that I probably won't be able to meet all of my expectations in life. Even if I practice Zen and practice well, I'll probably still fail. It's hard to admit, but I to think of this concept in the way that my freshman Texas Interdisciplinary Plan (TIP) advisor explained it to me. She equated it to a fallacy of argument referred to as the slippery slope; which assumes because one event happened, another is unavoidable. When I failed my first sociology test as a freshman I was understandably upset and was anxious about how the rest of my college career would turn out. But Dr. Harkins (no relation, by the way) knew I was a sharp kid and she understood my anxiety. She joking said to me, "So I guess this is the end of your college career, huh?" I suppose I could've been offended by this, thinking she was patronizing my or something, but she was simply trying to point out that, in fact, we all go through trials in life and there's no way that we can achieve success with every one. What is beneficial about these experiences is recognizing where we went wrong and how we can improve in the future. Using a failure to think or worry about future failures encourages suffering. As a Zazen student I constantly struggle to recognize when I am in a situation that I can apply my past experiences to without getting completely caught up in the outcome of those experiences. Rather, to stay in the moment, understand what I can do in the present to appreciate and enjoy the act of what I'm doing. After all, the effort, within itself, is important.

This brings me to my next point, knowing what's happening in the present in relation to all aspects of my life and of my own person. As discussed, mistakes are inevitable. Just as this is true, I probably won't be humble and loving all of the time. To attempt to be such would be futile anyway because I react to stimuli in an imperfect, ever changing world. I particularly struggle with resentment, though, in spite of my knowledge of this. I often sit back and think about a certain situation I was in asking myself, "Now why did I do that," or "why did I act like such a jerk?" In those reflections I try to be as honest with myself as possible and I often come to the conclusion that my actions were being ruled by emotion in the moment. You might ask, "But wait, I thought the whole idea was to remain conscious of the present?" and it is. When I look back on reactions I had to a customer at my job, or one of my roommates at home, or even a conversation with a girl, most often my regret comes from a response that didn't consider the full context of the moment it occurred in. Over the course of the semester I have been recording individual observations of my daily life as a reference of my Zen practice. One observation in particular was recorded in a confrontation with one of my roommates, Alex.

I noticed I had a thought, 'Alex is being a jerk when he is in the wrong". I felt angry in the moment after this thought. I had been talking to him about the fact that his lock for his bike had broken and how it happened. Since the lock broke he hasn't been able to lock his bike up at night so it's been sitting in our living room. When I suggested that he take his lock down to the bike shop on 24th street. to get it fixed he sarcastically apologized for not having done saying 'I haven't gotten around to it- sorry it's been bothering you' in a very sarcastic, snippy tone. When this happened and I had the above thought I immediately had an impulse to act on it. I wanted to cuss Alex out for not only speaking to me disrespectfully but also for trying to defend his action of leaving his bike in the living room for 2 WEEKS- plenty of time to go get a new lock. But I didn't. I simply said, 'There's no reason to get angry with me' and stopped the conversation. His bike is STILL in the living room.

It's clear that, even in my observation, I was still angry about our interaction. I often let small annoyances get to me without seeing the big picture and whether or not they actually matter. It only takes something small, which can be attributed to a particular person's fault, to trigger a larger, angrier reaction from me. So even though I admitted to having thoughts of discontent, I didn't really ask myself why I was thinking this way. There were other factors at play that were putting me in a bad mood; it wasn't just that Alex's bike was still in the living room. But when he understandably reacted shortly with me, in my head it only certified the fact that he was being a jerk and that I didn't deserve it. In reality, I had used loaded questions to get him to admit that he had left his bike sitting in the corner of the living room because he hadn't gone to get a new lock for it. The reason that I assumed so was because he was too lazy; when really it could have been any number of things, say money that was keeping him from getting it done. The whole point here is that while I thought I was staying grounded in the moment, my own personal biases were still at play- I just wasn't willing to admit it.

Understanding my own actions, even within the practice of Zen is hugely important because it allows me to see that in my quest to practice I have often tried to adopt a new way of life. This is again not the point. And as we continue to dive deeper and deeper, the nature of these situations in which I attempt apply my studies can turn out to be deceiving. I think this is true of any Zen student, and it is certainly a problem that many of my peers in this class struggle with. We have had such an emphasis on success and failure, especially in academia, that is it hard to admit when something didn't go quite as well as I thought it did and use that experience in a positive light. I enjoy the metaphor of food and Zazen knowledge that Dale Wright put forth in *Philosophical Meditations on Zen Buddhism*. He says, "Their insatiable desire to consume the texts leads to 'indigestion'. This is the crucial metaphor: sutras are susceptible to being consumed' in appropriate ways, with devastating consequences. 'Undigested' sutras are those from which we all gain and retain knowledge 'about' them." It is obvious from my particular observation that I was trying to recognize my feelings as "having a thought," without considering all of the reasons as to why I was having that thought and what other factors might be at play besides my own feelings about the situation.

Diving Deeper

It is especially hard for me to admit when I'm just being outright rude or mean, even when I cover it up with nice rhetoric. I realize can't be nice all the time. My annoyances and true feelings are bound to come out especially in response to other people's actions. Of course only I can control who I want to be. So I try as hard as I can to suppress my "natural" response to agitating situations. But while I am a genuinely easy person to get along with, I am in constant battle with myself in the comparison of others. Personal reflection can be healthy but it often becomes personal evaluation, especially in relation to others around me. I'll be the first to admit that, indeed, I am insecure about a lot of different things. Most people wouldn't have the slightest clues about my insecurities, even my closest friends, because, hey, I mean who really goes around shouting what they don't want people to notice about them? It's still very difficult for me not to lash out in some way when I see my own traits exhibited in others- especially those particular traits that upset me personally. So while my friend Alex is a very good buddy of mine, I sometimes come off as an asshole to him simply due to my own inhibitions. I observed at one point in the semester,

Today I found myself angry and annoyed while in the middle of a conversation with my roommate Alex. This happens all the time when we talk and so I asked myself why this was during our conversation today. My roommate tends to discuss his obvious opinions as if they were fact and further, he discusses everything as if he is the world-renowned expert on the subject even if he knows nothing about it. In several instances, in fact, someone else in the room will know something he has stated is factually wrong- but he'll never admit it. He just keeps arguing that he is right and this really annoys me. Most of the time I try not to get angry because we end up arguing over something I don't even CARE ABOUT. So Today when he started speaking in a ridiculous manner about the recent gun incident on campus (he was sure he knew exactly why the shooter committed suicide on campus because he "has studied plenty of psychology and read a lot of psychology books") I simply apologized for questioning his omnipotent wisdom and walked away. Clearly I was still angry and was unable to brush that anger aside. I think this is why I walked away, because I knew I couldn't let go of my anger in that moment

So why wasn't I able to just brush off the incident and let it go? If I'm truly honest with myself it's because I love to deliberate and discuss topics of interest with my friends, and while I really attempt to do so in a way that is conducive to healthy conversation, sometimes I feel like I'm being a "know-it-all." When I see this sort of trait in someone else (Alex in this case) it angers me because I try so hard to hold back that tendency of my own and it's being thrown in my face. But getting angry about it is of course not healthy, and even observing it as I did in this case isn't really helpful. For, as one can clearly see I didn't let it go or learn from it in that moment. I was still being hateful and sarcastic when I said, "I apologized for questioning his omnipotent wisdom." But it's very difficult to whole-heartedly consider someone else's perspective. Perhaps I should look at myself; the reasons why I sometimes had the urge to always be right; attention, maybe. Alex may have struggled with some situation in his past that made him feel really inadequate, unintelligent. This is so hard, though, to consider in the moment that such discourse occurs. I want to think about my reaction before I actually react, but this is so opposite of what I've known for so long. If I were able to more often apply this type of observation instead of reacting with emotional exasperation, I bet I could avoid a whole lot of self-doubt and suffering. What might be more beneficial to me is to understand that there are other forces at work besides the ones in your own life and to recognize that they are all in play in the present. The most adversity I encounter in my practice is through this very concept, however. Because I'm in my life, it's hard to step out and attempt to look out from other's eyes. Even when I am able to do so, my own biases are always present and I might my own reasoning to some experiences that I have no knowledge of. It's so hard to understand others when I find myself thinking, "Even so, I would've done this in that situation," or "I would have handled that pressure better."

The idea of understanding as I have come to learn about through this semester, is much different than the definition I held in my mind. I'm a rhetoric major, so of course I have to always be familiar with the opposing side's stance, view, and perspective- in order to formulate a well constructed argument that address rebuttals appropriately. But the understanding that Zazen preaches is much different than this academic view that is so ingrained in my mind. So much of what I know about the concept of understanding comes from asking, "why" and "how" in an attempt to formulate a situation that has(d) options. Zazen aims only to understand "what," not to judge, formulate, or provide opinions. "Understanding" is simply knowing. So as the end of the semester nears, it is becoming easier for me to live more passively; to take things less personally. I've noticed by doing so I have stopped reacting with such defensiveness when certain situations or even utterances make me uncomfortable. As I read *Philosophical Meditations on Zen Buddhism* I am encouraged by this practice, but it's still very difficult to genuinely take interest in someone's else's perspective without putting in some form of myself; my own perception.

Coming Up For Air

Zazen practice is difficult and it only seems to get more difficult as one continues to learn and practice it. At first, as many of my peers in the class began to recognize this and discuss it we collectively felt a little discouraged. This is normal, now I think, and good! It's good because life is complicated and there is no right answer for anything. What Zazen has taught me to do is to think about what's best right now, here, and how I can go about finding that path of success. Even in utter failure, this path can be found. And I would hope that this text doesn't come off as some vague rambling about feelings, but that instead readers will come to understand that Zazen is the practice of personal fulfillment. Not to be confused with material fulfillment or personal expectation, personal fulfillment should be the pursuit of genuine satisfaction. Even in times of struggle I find comfort in myself when I can say, "I have done everything in my power to better myself and those around me to the extent that is conceivable." I still make mistakes. I mean, are you kidding? I'll always make mistakes, probably until the day I croak.

But I'm certainly not going to let these mistakes rule my life. I'm not going to let my inner struggles rule my life either. Everyone has inner struggles, inhibitions that they share with no one else. Knowing this, being conscious of all the things in play at any given moment and in any situation, will help me, and anyone, react in a way that is favorable to who I really want to be; and ultimately what I want my life to be.

Sean Harkins is a third year Rhetoric and Writing major at the University of Texas. He is interested in law and business, particularly entertainment law, and plans to apply for Law School in the future. For Sean, music is an obsession and self-expression is constant. He grew up in various parts of central Texas, and is a true Texan at heart. With a love for water instilled from birth, he has always loved "sitting on the dock of the bay" and considers no time wasted as long as it is enjoyed.

Mindful Experiences of Zen
Ashley Underwood

Early Zen Reflections

Living a Zen life brings many words to mind: calm, serenity, peace, patience, dedication, and trust. All observations of Zen living at this point are, of course, based on a platform of un-knowing and bias as well as my cultural surroundings. In my first journal entry in this class I spoke of things which I related with Zen. One being a Zen garden manufactured and sold to corporate bookstores across the nation to show Americans you can manufacture peace in a box. The idea is that when one is stressed at the office, they can take out their miniature Zen garden and plow the small box of sand until they find peace again. I have some idea that practicing Zen as a way of life involves more than this.

As I am learning from readings and discussions in class, practicing Zen takes a certain amount of discipline and self-control. With this discipline comes the freedom of mind. As Steven Hagen in his book Buddhism: Plain and Simple states, "You are already enlightened... You only need to stop block-ing or interpreting your vision." This takes discipline. It is my personal inclination to let my mind be blocked by my thoughts, fears, and worries. If and when I can learn to take a step back from these thoughts and look through the perspective of the Buddha-dharma, it is then I will comprehend my enlightened state of being.

Now to delve deeper into the adjectives I described earlier. Calm, serenity and peace all coincide with this enlightened state of which I am referring. Because life is ever-changing and moving, it creates obstacles for one's own world. Most people in my American culture see these obstacles as problems. However, I am finding that in the Zen frame of mind, such problems and/or obstacles are dealt with at a distance. One who controls their reaction to obstacles and challenges of life has an objective, peaceful state. As a baptized Christian who prays on a regular basis, I know what faith is. I am also very spiritual. It is this worked on faith that I carry that brings me calm peace.

I personally believe in a life that practices Zen and Christianity together. They can co-exist without conflict. That is why I align very well with the practices about which I am learning. When one faces a challenge, there is a reason or lesson for such a challenge. That person may not realize it while they are in the "problem." But, at some point in time, maybe years later, they will look back and see the reasoning for why such a thing happened. That is when the word trust came to mind. One must trust in the outcome of such belief and practice in order to realize its full effects. Without the ability to trust, there exists no concept of understanding. Trusting a practice helps to guide one through the paths of comprehension. For example, I, for the first time, practiced the art of meditation in this class. I started off optimistic about the skill. I listened to what the professor told us to do; keeping our bodies still and focusing on one object while we let our mind wander. I then became sort of cynical wondering if I was doing it right. At the end of the meditation when the entire class discussed their sensory and emotional thought processes, I had a similar experience. It was this experience that then allowed me to trust what I was doing. I had the reaffirmation of a common goal, thus creating a sense of understanding. For the remainder of the day, because I trusted what had occurred during the meditation and saw it as truth, I felt that sense of peace, calm and serenity.

The next word that I spoke about was dedication. Even in

American culture, it is commonly understood that a platform for learning is repetition. To practice an art or skill once learned over and over is the art of perfecting. And, thus engraving such a practice or skill into one's system and perception means that one has fully understood such a skill. In the case of Zen, I am finding that this concept applies fully. In Hagen's discussion of the Human Situation, he recalls, "the eightfold path [to understanding enlightenment or the freedom of mind] also includes effort, mindfulness, and meditation" (23). Many people have studied Zen their entire lives and are still learning and growing in their path. One must have the desire to dedicate time and mindfulness and steadfast learning to such a way of life in order to attain it. This should be something easy for me to understand as one who lives in the American culture, where many dedicate their entire lives for the almighty dollar. I personally, would much prefer to seek out a life of depth and substance; something the insatiable dollar can never give. So with the dedication and discipline that was taught to me at a young age to have a good life for myself, I am finding that the dedication it takes to have a serene life; one of a Zen life is comparable and attainable.

In order to maintain such dedication, one must hold the power of patience. This is one I know I will struggle with due to my environment. My life, one that is filled with deadlines, technology and immediacy is one of a short attention span. I have very little patience for myself and only a little more with assignments and others. For instance, while meditating for just thirty minutes in the beginning of class, I became extremely impatient. This came out in the form of leg-tapping, eye wandering, and focus going off of the meditation and on to my "to-do" list. Patience will need to be learned because the art of Zen meditation and feeling enlightened means slow, well thought-out reactions to life's issues, not fast, immediate decisions and outlooks from what I can tell in this early part of my journey. Author Steve Hagen focuses on the "uncluttered, original insights and observations" of Buddhism. Such observations take patience, and such patience takes time.

As I am in the first weeks of the class, I feel like a newborn opening her eyes for the first time to this foreign experience that is Zen. I am unknowing of where these lessons and practices will take me, but am as anxious and excited as ever for the path I see ahead.

A Deeper Understanding

Now in the midst of the semester about seven weeks past, I go further into the uncharted waters of my enlightened path.

"The purpose of studying Buddhism is not to study Buddhism, but to study ourselves" (Suzuki 76). That is a mantra that resonates well with me having practiced more these past weeks. Digging a little deeper into the great wealth of knowledge on the practices of Zen, I have retained an understanding of the concepts and practices. Greatly due to the ability to relate Zen so much with my life and daily occurrences, I move forward in learning. The emotional awareness that arises from Zen brings a value system of truth and being "awake" to my life. This sensory experience has struck me deeply expanding my own mental and moral awareness of my life. I have a better grasp that the practice Zen allows for a more tempered mindfulness that brings about true happiness and contentment. Hagen and Suzuki contribute much to the breadth of analogies and passages. These serve as the underlying reason for my comprehension. But the best method of my learning and education in Zen comes from real live practice and application. That is what I will discuss in this paper; the vast understanding of Zen that I have gained through my personal experiences with reference to the authors, of which I have read.

First I will refer back to earlier reflections in my learning. I have always felt I am aware due to my ability to talk to most people, including strangers, openly about topics of their interest at any one moment. Most of the time I am witty and in the present. But sometimes I do go on autopilot. Being sleep-deprived or drifting in my thoughts makes me this way. However, I demand a lot from myself during the day. This keeps me engaged and always eager to keep my eyes open. I constantly observe the experiences around me, almost from a third person perspective. I consistently analyze and overthink situations, even perhaps to a fault. This analysis and eager readiness helps me with my experiential learning of Zen practice. It is my understanding that Zen provides the deep consciousness of the mind. You are aware of your thoughts and let them float by the forefront of your mind or you focus on certain thoughts. Such focus causes a chain of thoughts stringing together to create a certain outcome, of which you can choose to take action or keep thinking. The entire process brings you to a contemplative state from a perspective of the mind looking at itself. This happens a lot during the process of meditation. Now that I have a fuller comprehension of the purpose and practice of zazen, I am having an easier time getting more out of sitting.

For instance, during a meditation I attempted solo in my bedroom before going to sleep, I was at first uneasy. As I wrote in observation, "I was at a time when I began to make sense, on my own revelations, of Zen lifestyles." I sat in bed and it was near 11 p.m. My mind was spinning and grinding like a squeaky machine in need of oil replenishment. Being Sunday, I knew I had a lot coming for me this week in the area of work and school. I trembled as I realized my weekend of limited freedoms is ending and I face a scheduled five days of every hour occupied. It is not that I despise my self-created schedule; I just did not want to think about all of my to-dos at a point when I would like to be at peace and stay restful. It was that spinning state that prompted me to meditate as I lay there. This was so helpful because I began to slip into a calm state free of worry. I started to focus purposefully on my breathing, the elements of the room, and then back to the thoughts of my mind. The focus on those thoughts brought a sense of awareness to the present forefront. I was then able to focus deeper on which thoughts brought me a sense of serenity and let other mindless, busy triggers float on by the clouds in my mind.

As Suzuki states, "If you want to obtain perfect calmness in your zazen, you should not be bothered by various images you find in your mind. Let them come, and let them go. Then they will be under control" (32). After reading this passage, I related it to the real life practice of meditating I had experienced before. The sense of control I felt became rather uplifting. I then felt powerful, as if just knowing I had the ability to control what thoughts I could think about and categorize in my mind brought a sense of overwhelming freedom. As more meditation sessions continued, this sense of freedom by control in my mind began to glow. I am more able to harness the thoughts in my mind so that I am not so easily reactive.

Living a "stressed" state of mind is a part of my nature due to my upbringing. Before the opportunities presented in this class, I felt it was a necessity to consistently and overwhelmingly consume my thoughts with busying thoughts of stress, to-dos, and worries that drained a lot of energy. Many times throughout the day I allowed my mind to wander through its chains of thought reducing to an outcome that caused me grief. For example, my interaction with a friend was played over and over in my head. So much so that I began to question what I said and what she said to a point of insecurity and negative outcomes. Misreading, judgments, and hidden motives were sure to ensue. All the while, I could have been focusing on how beautiful the day was outside or how fresh the air felt against my cheek, which would have brought me calm contentment rather than suffering.

The daily dialogue of wonderment and chained together strands of thought frequently produce wrongful conclusions in my mind about situations which contain no "problems" whatsoever. Delusions in my mind due to my own insecurities and mind chatter could have been prevented with the art of Zen. Capturing the ability to categorize thoughts in my mind to a point that my awareness of them allows me to take a step back, identify what is triggering these negative thoughts and fears, and then move forward with a more reasonable sense of understanding about a situation or conversation.

After tackling the ability to control the thoughts in my mind via meditative practices and readings, I still struggle with the task. As Suzuki says, "This policy is not easy. It sounds easy, but it requires some special effort" (32). Recently however, I felt very positively about my depth of learning when I was able to speak wisely on a situation my brother is going through. As if to spread the teachings I have learned from Professor Syverson, Hagen, and Suzuki, I spoke with my brother on topics bothering through a Zen-educated lens.

He came to me all frazzled on the phone worrying about his relationship of eight months with his girlfriend. She had just gone on a three-day trip and was seemingly distant. He went on and on about his curiosity and grief regarding his self-directed conclusions about her desire of him. He was convinced she was having an affair at the start of the conversation. Then he went over his chain of thoughts vocally on the phone with me. I simply sat and listened. He told me the context of the situation, how he came about thinking such suffering thoughts and the reasons he thought them. He then explained his own anxieties in his "mind chatter." He told me that he worries about his perception simply being skewed and that he might be making a huge mistake.

For the first time, I did not have on overly thought-out emotional answer for him which might hurt all parties in the end. I deducted that every time I see him lately he is very stressed out and then he would benefit from clearer thinking. I told him that whenever his girlfriend did certain actions, these actions act as triggers. Afterwards, a chain of thoughts react in order, producing a grief-filled conclusion. I told him that through the practice of meditation, he would become more aware of such triggers and thought patterns. So much so that he could then learn to recognize them before they are even fulfilled as thoughts. He could understand why they are happening and let the thoughts float by in his mind to create a better sense of perspective. This awareness would lead to a more "awake" and "real" understanding of the situation, while also keeping him calmer and wiser through the entire process.

I could not guarantee that my brother's initial conclusions were incorrect. Nor could I guarantee his mind chatter would go way instantly. I told him that through the practice of meditation, he will reach a state of content serenity, just as I had experienced. And with further practice, he will be able to see things without the fog of his own fears and personal interpretations. After we got off the phone, he went and meditated. I did not feel any sort of self-righteousness, but rather a sense of joy. I knew I had helped my brother due to the learning I had the opportunity to experience because of my training in Zen. Though I will always be on a path of learning, being able to share such goodness with others so that they benefit made me happy. I had given to someone else.

Suzuki mentions giving a lot in his readings. As he states, "But as everything is originally one, we are, in actuality, giving out everything. Moment after moment we are creating something, and this is the joy of our life... when you give something you feel good, because at that time you feel at on with what you are giving" (65). This is exactly how I felt after speaking with my brother on his conflicted issues. I felt one with Zen practice as if I had understood it fully. That moment, coupled with many other experiences from class lecture and meditative practice has compiled together to create the epiphany of my deeper understanding.

I can only hope that in my furthering curiosity I have more epiphanies such as these. To be enlightened is a state which takes much practice, but one that is practiced for habitually every day. A lot of the readings spoke of not striving or leaning too far for or against something; this seemed hindering in my development as a human being. I have come to understand such notions as the art of ridding one's self of insatiable desires and non-realistic goals which cause grief. My family being very close to me, I have found many great analogies from them. My father, for instance, struggles with the "self-centered dream" Professor Syverson refers to in class. He is always seeking and striving to the future for new dreams, new material possessions, and new places he will live. As the saying goes, "The grass is always greener on the other side." This is a paradoxical idiom that expresses the human desire to want what we do not have. Such desire can be destructive and insatiable; never-ending. I wish my father could reach a calm state of contentment so that he is not running all the time; running from his own state of mind. The self-centered dream is one I need to learn from as well. Coveting and wanting more out of my day than the day allows is something I do constantly; it was probably inherited. I hope to grow from such destructive striving in my future learning of Zen practice.

Overall, these past weeks have been moving me forward in my path to enlightenment. The books by Hagen and Suzuki are informative and provide a great cushion for my experiential learning. Class and Professor Syverson's talks, as well as my outside experiences with reality have truly developed my sense of learning in Zen. I look forward to what the future holds.

Later Reflections of Zen

Now in the last part of the semester, I reflect on my time in the class realizing I have so much more to learn.

"Zen is less a religion than a way of looking at life" (Kennedy 12). Among other revelations these past few weeks, I have identified very well with the above passage from Robert Kennedy's book "Zen Spirit, Christian Spirit: The Place of Zen in Christian Life." I have also humbled myself a bit since my middle glimpses in my early Zen experience. I realize that my own journey is one that needs the most focus and should be studied upon. That is not to say I have not helped others in the process, but this was not an aim for me. It was more a surprise. Much like what was learned from Rick Hanson's *Buddha's Brain* as well as class discussion, revelations and learning in Zen comes through experience in the natural setting for our own lives; nothing artificial or temporary, but lasting tidbits that make up a whole and stay with one's own self forever. I would like to first provide some insight into my own personal experience via my background and relationships with others at the moment. I will then apply my learning to concepts learned during student and teacher discussions as well as the readings of *Buddha's Brain*, *Meditations on Zen Buddhism* and a book I researched myself. The book is about being a Christian and living a Zen life simultaneously.

This particular year of my life has been difficult due to a pending breakup in my family. For years we have been a foursome that travels together, eats together and laughs together. As we all get older however, it is not only difficult to have this static contact between us all, but it is also very difficult for my parents to cope with the "empty nest." My brother and I are off at college living our own lives no longer under their wings. I used an analogy with a friend of mine to describe their situation. It is as if my parents were working horses that grew accustom to carrying a carriage behind them for years and years until someone took that carriage away. They are two horses who have been doing the same routine for so long they feel lost when their duty has been served and they are free from the responsibility. Then it comes time to create a rebirth in their individual lives. This is so they can be enriched and challenged as before, but in new and various ways. Such fulfillment in life may only be reached after a realization that these two horses are lost together. They both feel the need to take dire measures to change their lives. Due to lack of understanding and lack of compromise, they both decided the best way to deal with the change was to live apart from each other. For months, not a word was said to each other. As unbiased as I wanted to remain, I still had to intervene. Zen tools and practices I was learning in the class forced me to be involved. I started off by pushing the practice on both my mother and father. That was not nearly as effective as just using the practice in my own life and letting them recognize my own changes.

It does not matter how old a person is, when their family breaks up it is painful. People can deal with pain in many ways. My brother tries not to deal with it. I was busying myself so much that I would not have to deal with this pain either. The problem with these, as I have learned through the class, is that you are never facing your individual fear or emotion having to do with such a pain. The triggers that draw up different mental synapses are pushed aside and pushed aside just building up for a later explosion.

To give a playback on the details of the situation, I will go into how I first reacted. My first approach after discovering more about being Zen was, as I said, to push this knowledge on those in my family who I know were in pain; those such as my brother (mentioned earlier in the chapter) as well as my parents. My mother was more receptive at first; listening to what I had to say and agreeing with it fully. I would talk about the ways in which to deal with problems, that it is incredibly important to segment issues one is facing into different regions and tackle the thoughts head on as they come. This is with a background understanding that you control your own mind and not vice versa. Hanson in his book calls this taking refuge. As he states, "Taking refuge pulls you away from reactivating situations and concerns, and then fills you with positive influences. As you rest increasingly in a background sense of refuge, neurons are quietly stitching a safety net for you... At these times [of darkness], your refuge will catch you and help you ride out the storm" (Hanson 94). This all made sense to me and I found it fascinating that all of these things were going on in my brain physically, while I was only mentally and emotionally connecting with these experiences. I would go over and over projecting my newly learned knowledge on others feeling gratified in me and my path. It was not until Professor Syverson pointed out that this is common for new practitioners of Zen that I halted and had a revelation.

I realized I was again focusing on others paths and trying to help others so much so that I would forget about my own self. It was after that very class at the end of October that I realized my experience with Zen could not be measured by my ability to help others in their daily dealings and relationships, but rather it was time that I help myself in my own path. Little did I know that this inward focus would spread outwardly in an incredible, positive way.

The first thing I did to focus more on my own path was to practice meditation on a more regular basis outside of class. The more I sat focused and not falling asleep, the better I became at mindfulness mediation. A way of sitting that made me feel more resolved and happy about my own world. Due to my inherent nature to overcommit and cram my time to the max, this particular fall has been incredibly hard to stay focused and tackle my day with confidence. I have really just been falling in a heap everyday feeling like I am drowning in my own To-Do lists. Not only physical improvement of posture, but also proper hand positioning and breathing slowly has been essential to my mindfulness during sitting. I find my mind is increasingly alert as I focus on thoughts as they float in and around my mind. I love what *Buddha's Brain* talks about while describing the book, "By combining breakthroughs in neuroscience with insights from thousands of years of contemplative practice, you, too, can use your mind to shape your brain for greater happiness, love, and wisdom" (Hanson). Reading such a statement one unfamiliar with the art of Zen might be left perplexed wondering how or if that is even possible. But I read the statement and know that it is very possible, having practiced such an art.

After several small sessions of sitting, I began to feel more serene and at peace with the choices I have made during my day. I also do a good job of fragmenting my day into what I like to call "baby steps." Such constant mindfulness and atten-tion to the way I approach my day has really been essential to my experience with Zen. Suddenly, talks with my parents and friends about their individual pain would first be focused on the way I deal with my own issues. Simply telling about my own coping with real life struggles somehow became a refuge for my mother and father. My Dad who is a little resistant to the practice noticed how happy and peaceful my approaches to his questions became. He right out asked me what I was doing differently and I simply said that I was using the practice of Zen to shape my thoughts in a way that better improved my outlook on life.

My mother started reading some Christian Zen books and began mindful prayer meditation. As a way to protect herself from her own pain, her form of sitting is to literally chant a prayer over and over while sitting until reaching a place of calm. I found this absolutely fascinating and that is when I took on the task of researching being a Christian and living a Zen life. I read up on the book, "Zen Spirit, Christian Spirit: The Place of Zen in Christian Life" by Robert Kennedy. As a person who was never truly fulfilled spiritually by organized church alone, such studies resonated so well with my life. As Kennedy states, "So I do not relate to Zen as an alien religion, but as an opportunity to share with like-minded men and women of many religions a way of being human" (14). Kennedy worked with Yamada Roshi and many other Zen teachers. He says that they never once asked him about his faith, but how he sat, how he breathed, and how he saw the world. This is to be acknowledged. The no-motive nature of Zen is one of the reasons it appeals to me so. It is about the nature of one's own experience and their ability to reduce the suffering and cope in the presence of their own individual lives. Such coping calls for an awake state of mind. This takes much practice to obtain.

I have always felt spiritually connected to nature and God and pray a lot. However, I am also moved by music and the ability to have faith and maneuver my life to where I feel peaceful regardless of what may be going on around me. Having practiced and studied Zen, I realize that my spiritual side is only better improved and focused upon through zazen. It is like having a skill to paint that one would utilize casually until having the opportunity to flourish at an art school where such skills are challenged and pushed to an entirely higher level. Zen is my art school and I feel I am flourishing. I only hope to continue in this journey so that I can reach deeper and deeper level of understanding of the Zen practice.

Works Cited: Kennedy, Robert E. Zen Spirit, Christian Spirit: The Place of Zen in Christian Life. New York: Continuum International Group, 1995.

Ashley Underwood is a senior dual-majoring in Rhetoric and Writing, B.A. with Public Relations, B.S. and a minor in Business Foundations with the McCombs School of Business. She is from Austin, Texas and lived in Santa Fe, New Mexico for four years. This is where she identified with nature and the balance of the world around her. Her creativity and love for Zen stems from the Land of Enchantment and Professor Syverson's class.

Classical Gentleman in the Modern World
Logan Ross

Before

I began readings of Suzuki during the summer or 2009 before going to Taiwan to study Chinese. I was impressed by the clarity, simplicity, and rigor of his thinking. The way he determined and offered a definite idea of what is "right practice," and the definite way with which he handled situations of aporia (e.g., the good horse, bad horse analogy)—all were impressive and became simple tools I could carry with me in my studies. In Taiwan, the spiritual culture is so very different than ours. It's Confucian, but it's also Buddhist, and Daoist as well. There's also a Christian element, brought in and cultivated by foreign missionaries. To note, while I anticipated the encounter of the new 'religions' to be exotic or strange, it was my own culture that became incredibly exotic, strange, and complicated, while the new religious perspectives appeared increasingly simple, domestic, and tame. All throughout this experience with Zen and non-American culture, was the influence of Socrates. Plato, more so than any other 'maker' of media, influences and enriches my exploration of the world of ideas. Furthermore, Socrates and Plato are surprisingly in tune with Zen and Ancient Chinese philosophy.

First

2010: I signed up for the course "Non-Argumentative Rhetoric in Zen" because I was working on a project which focused on the 'roots' of language. I felt that a study of Zen would refine my sense for those core shapes and movements in language. Something I didn't take into consideration, to my fault, was that I'm not exactly the normal undergrad (I'm 28, for one thing), and not everyone in class would be as prepared as I was to leap into the fray. I certainly wouldn't have been 8 years ago. The course, though, is set up to introduce Buddhism with one text, then study Suzuki to introduce Zen and mark it's sovereign place apart from Buddhism (though Buddhism needs Zen, Zen does not need Buddhism), then, we studied a scientific text which discusses the neurology of meditation; finally, we studied a more academic text which dealt with questions of textual practice in the study of Zen. Alongside the reading, we use a website to log weekly observations, post questions, respond to questions, etc. This was something I really had trouble with. I often became uncomfortable and impatient when dealing with the computer side of the course. This most recent summer, I decided to work only with paper, and studied characters, researched, and wrote intently. I knew that I was going to have to return to the computer-world, but also knew that I had to stick with the paper because the results I got were so positive and focused. So, when it came to navigating and keeping up with the course website, I was out of my element, and never quite got the hang of it. However, the way the course website was organized was much more carefully structured than others I've had to interact with. Even though I wasn't very good at it, I found myself wondering how I might employ the course-website structure in future classes.

The actual class, occurs two days a week, and we begin with a 15 minute meditation, followed by 5 minutes of free-writing. I found the meditations to be crucial, and I don't think I'll be able to fully appreciate this until more time has passes and I've digested all that's gone on this semester. The text which focuses most directly on sitting is Suzuki's, and it is no coincidence that this text is so straightforward and applicable to my day to day interactions. Suzuki will often begin a sentence with something like, 'So, when we sit..' As a reader, this acted as a kind of subtle corrective mechanism in my activity. When I'm reading, I'm usually sitting, and so Suzuki's message maintains an immediacy of presence; it's like having a teacher check in on you while you're at home studying. Instead of staying off in thoughts and intellectualizing, I would get drawn back to my immediate physical experience of sitting down, reading. As the semester wore on, other classes and projects began to pull and push at my time and attention, and I found it was much more difficult to maintain genuine attention (as far as my own brand of it) to Zen study. I could read the books, and meditate on the concepts, but not in the same focused way I could in the beginning. I felt I had to dilute my interest/engagement in order to survive my college coursework.

Study Practice

While it may not be the most fascinating or potent issue drawn from our study of Zen, the question of what distinguishes practice from study is the one which I feel must take priority. The foundation of Zen practice is sitting, and sitting is just sitting. Studying Zen becomes complex when it becomes clear that reading and writing and intellectualizing are not *zazen*. Buddhism, we learned, has a more deliberately structured system of ideas, but Zen is about practicing sitting. Of course, a great deal more goes into it, and there are texts and a wealth of ideas which come from Zen practice, but engaging a study of Zen in the same way one might study Political Philosophy or Christianity is inappropriate, while a study of Buddhism could be carried out within such a framework. In Zen, there are no set ideas or external constructions which regulate and/or direct Zen Practice. There is a tradition, yes, but when it comes down to it, zen practice is sitting down in silence for a time and letting your mind do what it needs to. What is it exactly that the mind need to do? No one really knows.

We read about the ways the brain works and develops

from meditation, but we don't know exactly why it is that this one practice is so effective over others—a pill, or academic or physical-athletic regimen for instance. What we do know is that this practice tends to bring people closer to who they truly are, closer to health, closer to a balanced and harmonious state of being. That may be a broad sweep, but we're talking about a very simple thing—sitting. Is is really so strange to find such benefits in that overlooked first step to rest? So, how do we study Zen in a way that does not lead us farther and farther away from experiencing Zen practice? I am very glad I don't have to come up with the answer to this question, because I have no idea. It's tricky; and this is the way of this course. Fortunately, our instructor is very experienced, practices Zen professionally, and also practices study professionally.

So, there is this kind of balance between aesthetic philosophy and textual practice. Because it truly is a tricky thing to balance, I certainly experienced some slipping and sliding while navigating between the somewhat anti-textual or textual-indifferent nature of Zen, to the textual-heavy practice of reading modern books, using websites, keeping a regular observation log, etc. If I go too far in the direction of Zen practice, I can't possibly keep up with the many textually-governed realities of my life in a city, at a university, as a student. Meditation becomes a "hiding" as opposed to a practice. If I go too far in the intellectual direction, I begin to presume knowing when in fact I'm mainly recalling and reciting textual experiences. This brings me back to Plato/Socrates.

In the Republic, Socrates leads an inquiry into aspects of life in a city, how a city can begin and grow, and what can result from people's desire for "relishes" in a civilized setting. There's no way I can capture the full scope of this inquiry here, but I do want to refer to his handling of text. Socrates and his companions decide that in their city it will be best if poetry and the arts are regulated so that makers (the word for poet literally means maker, and I like to press the term because in Chinese, the word for writer translates to "professional maker") only be allowed to create representations of good and simple people, and that the performances of poetry be the same—so that the performers do not have to imitate behavior, people, things, animals, etc which are not simple and good ("good" is something I trust we can have common understanding without a complex philosophical investigation—don't steal, do your duty, take care to be honest, don't be too much of a hard-liner, etc.).

Working within this framework is a rawer model asserting that text and the arts and those intellectual creations of man have the potential to sharpen the mind while nevertheless taking it farther and farther away from what is truly nourishing and preferable. Now, the concern I and students like myself often have regards how we can study something and also experience it fully. If the dynamic is harmonized, we achieve a kind of balance of limited results; we do not get the full studiers' boon of info and textual agility, and we also do not get the full practitioners' boon of hands on experience. However, through harmony, we can acquire the new material in a way that does not leave us with intellectual indigestion (something we touch on in Wright's book). This is a fascinating and important challenge in education. This semester, my experience with RHE330 was to go through a standard-style (one semester, midterm, final, etc.) course-format that in every way sought the harmony I just mentioned. It was one of the most effective attempts I've experienced, and I imagine my classmates would agree. There's still the University setting though. It's the elephant in the room. There's no getting around it. Every student is taking other classes while taking this one, perhaps working also, balancing efforts at finding a social community, etc. My experience was to routinely find myself obstructed from digestion, not by my particular class so much as by the institutional constraints of the University. I find I simply do not have enough time/energy to fully engage and digest what I was studying. To use an analogy, it is often like we are doing agility drills which train our ability to do agility drills more so that they truly train our agility. This is not something I see as being bad or good. I just notice that often grades depend mostly on the ability to adapt to and engage various drills or clerical procedures. This pull towards drills is something I struggle a great deal with, but I understand it is a necessity in an environment with strict scheduling and time constraints. The way I struggle with the University climate is relevant to our discussion, and greatly impacts how I've been able to engage the study of Zen

Some questions require longer than others to appreciate and digest, yet I'm beginning to understand why some people regard the recognition and appreciation of important questions as more of a burden and disease than valuable capacity. I mean, I can talk about what I'm learning, and I can navigate and manipulate the information of texts and lectures, but as for digesting and fully experiencing study/practice, the more I remained loyal to and focused on a vigorous harmony, the more ridiculous and "washed out" I became. As the semester went on, I found myself becoming thin in my intellectual vigor. This is due to an inability to compromise on my part. I don't know how to 'turn off' the recognition and appreciation side of things, and I am never willing to take shortcuts in understanding for a grade. I wish I was! This brings me to the final knot in the line of my experience: Though my approach has been incredibly nourishing and beneficial in some respects, granting me a kind of "skeleton key" whereby I can walk from school to school, from issue to issue, from subject to subject, etc with relative ease, I generally encounter distrust suspicion or resentment when I use the things (I don't if I can even call it 'things') I've learned. As we approach the end of the semester, I am no closer to understanding what this is about. I take for granted that, as a classmate of mine (he also gave me the title for this chapter) told me this semester, "Yeah, I mean, that would be a great way to learn this, but not everyone wants to bang their head against the wall engaging such difficult passages/questions." What I am coming to believe is that it is more in my interests to take steps towards silencing my curiosity and stopping myself from flexing and stretching out my intellect. I don't want to be an outcast or oddball, and I see now that the more intent I am on seeking the full appreciation and digestion, the farther I slip behind, and the more dismal my future becomes in every practical, economic, and social respect. I am very concerned that I will cause distress for myself and my family if I do not "shape up." I imagine this may come across as combative, but that's by no means my mode as I write this. I find that when I flex and stretch and settle myself into thorough inquiry, I get trampled and swept away in terms of grades and scheduling and social connections, and the things I was able to do and achieve through study are... irrelevant, unnecessary, and of no value to others. I can't argue with this, and I don't want to anymore. Zen gives me a perspective of how to "drop it." I never thought I'd say this, but I'm close to being ready to drop it, press to graduation, and just be a regular guy who might meditate and do community service. I feel this is not such a bad thing, and the only concern would be over whether leaving my projects behind will result in painful atrophy. I really don't know, but I'm definitely interested in hearing ways I might compromise and bleed myself of whatever it is that makes me take inquiry so seriously.

PS: Ancient Stuffing

Throughout the semester, I found myself constantly wanting to bring Socrates into the discussion. In *Symposium* , Socrates, before going into the party, suddenly stops and goes out to a balcony and stands in silence for some time, just staring off into space. Apparently he was known to do this often; and, the practice amounts to a *standing zazen*. Also, in *Phaedrus*, he describes the soul—first, as being impossible to describe in actuality; then, he goes on to try describing "what it is like." He says the soul is like a chariot team of driver and two winged horses. One horse is of good stock and well behaved, the other is of bad stock and will pull the chariot off track if the driver does not carefully attend to the *driving*. What I just wrote was a coarse and impoverished summation, but you get the idea. Now, similarly, in the book *Buddha's Brain*, the authors include a section where they describe the Native American frame of "two wolves" within the heart, and ways they drive and can also trouble us. Then, one of my favorite passages in Suzuki is where he uses an analogy of good and bad horses, and suggests that we must be careful when attending to notions of "good" and "bad," since there are times, *sometimes*, when the worst horse is also the best horse. Plato's resonance with Zen philosophy is, at least to me, very interesting, useful, and important. This semester's coursework has carved out another line of study which I hope continue into the future. It would not be fitting here to attempt a full discussion of the resonance between Zen and Socrates' practice, but I did want to at least touch upon the beautiful ways with which ancient schools of thought intertwine and 'speak' with each other, and the ways those ancient schools remain, in my opinion, steadfastly applicable to humanity regardless of time passing.

Actually, I feel that the ancient schools of knowledge are in fact clearer and closer—though challenging—to the truth than modern attempts at creating a "complete" understanding. The move away from studying the classics or ancient traditions is something I sense comes from efforts to make academics easier, more comfortable, and, especially, more accessible. I think this is unfortunate, in my opinion, but can't say I know whether it is a bad thing.

Logan Ross is from Austin Texas. His family is from Texas and Oklahoma, and he is 1/16th Cherokee. He is Junior studying towards a double major in Chinese and Rhetoric. He has a very low GPA. He is 28 years old. His interests are philosophical inquiry, studying Chinese characters, playing soccer, playing music, and spending time with family and friends, and cultivating 君子。

Practicality
Heath Cleveland

I don't think I would have taken this class if I had not needed an "Area E" requirement to graduate. I've always made a habit of taking writing classes that I felt had "real" practical purposes, and a Non-argumentative Rhetoric in Zen class seemed to entail everything but little did I know the range of practical implications Zen would bring.

Before this class, I would liken my day-to-day experience to that of a caged hamster who thought he was being forced to run on the hamster wheel. My point of view was skewed, and so fraught with mixed expectations that, no matter what I was doing, I was dissatisfied.

It's October 30th, 2010, the day before Halloween, but the night of Halloween celebration around the UT campus, and I'm at Zach's coop in a study room by myself. I feel isolated, alone, and like there's something I'm missing out on - but none of that's true. I'm in a building bustling with people preparing for a huge party, Zach's downstairs taking a nap before we prepare our amazing costumes and go out for the night, and I thought it would be the perfect opportunity to do some writing and reflection. By all means, I wanted to be here in this spot, right now, doing exactly what I'm doing. Nothing's wrong, but my shoulders are tense, I feel anxious and depressed, and I keep looking to my left out this 6th story window as if something between the unflinching darkness, treetops, and the UT tower will show me evidence of everything I think I'm missing.

Fortunately by October, I was at least realizing I had this tendency. Reflecting now, I can see some of the reasons that I often feel this way. For one, I have a tendency to strive for perfection. Even when I first started studying Zen, I was striving to attain this omnipotent point of view that would allow me to know the "right" course of action in any situation.

So far my exposure has been minimal, but – at least after reading Hagen's *Buddhism Plain & Simple* – I feel like I began receiving an education in Zen (or Buddhism) long ago. I find myself searching through old memories, and reorganizing my life story into a series of events that culminate into a kind of Zen understanding. In the present, I'm struggling to find clarity, and I cannot seem to find a reference point that provides me an appropriate purview for my day-to-day life. The oddest part of straining to see the world for what it truly is while simultaneously restructuring my past experiences is that both are taking place in the present. It seems counter to Zen to spend so much time reflecting on the past.

I remember at the time I wrote this, that I seemed to think that this process would stop eventually, and I would reach this "perfect" understanding. I no longer believe that I will ever reach a point where reflection isn't necessary for my Zen practice. Unsurprisingly, my Zen practice isn't the only place where I've strived for a false idea of perfection. My short exploration in Zen is very similar to my attempt to find 20/20 vision. When I was younger, I used to have perfect vision, but when I was in the fifth grade I got my first pair of glasses. From there, my vision only worsened. By the time I was 14 years old, I was legally blind, and by the time I was 17 years old, my vision could no longer be accurately corrected with contact lenses. The best I could see out of each eye with contacts was around 20/50, but because I had astigmatism, the contacts would rotate, and I often couldn't even see that well. Even though I could see better with glasses, I refused to wear them. They were very thick and they magnified my eyes in such a way that they looked oversized and lopsided. I was already heavily made fun of at school, and I was not about to add fuel to the fire.

I remember feeling so unfortunate and angry because of my bad eyes. To me, the eye doctors were stupid, my glasses were stupid, my eyes were stupid, my parents were stupid for sending me to stupid eye doctors, and there were 84 reasons why my eyes weren't being fixed. I never once appreciated the fact that my vision could be corrected to the extent that it was. No, I only cared to see the flaws. I would waste so much energy thinking how my life would be better if I had better vision, and I never thought to put any of that energy towards adaptation. It seemed incomprehensible to me that my vision was as good as it could ever be.

In my last bout to achieve perfect vision, I had Lasik eye surgery the day of my 18th birthday, but Lasik was not the cure-all I had expected it to be. My vision wasn't perfect afterwards, I became night-blind, and my eyes became very sensitive to light. Of course, I went through the same emotional process, blaming the doctors, my parents for sending me there, etc. In reality though, I would have gotten the surgery anyway – even if I had known the negative consequences ahead of time.

I didn't really start to understand that my eyes were about as good as they were ever going to be until shortly before my 20th birthday. Most doctors that perform Lasik have a policy that if someone has Lasik and that person's vision isn't 20/20 afterward, then he or she can come in for a free touch-up as long as it is no more than two years after the initial surgery. Since it had almost been two years, my doctor called me to remind me of this deadline. He also told me that it wasn't medically recommended to get Lasik more than twice in a lifetime. Since my eyes were still changing at the time, they would almost certainly change after I had the surgery. Finally, I had exhausted all my options, and realized none of them would get me the perfect vision I had strived for so long.

Before this experience, I had never come to terms with medical cures not being perfect cures, and that some things might never be perfect. It's strange, but I was allowing myself to hold others culpable for not being able to fix my eyes in the way I imagined perfect vision to be. Even though my vision was being corrected as much as possible, I wouldn't let myself see it for so long, and I caused myself a lot of suffering. Now that I've accepted that my eyes are functioning at capacity, I don't feel nearly as much frustration related to my inability to see some things.

That isn't to say though that I don't feel any frustration related to my sight. I think that, for me, this frustration will never really go away, and I will always have to practice dealing with it in a positive way. In order to do that, I've started reflecting on the times when I notice that something irritates me. I first got the idea when reading Hagen's discussion on the kinds of pain we inflict on ourselves. In a situation where I felt emotional, I would ask myself where that feeling came from and how it started. Sometimes, I would even be able to pinpoint what exactly triggered those thoughts, and then I'd start to see patterns. For example, when I'm reading with other people, I start to become much more conscious of the vision problems I have. I'll begin to focus on minute details, like how much more quickly the other person reads than I do, or how the words on the page always seem a little bit blurry to me. Then I'll start to feel the need to rationalize why the other person reads faster than I do, and I'll come up with reasons why my eyes are the cause. Afterwards, I'll feel anxious and uncomfortable, and I won't be able to focus on what I'm reading. Upon reflection, I started to realize that this kind of pain comes from a tendency to compare myself to others, just like Hagen discussed. I realized that it was happening in a lot more than just reading.

Whether it is about health, mental capacity, physical appearance, or life-obstacles, I feel stress related to jealousy, inadequacy, and a need to have some superiority over others. I just don't respond well when someone has something that I don't, and I experience the same emotional responses that I did with my bad eyes. I feel like the farmer in Hagen's novel that always felt the need to comment on his neighbor's good or bad fortune, but the value judgments I bring in only seem to waste energy. Who can really say what's good or bad?

It's a fact that I will never be able to see perfectly, in practicing Zen or using my eyes, and I think that, for me, value judgments will be one of the biggest hurdles to "seeing" in the sense that Hagen uses it. I don't have to have perfect vision to see and experience the world around me for what it truly is. I think that ultimately, my experiences are more limited when they are muddled with thoughts about how they could be better, rather than by my vision itself.

I had an experience earlier this semester where I noticed my mom was doing this very thing.

> I went to visit my family in Port Aransas, but I got off to a late start on Saturday and my mother was frustrated. My family and she had presumed I was going to arrive sooner than I did, so they waited for me even though I wasn't going to be there when they expected. My mom was understandably frustrated, but when I got there an hour after they arrived at the beach, she still seemed upset. On a beautiful sandy beach, she had two things on her mind that were ruining her experience: that she could have spent more time at the beach, and she had seen a dog defecate nearby and its owners didn't bother to clean it up. She couldn't enjoy her time at the beach because she was too focused on the time she had lost, and in the vast expanse of everything beautiful she could have chosen to appreciate that day, she instead focused on a small piece of dog feces located – somewhere – about two hundred feet away.

Not to rag on my mom, after all, we are related and, as I've pointed out, I have a tendency to do similar things. The experience just made me wonder about what I'm really missing when I'm distracted by everything an experience could be.

In the movie we watched about Joko Beck, she told her students something along the lines of, "Work with what you have, because that is your path. Don't think about what you want your path to be because you already have one." I think that doing the best with what I have, not what I wish I had or think I should have, and being truly at peace with that, is a very important part of Zen. Now, when I think about my vision, I think about how even though most of the things I see look very hazy to me, my sight is adequate for most things. I can even see about 20/20 on an eye chart. That's good enough. What matters it that, at the end of the day, I can still see pretty well, and maybe seeing hazy has its benefits sometimes.

I wish I could say that if my vision were to become worse, or that if I were to become blind, that would be good enough too, but I can't. For me, it seems that changes induce the same kind of emotional responses that I feel when I think something could be better. In a nutshell, instead of comparing myself to other people, I compare my circumstances to what they were in the past. It's still a comparison. The big difference being I know for a fact that something is or isn't possible because I lived it. When comparing myself to others, however, there's always a level of uncertainty. This small difference seems to make changes into emotional situations that I have quite a bit of trouble handling positively.

For example, a couple of months ago, I had an emotional encounter with a friend.

He and I used to be close, but lately he has been distant and we haven't been on good terms. As a solution, I wanted to try and spend some extra time with him, because the problem seemed to be worsened by the fact that both of us are very busy. Despite me spending the extra time and effort though, he didn't see it or appreciate it. He became very bored, acted like he didn't want to talk to me, and was very anxious to go and carry on with the other things he had planned that day. To me, it seems like I was doing him a favor. He had to be where he was at the time because of an organizational obligation we both had, and since I had already completed my required hour,

I was taking extra time to keep him company. Much to my own shock, he ended up leaving early and leaving me at the coffee shop, even though he knew he wasn't supposed to, and he left me there by myself. I had no reason to be there besides him, and his complete disrespect for my feelings made me very upset. He knows I was trying, but he doesn't seem to care.I put off some of my obligations to spend time with him, and I expected him to return that in some way. I know that I shouldn't have expected anything, but I found myself flooded with anger and anxiety. I couldn't seem to overcome it, or clear my head. In a short amount of time, I became completely consumed by my emotions, and I felt like I was stuck in a hole.

These are the typical feelings I had when I would think about how my friendship with this person seemed to be tanking out of my control. I don't think I mentioned it in the excerpt, but whenever I feel like a situation is out of my control, I have a tendency to feel very helpless. That feeling of helpfulness greatly contributes to the anxiety I feel.

At this point in the class, we were reading Suzuki and Professor Syverson was talking quite a bit about how meditation can often help a person calm themselves in a stressful situation. For the first time ever, I tried meditation as a method for dealing with my overwhelming emotions.

So, I did exactly what Professor Syverson and Suzuki said to do. I found a nice quiet place, sat up straight and comfortable, and I focused on my breathing. Any time my mind would sway, I would re-focus, but after the first minute, my thoughts about my friend, and the hopeless emotional state I had fallen into, subsided. I stayed, until I felt I was done. My head never completely cleared, and I'm still coping with the situation between my friend and I, but the emotion no longer consumes me. I'm aware of it, and I'm addressing it, but it's not taking control.

My emotions related to change are often the most disruptive to my every day life. When I realize that I'm aging, that I used to do better in school, or that I'm not as cool as I thought I was, I can lose myself in an instant. To the same effect, if I realize that I'm smarter than I used to be, or much more accomplished, I find myself flooded with positive emotions that are just as distracting from the reality of the moment. I don't deal well with change, and it seems like any major deviations from something I've come to take for granted cause me to go through the same emotional responses.

After having that experience with my friend, I started to notice just how narrow my world would seem whenever I felt emotionally overwhelmed, and how much it would expand when I'd sit in zazen. Realizing that turned out to be very important when I read *Buddha's Brain*. In *Buddha's Brain*, Hanson talks about how the brain creates neural pathways for certain activities, and the more often those pathways are used, the stronger they become. I began to notice that whenever I would have a bad reaction to something related to change, I would be experience similar emotional responses. To me, that signaled that some of my negative neural pathways had become too strong. Zazen has helped me to promote an alternative response to those emotional situations, which will invariably weaken that negative pathway.

Dr. Syverson also spoke about how humans sometimes create mental barriers in order to make the world around them easier to manage. When reflecting on my own mental barriers, I noticed that they often go hand in hand with my expectations in certain situations – along with the strong emotional responses I often have. I had a particularly eye-opening experience with this kind of idea not very long ago while at a dinner party with my friends. My friend had a really spacious backyard, so, I decided to go experience it. Much to my disappointment though, it was much more cramped than I had originally thought. To me, the fences seemed to be the problem. I thought that, without fences, that backyard would have been so much better. But then I realized that houses would still be in the way, and so would other buildings and roads. So, then, I thought that I really I wanted a vast expanse of totally uninhibited nature, but, that really wasn't it either. What if I got attacked by a bear or something? It seems that, what I wanted to experience wasn't really completely uninhibited nature. In fact, I wanted it to be completely controlled, but I just didn't want anything manmade to be controlling it. I was striving for something completely unreal, like when I was trying to achieve perfect vision.

Just like I realized fences can limit an outdoorsy experience, I noticed that my mental safeguards and strong neural pathways can sometimes serve more as barricades to my understanding rather than tools when striving for a false ideal.

> Walking through Misha's backyard, I wonder about the barriers humans create to gain control. We build houses to control our environments, right down to what enters and what exits. We design, manufacture, and regulate small pieces of the world just for ourselves – homes – and those pieces become ours – ours only – to inhabit, control, and change. We come to depend on our homes to be just what we expect, but to some extent this idea is naive. We know everything changes, but we often live our lives as if they won't. We place objects in particular places for particular reasons, most often perfunctory or decorative. We design and manufacture a piece of the world customized just for us. Sometimes, we cut off ourselves from the world so much that our expectations become reality. The great outdoors becomes our backyard, and we forget what the difference really is. Just like we create physical barriers, we create mental safeguards to regulate what comes in and what comes out. What we can handle and what we can't. We need to understand the strengths and weaknesses of safeguards. They're not always ideal, but often exactly what we need.

After this experience, I began to question the things that I would always assume. For example, when crossing a busy street at a busy stoplight, I assume that I'm going to be safe walking across as long as keep an eye out for dangers and only go when the red hand changes to a white-lighted figure of a person. In all probability, I will be fine, but there may be something out of my control that happens. That lack of control seems to be the wild card that makes me feel so helpless some times.

In *Buddha's Brain*, Hanson talks about how humans have developed a natural inclination to stabilize what's changing around them, and that this can often cause pain. I've noticed that when I experience negative emotions related to change, I almost always feel a great angst about the change and I dwell on what I should or could be doing better to solve the problem. I think this has its benefits for survival, but I've observed that I often don't know where the line is between what I can control and what I can't. Often times, just like with my eyes, I'll pour a lot of energy and emotion into something that's not even achievable.

I think Zen can be used to draw that line, and that zazen reflection can be used as a litmus test for what's working and what's not.

In college, my biggest challenges have been time management and understanding my limitations. I like to keep myself busy, but almost every semester, I've ended up over-committing myself. Regardless of what it has been, I've never had enough time to commit to everything I want to do. My freshman year, I spent too much time with my girlfriend, too much time studying and too much time being involved. My sophomore year, I spent too much time being involved, too much time with my boyfriend, and not enough time studying. My junior year, I spent too much time being involved, still too much time with my boyfriend, not enough time sleeping, and not enough time exercising. This year, it's been a lot of the same. I've tried many different solutions to these problems but nothing seemed to make me good enough to do everything I thought I should be able to do.

Somewhere along the way, I started trying to change myself in order to become someone better. I was so jealous of the people who seemed to never sleep or exercise but could manage to accomplish more than me and stay in better shape. I decided I needed to make myself more like them. In order to do that, I forced myself to sleep less, and I made myself exercise less. To sleep less, I started having coffee, and lots of it.

Around the end of my sophomore year, I started to notice that, despite my best efforts, I was just not as efficient as I thought I ought to be. So, I went to the doctor, and got a prescription for the medication usually prescribed for ADHD, Adderall. Since Adderall causes people to lose their appetite, I stopped eating as much.

Even after all of that though, I still wasn't becoming the superstar person that I was striving to be. I didn't know what was wrong with me. I would think that I must not be as good as those other people, and I would think that I just had to try harder. To me, this meant less sleep, more caffeine, more Adderall, and more self-sacrifice.

Eventually, I started to notice that my health was deteriorating. In general, my quality of life was just bad, I never felt well and I had somehow gotten wrinkles, pains and aches that I never had before. At that point, I started to realize the consequences of what I was doing to myself, and it made me feel even more inadequate that I couldn't handle very much. I felt fragile, and helpless. I hated that I had to sacrifice my accomplishments for my health.

Reluctantly, I started exercising and sleeping more. I didn't quit taking Adderall or stop drinking coffee though. If I didn't have those, I thought I would never be able to accomplish anything.

But this semester, because of this class, that changed. I started to pay more attention to my emotional responses in situations that made me feel anxious, overwhelmed or stressed. I began noticing that any time I felt overwhelmed with an assignment or a task, I would immediately think that I needed to have more coffee and more Adderall. I would just assume that I wasn't capable of doing it on my own, and the more that I fell into that pattern, the more that belief.

Recently, I decided to completely cut Adderall and caffeine out of my life. It was difficult at first, especially because of the caffeine headaches, but it has completely changed my life. It turned out that my frequent trips to the coffee shops were really cutting down on my efficiency, and Adderall was actually interfering with my ability to learn more than it was helping.

All this semester, I've felt like Zen was something that I couldn't do well while simultaneously keeping up with all of my commitments. Before weaning myself off of Adderall and caffeine, I thought that I had to sacrifice my health to achieve what I want in life. Since I consider my Zen practice to be beneficial to my mental health, I operated under the assumption that the two couldn't be reconciled, and I had quite a bit of trouble uniting them in my life.

Because I assumed I wasn't capable of some things on my own, I blocked out some of the whole picture of what Zen practice really is—just like a fence can limit out an "outdoorsy experience." I walked into this class half-expecting everyone to be deodorantless, wearing ponchos, and experimenting with psychotropic drugs for homework, but what I got was actually very ordinary. I've been searching so long to find something that would take me beyond my day-to-day, hyper-stressed life, but little did I know that all I needed was to experience just that.

Through Zen, I've discovered that I have a haven within myself, and that I can gain control over emotions that are out of control. This experience also helped me to realize that taking control of your mind isn't like saying to yourself in that situation, "stop being emotional, or "stop thinking," that's forceful. Taking control requires addressing exactly what you need, and being willing to take stock of what that might be in a given moment. It's funny how often that doesn't happen.

What a practical application.

Heath Cleveland is a mathematics and rhetoric and writing senior at The University of Texas at Austin, and a new Zen practitioner.

Origins of The Holy Act:
Reflections on Observation
David Daniel

"We are all looking for Answers. The Answers are easy. The Doing is the Work." – Monty Galloway

Preface

What follows here are a series of inquiries chiefly into the efficacy of both Zen rhetoric and Zen practice. Though what you are viewing now (this Preface) comes first in the reading, it was written last. Similarly, though the inquiries below are presented in a particular narrative form, the form should not be considered to be the "truth" of the inquiry, but rather the processed and refined thinking of several weeks, distilled and packaged in a way that will allow you, my reader, to journey on the inquiry with me.

I have chosen as the testing ground for these inquiries the experience of my life while I have undergone the process of writing this chapter, and it is an effort to contextualize this time for you that prompted the addition of this late section to the text.

The first and likely most salient fact that comes to mind, is that I am a student at the University of Texas, as indeed all the authors of this book are. I am attending a class on "Non-argumentative Rhetoric in Zen Buddhism," as all the authors of this book are. I am a senior in Rhetoric and Writing, as many of the authors of this book are. And I am a student of middling performance, who makes great grades in my own field of study, and frequently has to repeat classes like Biology and Japanese, as some of the authors of this book are.

Beyond these things, my similarities to my peers begin to wane, as does theirs to me. And it is these differences which I hope make this book both relevant and interesting to you. I am a gay man, coming from a Christian faith background, and now a practitioner of Native American shamanism and Fourth Way esoteric psychology (much of which is influential to my writing, but not foundational, and so left little explained). I generally vote Democratic, though I consider myself more fiscally conservative. I chiefly get my news, like most of my peers, from comedy sources like The Daily Show with Jon Stewart. I am involved in a serious relationship at the time of this writing. I am an aspiring writer of fiction and biography. And I am an avid video-gamer in my spare time. All of these things and more shape my inquiry, as the Buddhist doctrine of "dependent origination" would teach. But they may also shape your reading. And as you read, I encourage you to use the reactions which my writing draws forward in you, not only to agree or disagree with my words, but also to illuminate your own experience.

This text is but one step on a journey of education for me. And it is a step I hope to share with you my reader, whether you are a practitioner of Zen Buddhism reading this book to better inform your own practice or teaching, or a parent of one of my classmates whose chapter mine happens to follow, or one of my own friends or family whom I have no doubt given this book to as a, perhaps narcissistic, but still poignantly well-intentioned Christmas present.

Above all what I hope this chapter demonstrates and advocates is a capacity for self observation, which brings with it the possibility of freedom from the tyranny of anger, fear, and anxiety. Buddhism, and in many ways all systems of spiritual thought, chiefly advocate the alleviation of suffering. It is that work which I hope is most represented in what follows. The prose is necessarily disjointed in places, and sometimes rambling. This, I have found, is a good sign of genuine self-reflection and inward turning. I have left it intentionally. The inquiries are presented in chronological order, so that in fact, one was not occurring simultaneously with the others. And this is intended to help give you a sense of my growing familiarity with Buddhist teaching and practice. Though I chiefly reference two of the course texts in the chapter work itself, much information and teaching from the others touched and shaped my understanding as well. Finally, the inquiries are based around a single question, presented at the beginning of the section, and which arose in all instances from my participation in class discussion and from the particular readings at that time. As such, the inquiries do not intentionally build upon one another, but rather interrelate only in the connections which you, the reader, draw between them. What follows can be as much your journey as mine, and I hope that you will find it, at the very least, worth remembering, and at best, a contribution towards your own enlightenment.

Inquiry 1

I sit upon the dock and contemplate the question, 'What is my opinion of Zen Buddhism'. I am unsure. I have come here, to my Sacred Space, a fetid tank of pond water squatting just east of two dilapidated "single-wide" trailers and about thirty miles north of College Station Texas, in order to observe my answer to this question. I find myself wrestling to move beyond my opinions and into what I would consider a more broad and objective inquiry. I do not seek to overcome my opinions only because Zen Buddhism teaches that this is crucial to observation and inquiry(and it does), but rather, because the man who purchased the land this fetid tank sits upon (with money he got as compensation for sacrifices he made in a war some thirty years ago) taught me the same thing. But this is where I must begin; with opinion.

My opinions of Zen Buddhism are varied and often times extreme. As a student in the Japanese Language program, I have some knowledge of Buddhist holidays in Japan. As a former

Christian, I am aware that much of the Buddhist practice is now being studied for concurrent inclusion with Christian doctrine. As a consumer of mass media, the rise of the phrase "I'll be Zen soon," and the consequent "verbification" of an entire school of religious thought, taints my view of Zen and adds a bleached blonde female with a soy foam non-fat latte and the cadence of an airhead to the cast of characters I associate with the practice of Zen (previously limited to bald Japanese men, and aging hippies). But as I examine each of my associations two things become clear to me. The first is that little of my opinion is based upon any sort of knowledge or experience with Zen itself. The second is that, overriding all of these assumptions is a somewhat dour and even negative shadow. It seems to me that this shadow comes from a deeper part of my life.

I have been a student of Fourth Way style esoteric spiritualism for the better part of six years. What I mean by Fourth Way is a system of thinking advocated by several different early to mid 20th century philosophers and championed most famously by one George Ivanovich Gurdjieff. A figure of some controversy during the early years of the previous century, it is not Gurdjieff I follow. Rather, I followed for a time Monty Galloway, a little known author and thinker who became my direct mentor and guide in 2001. He recommended Fourth Way thinking to me, and even invited me to be part of his institute, which was small, but cozy, and heavily influenced by Fourth Way.

This is important to my opinions of Zen Buddhism because the central tenets seem very similar. In the first text I read on Zen Buddhism (*Buddhism Plain and Simple* by Steve Hagan) the author states that Buddhism is simply the practice of being here, now. In Fourth Way, the object is to be fully present in the moment, and to observe with complete objectivity (or as close to it as one can get) what is actually happening. So my opinions of Zen Buddhism, I am finding, are colored directly by my experience of my previous Work. Rather than arousing curiosity, this draws out in me a strong state of agitation. At the surface, this agitation seems to derive from a need to provide adequate defense of what I have experienced, a justification for why Fourth Way is "better" than Buddhism. This is silly. Gurd-jieff himself claimed to have created his system based upon the great traditions of the Eastern World. It should be a good thing to find the central tenets to be so similar.

But if I sit with the emotion of agitation, and observe it, as Fourth Way and Zen Buddhism would teach me, what I find is a connection to deep grief inside of me. A year and a half ago, my mentor, Monty Galloway, passed away unexpectedly and in my presence. This was a tremendous loss for me, and one of the ways in which I have made my peace is by adopting and advo-cating his work to others. My agitation is not born from a rivalry between Fourth Way and Zen Buddhism. In fact, there can be none. Zen Buddhism is recognized the world over, practiced by millions currently, and billions historically. Fourth Way is a little recognized system. And further still, the unique blending of Work which my mentor taught is smaller even than Fourth Way. The agitation comes from a fear that the immense and ancient tradition of Zen Buddhism can, in some way, invalidate or lessen the meaning and wisdom of a man who I credit with saving my life (a longer and more dramatic story).

The freedom that this observation gives me lies, for me, chiefly in the ability to now speak to this voice of discontent inside of me. I can tell this fear, for instance, that in Hagan's book, Buddha is described as one who is "awake" and further, Hagan says there have been many who are awake throughout history. I can assure the fear inside of me that it is quite possible that the Monty I knew was perhaps "awake" himself. Or not. But Zen Buddhism would not in any way conflict with the ex-periences I have had. And in fact, it lessens those experiences to require that Zen Buddhism validate them in some way. My memories are mine, and what they mean to me is up to me. I can set this emotion aside now.

This setting aside begins to open up for me a new space of inquiry. No longer are my thoughts held captive by the tyranny of my own opinions, but rather, those opinions can form a sort of platform from which further inquiry and new insight arises. And, because I now have control of my opinions, I am also free to change them, and rearrange them, in ways that empower me and leave me positioned for action. This is freedom from suffering. It seems to me that the truly insidious nature of suffering is not the pain it causes, but what it attaches itself too. The suffering caused by my attachment to my opinions tells me that in order to be free of the pain I will have to give up my opinions. But this is a lie. A lie which becomes clear as I sit with the emotion. In truth, what I must give up is the feeling that my opinions are correct and in need of defense. When I let my opinions become mine again, bound by the smallness of my human condition, as am I, then they become tools for me to use how I please. They become more useful in their smallness. And the suffering disappears, while the opinions remain. Perhaps there is something to this practice of Zen Buddhism.

Inquiry 2

I sit upon the dock and contemplate the question, 'What is my opinion of Non-Argumentative Rhetoric in Zen Buddhism'. I am sure of this. It is a loud opinion, which in this stillness, I find nearly deafening. I do not believe that non-argumentative rhetoric exists. All rhetoric is argumentative. In my view it would be more accurate to call it "thickly obfuscated argumentative rhetoric." Whether you move someone towards your own opinion, or some more murky sense of his "appropriate" path of self-expression, you are moving the listener. Further, to present the rhetoric of Zen as non-argumentative is unethical, because it encourages listeners to view the rhetoric of Zen outside the normal filters of critical thinking with which all Rhetoric Majors (and really all listeners period) should view attempts made to persuade them of anything. The word non-argumentative itself seems overtly eulogistic. The portrayal of the rhetoric of Zen as fundamentally non-hostile, in the sense that it does not attempt to persuade the listener of a particular course of action, seems not only impossible but immoral to me.

And this is where I find I must begin. As I observe the seething emotion underlying my opinion, and listen to what it has to say, I find that there must be a reason inside of me for its fury. I realize that it is related to my sense of identity. I am a Rhetoric major. I listen to the reasons, to the justifications, to the complicated tangle of concepts that construct this identity. I chose to be a Rhetoric major based upon a feeling of inspiration I felt when I was in a class that studied the practice of demagoguery extensively. In particular I was inspired by the study of counter measures to Hitler's brand of fascism and all the various thought tools and means of argumentation that can be used to effectively neutralize the effects of this sort of tyranny. For me, argumentation (as understood to be the crafting/discovery of ethical and effective syllogisms in order to combat "evil" men) is a heroic and noble practice. To consider a system which eschews the very heroism to which I aspire generates a feeling of righteous indignation.

But this emotion that speaks to me is blacker than that. It is more than anger, it is spite. It is near vengeance. Not only do I want to prove the advocates of this so called Non-argumentative rhetoric wrong, I want them to be humiliated for even having suggested it. I conjure the faces of those I want silenced in my mind, and I place them in a group with others like them. Things become much clearer then. My mind has placed them in the company of the Evangelical Pastor of the church I attended as a child, and their voices speak with the voice of one Dr. James Dobson, a nemesis from my adolescence. I realize now that for me, argumentation is the method by which I was able to win self-acceptance. As a homosexual raised in an evangelically Christian home, I have the experience of deep self-hatred haunting my teenage years. And for me, the tyranny of that mindset did not end until the above mentioned class in which I learned how to respond internally to demagogic rhetors (such as James Dobson). I realize that the concept of Zen Buddhism has become unintentionally aligned inside of me with other organized religious movements, and that the strong negative experiences of my childhood taint my opinions of the proposition that non-argumentative rhetoric exists (anywhere, or in Zen Buddhism).

Again having identified and observed the source of my

emotion, I am free now to dialogue with it. I can tell this deep emotion, whose chief concern is really that I never have to experience the negativity of my past again, that Buddhism does not seem to advocate blind faith. In fact, according to *Buddhism Plain and Simple*, "The Buddha repeatedly emphasized the impossibility of ever arriving at Truth by giving up your own authority and following the light of others... The message is always to examine and see for yourself." (Hagen, 9). I can also assure this emotion that the exploration I am now embarking on is just an exploration. I am in no danger of being forced to do anything. I am merely examining a different style of rhetorical maneuvers. I do not even have to agree with the label "non-argumentative."

The opportunity I have here is not to set aside anything I already find valuable, but to expand my horizons of knowledge to perhaps discover new value. And in truth, being bound up in the idea that something is "wrong" is just as choking as the earlier explored idea that my opinions are "right." They are two sides of the same coin. When I realize that I have the freedom to examine anything, just as I have the freedom to believe anything, then my examination becomes an act of curiosity and not aggression. I am not looking to prove anything. And I am not trapped between the two polar extremes of agreeing or disagreeing. This black and white world seems to be another popular refuge for suffering, and in completing this inquiry, what I find is the possibility of freedom from polarity.

Inquiry 3

I sit upon the tailgate, and consider the question, "What does it mean to live free from leaning?" I have come north, across the mighty 35th road of Inter and State to the land of corn and Cornhuskers, invited to join the family of my dead mentor, Monty, in an annual pilgrimage of fellowship and carnage known as a hunting trip. Nebraska is dry. Hot, and then cold, as night follows day, but ever dry. I have never been hunting, but I desire this connection to my mentor and his past. As I sit here on the Ford, my hands sticky with Grouse blood, I find the words of Shunryu Suzuki coming to me now. "In everything, merely work with no gaining thought." Is this trip, this pilgrimage, a leaning? Is it attachment, to come to this place, seeking the roots of my friend?

To live without leaning seems so hollow to me. To distill the vast breadth of human experience to a ceaseless form of sitting and breathing, as Suzuki seems to argue that we should with his presentation of zazen(a technique of meditation in which one sits and breathes), is both invalidating and insulting! I know that desire is the cause of the Arising of Suffering (The Second Noble Truth), but what is the value of love then? Is the life well lived only one spent staring at cave walls or monastery gardens or cow tanks in the Nebraska autumn? How can the path to enlightenment require the sacrifice of all the good which we expect an enlightened soul to bring? Didn't Monty bring love and life back to my life? In fact, love seemed to be his only intention in life. Would Zen Buddhism require the sacrifice of love to be free from suffering?

But in his seminal text, *Zen Mind, Beginner's Mind* (a text which has indeed inspired this very book, this very inquiry), Suzuki addresses love. He says, "Recently the younger generation talks about love. Love! Love! Love! Their minds are full of love! And when they study Zen, if what I say does not accord with the idea they have of love, they will not accept it. They are quite stubborn you know." Of course, he isn't talking about me. He is talking about those pot smoking, bra burning, proto-anarchist hobos affectionately referred to as "Hippies." That's who he was speaking to, in San Francisco, sitting in his zendo, or in his mountain school. Surely he wasn't talking about my love, or the love of my mentor.

And I sit awhile longer, paying attention to this emotion (for it is speaking to me, sitting on the tailgate, covered in grouse blood, staring at the cow tank in the dry Nebraska autumn). What if Suzuki was talking about my love? I am reminded in my thoughts of something my mentor taught me. He spoke to me of the Lakota-Sioux Medicine Wheel, a Native American tool for understanding life. The teaching goes that all which exists in creation is mirrored in the Medicine Wheel. At the center of the Medicine Wheel sits the Great Mystery (or Wakan Tanka) around which all life dances, trying to see what it may see of this unknowable something. This is life. To dance and to know. I can remember suddenly the voice of Suzuki, "If it comes out of nothingness, whatever you do is true naturalness." All of nature may be reflected on the Medicine Wheel, and there may be much to see (good and bad), but if I hold tightly to some idea of how things must be or should be, then I have the danger of missing what is. Natural Zen "nature" is to be true to yourself, as you really are. And to be true to others as they truly are.

So now I can speak to this emotion. I can tell it that the love which my mentor gave to me, and the love which I carry forward in my life, comes naturally. I do not have to strive for it. It is there. And to live from love is natural; as long as it is natural. When love becomes a part of my life that must be, then I have placed it outside of myself. When I say that the love my mentor had for me must have value, then I diminish the value it actually had. When my view of what I see on the Medicine Wheel is clouded by the way I think it ought to be, I stumble in the dance. I do not have love. I have the desire for love, or the longing to have a particular love return to me. And from this arises suffering.

But if I can sit with myself, in stillness, and become the love that is naturally inside of me, then I have love. And others around me have the possibility of receiving that love from me. This seems to me to be related to Suzuki's assertion that "you must be enlightened to attain enlightenment." It is not that love must be given up, but that leaning for love you do not have must be eschewed. If I have love inside, then it is natural for me to love and be loved. If I do not have love inside, that is ok too. Because Suzuki says, the fundamental truth of Buddhism is that "all things change." If I have love, I have love. Maybe one day I will not have love. And maybe one day further I will have it again. But I do not have to diminish the experience of the love that I have by the fear of losing it, or the fear that someone else may demand that I give it up. Be with what is.

Inquiry 4

I sit upon the tailgate and consider the question, "What is the relationship of desire to action?" I know that it is important simply to have the experience in which you are living. Yet I find, even still, there seems to be no action implied by Suzuki, or Zen Buddhism as I have studied it thus far. I know now that I can have the experience of love, and not love, and let those two states come and go naturally. But what of effort? What of working hard, building up, saving the day, standing for what you believe in, and living a life full of rich experience? Aren't those things what it means to be alive? Or even if they are not what it really means, don't they produce a life full of good times and good company? What is it that Zen Buddhism wants us to do? At first glance it seems like a life lived in an enlightened state is one spent in constant inaction. But if that inaction is what is truly advocated, how could anything ever be accomplished, even daily tasks like preparation of food or hygiene?

But this thought is backed, as always I am beginning to find, by a dark cloud. There is a bitterness inside of me as I consider what I perceive to be a life of stillness advocated by Zen Buddhist thought. What good has my life been for then? What good is any life for? What has all my ceaseless struggling and striving been for? Have I climbed the mountain only to be told enlightenment is found sitting in the field below it?

And then I remember that desire is the Arising of Suffering. I can taste the suffering inherent in the desire for my life to be a "good" life. I want what I have done to be meaningful, and if not important, at least well executed. And in wanting to have my life be significant, it becomes insignificant because the desire for significance is an insignificant action to spend the moments of my life upon. I can hear the insignificance I become when I use my voice to say, "But look at me! I'm important!" Rather, to live in a state of enlightenment would be to constantly act.

As Suzuki says, "Naturalness is the seed sprouting into a plant in the Springtime." To practice zazen, this art of being awake in this present moment, I can act from my nature. That is to say, that it becomes possible for me to actually move towards a life of courage and action because I am awake to the presence of courage and action inside of me. I do not waste any time wondering how I should act, or if I should be courageous now. I act courageously because that is my nature. As Suzuki says, "Those who have attained enlightenment are incredibly straight-forward." And this hungry wolf inside of me called Turmoil, who so often masquerades as the sheep called Reason, is anything but straight-forward. However, if I pause and remember, both Suzuki and the teaching of my mentor, I know that life is simply to dance and know. Act and observe. Act within observation. And for awhile, perhaps it helps to sit still, and listen in zazen so that I can learn to identify this Turmoil wolf before it devours the very good things I have the possibility of bringing forth.

I get up from the tailgate, walk to the cow tank and wash the grouse blood from my hands.

Conclusion

Thank you for sharing this part of your journey with me. If my various inquiries into Zen Buddhism have taught me anything it is to live, right now, the life that most inspires me. Of course, this is tempered with the knowledge that often what will most inspire me will be to come inside on a cold winter day, make myself a cup of coffee sweetened with instant Hot Chocolate and spend the afternoon playing games on my Xbox. And this is all right. If anything, what I hope to convey with these inquiries is that freedom is possible, and self-compassion is always helpful. That is the final message I hope to convey here, to you. You, my reader, no matter who you are, are a complex collection of messy mixed-up experiences which gets more complicated and messy every day. And that is what makes you priceless. Just as each chapter in this book is a unique snapshot of life in the heads of very different college students wrestling to make sense of an ancient contemplative practice in a manner which will both entertain our readers and elicit a satisfactory grade from our instructor, so too, are you, our readers, an integral part of this journey. Whether you know it or not. And it is my wish, since we are so connected, that you would treat your own experience with deep compassion. After all, our experience is all you or I will ever truly have.

David Daniel is a senior in both the Rhetoric and English programs at the University of Texas. Originally from Rockwall, TX, he has lived in three different states, and visited four European countries including England, Greece, Denmark, and Italy. He is a Personal Growth Instructor, teaching under the guidance of Master Teacher Kenneth Galloway, and has accepted students since 2008. His interests include literary and rhetorical theory, spirituality, and creative writing. He is currently working on his first novel, and all the self-doubting anxiety this entails. He speaks Japanese. Poorly.

Buddha Beginner
Louis Baker

In order to understand the idea behind Zen Rhetoric, you must understand, or have some general knowledge about Zen. In order to understand Zen, you must have some knowledge regarding Buddhism because not all Buddhism is Zen, but all Zen is Buddhist. Simply having that bit of understanding organized in my brain is already leaps and bounds from where I stood at the beginning of this class.

Day 1: Oblivion

Zen was definitely something that I was unfamiliar with. Not having studied anything about Zen or even anything Zen related, I couldn't help it that all my preconceptions were bogged down with notions of spirits, magic wishing rocks, out of body experiences and a lot of Indian-style-sitting. The things I heard about and what I saw on TV were all the input that I got. And it was always a little unclear.

I genuinely had no idea what Zen was, much less what Zen Rhetoric represented. My initial questions were, "Is it a religion? If so, who am I supposed to pray to? Do you do any praying at all? Are there Zen worship temples? Would they be called "temples"? Who's the leader of the Zen people? Do they have a Pope or a Jesus or anything similar? Is it just a state of mind? Can one be in a state of "Zen" without even knowing it? How would you know? Can anyone do Zen? Could one be Christian or Jewish or Muslim or Hindu and still practice Zen?"

Needless to say, I was a bit uneducated in this particular field. The majority of the information I had about Zen (before I did any research) was from a friend of mine that claims to practice Zen. I've never asked very many questions about it though, mainly because her methods seem... let's just say, unorthodox. She has a small, shiny, wooden box with a tiny, gold lock on the pad. Inside this box is what she calls, her "Zen tools." Now before I go any further, I just want to say to all the true Zenners out there that she probably isn't a by-the-book kind of Zen practicer and I really didn't think that this was how one typically goes about performing the Zen rituals. So please don't get offended. To me, the contents seemed a little more like they pertained to witchcraft than Zen which sheds a little positive light on my sense of reality (but, not much on my ability to choose friends... odd lady.) But then again, I had no other frame of reference other than TV, so this could've all been legitimate. I really had no way of knowing.

Anyway, what I saw inside this box were three small grey feathers, plucked from what I could only guess to be a tiny pigeon. Next to that was a metal cauldron with a pile of ash in the bottom. The feathers are supposed to be used to fan the positive energy (or smoke, as I like to call it) all around the house or room or closet, released by the flame inside the cauldron so you can bask and meditate. A velvet sack of black powder was wedged underneath and lying next to that were a variety of rocks: black, red, dull, shiny, smooth, jagged, etc. Apparently, there were only a select few that I was allowed to touch, mainly the jagged ones. Smooth was, apparently, very personal. And if I were to touch the "forbidden" rocks (the smooth ones), they would lose their energy and have to be discarded and replaced. I was actually pretty disappointed as to how one performs the "discarding" process. I hoped there would be some involve-ment with a burial and a dance or a chant. But, apparently you can just throw it in the yard...

6 Weeks In: Light at the End of the Tunnel

After being in the class for several weeks, I reassured myself that the contents in the box do not come standard with a Zen kit. But in actuality, I really didn't know what to expect. I didn't think this class would involve shaving our heads, wearing robes and sporting sweets golden medallions. But, rather than just being a lot of background information on Zen's history, it turned out to be much more interesting and involving than I had initially thought. Each class day begins with fifteen minutes of silence and stillness. Nice. I usually do that in all my classes until I snore myself to consciousness or have one of those dreams where I'm falling down and knock my coffee twelve feet across the room. But in this class, eyes must stay open. Your feet should rest flat on the ground and your back should be straight. Though it's extremely relaxing, I couldn't stop my brain from working overtime during the meditations.

I started discovering certain things about myself that I never really knew. How significant they are, I really can't say. But it's interesting, nonetheless. For example, I noticed that no matter where I meditated, I never thought about anything past the next 24 hours. That being said, I only thought about things that related to my environment. If I was in class, I would think about the reading and writing assignments that were due the next day and would map out, or outline, how, where and when I would get it done. However, if I was at home, I'd do the same thing, only instead of schoolwork, I'd outline the order in which I'd clean my apartment. Usually it started with dishes, then laundry, then vacuum, clean the sinks, clean the bathroom, make the bed then turn on the speakers that were connected to my iPod and cook dinner. Sometimes I'd even specify the recipe in my head while I was meditating.

I didn't know how useful any of this would be, if this was how I was supposed to meditate or what I was supposed to learn from it. But I kept a record of my thoughts, hoping that by the end of this class it would all make sense, or at least maybe I'd learn what kind of "sense" was supposed to be made. But six weeks of class and two books in have broadened my understanding immensely.

Hagen's Buddhism, Plain and Simple highlights the basic elements of the religion/philosophy. The first of these elements were the 4 noble truths. These were the lessons given by the Gautama Buddha after he experienced enlightenment, or Nirvana. The first noble truth is Dukkha, or suffering. Hagen explains how all existence is characterized by some form of distress, hardship or "suffering." It is the cause of our anxiety, our issues, and our confusion about anything, really. "The first truth of the buddha-dharma likens human life to [an] out-of-kilter wheel. Something basic and important isn't right. It bothers us, makes us unhappy, time after time. With each turn of the wheel, each passing day, we experience pain." And this pain/suffering arises from a desire to attain something. Often times we idealize our lives and strive to attain this in its entirety. But we are never able to acquire this perceived perfection which, in turn, leads to Dukkha.

The second noble truth is called Samudaya. When Dukkha arises, when we finally "see" the source of our angst, we face it head-on. We acknowledge the fact that it exists and recognize its impact on our lives. Only until this happens can we move on to the third noble truth, Nirodha (Nirvana). This is where the 4 noble truths become a bit more blissful. Nirodha is the cessation of suffering. You've heard the saying, "What goes up must come down." Well, the same applies for Samudaya. If Dukkha can arise, it must also have the ability to dissipate or cease. Now, this path to the cessation of your suffering is the fourth and final noble truth, the 8-fold path to Nirvana. Each of the 8 "folds" refers to the "right" way of living in order to achieve enlightenment. "This is not a path we can take to get from point A to point B. Its peculiar nature is that the moment we step on it, the entire path is realized at once. Still, with each step we take we can deepen our understanding." These 8 "rights" are right view, right intention, right speech, right action, right livelihood, right effort, right mindfulness, and right meditation.

Personal Reflections

It's absurd how relevant the 4 noble truths become in your own life when you start looking. This class is on Mondays and Wednesdays for an hour and a half each day. On the Tuesday night of October 12, 2010, I checked the assignment page on the course wiki before I went to sleep to see what we might be talking about in class the next afternoon. My jaw dropped when I read on the Wednesday due date, "Midterm Learning Record, Part B1 and C1." This was a major part of our grade and it's NOT an easy task. Learning records take a lot of time and deep reflection... so much for going to bed now. I was about to be in for the long haul.

I had no idea what to write about. I hadn't learned a whole lot except for some book report Zen facts, or so I had thought. My first reaction upon seeing the assignment page was that nervous feeling in your stomach where your ears and face get hot. You know what I'm talking about. Then, I immediately reverted to anger towards my professor. She hadn't said anything about this thing on Monday. Who does that? Did she do it on purpose? She probably purposefully withheld that reminder so only the good students would remember and the rest would fail and learn from their mistakes. I genuinely thought to myself, "I'll stay up all night, knock this assignment out and throw it in her face! Booyah." And that's when it dawned on me.

Whose fault was it really that I waited this long to see when that assignment was due? They've been posted on the wiki page since the class began two months prior and the content is easily accessible. The anger I was experiencing was simply a mask covering my own personal guilt for procrastinating so long. And I've felt this exact same feeling before: pulling the all-nighter to spite the teachers' refusal to forewarn us of upcoming exams and papers. What was the anger I was experiencing? Dukkha. What was I experiencing when I realized the ultimate culprit (me) of the problem? Samudaya. I felt a vast sense of relief and understanding wash over me; Nirodha. That was what I needed. I needed that sudden catharsis to spark my train of thought on how I would approach the assignment. But most importantly, I needed it for my understanding of the class objective and my journey through Zen practice. I slipped on my readers, settled into my chair and started typing.

Suzuki: Master of Confusion

As the semester progressed, I started learning more and more about Zen Buddhism. However, the more I learned about Zen Buddhism, the more my brain wanted to explode. "We are not a human being anymore, but we do exist. When Zen is not Zen, nothing exists..." What? Shunryu Suzuki's *Zen Mind, Beginner's Mind* is chock full of these confusing little numbers. Something is, but at the same time, it isn't. If you do, you don't. If you don't, you might. A lot of it seems like one big riddle. And then, just to piss you off, he'll hit you with something like this. "When my talk is over, your listening is over. There is no need to remember what I say; there is no need to understand what I say." Well that's just great-even the writer knows I'll never understand it.

But to truly "get" what zazen is, you can't just read a book about it or ask a million questions. In fact, even the book says that it is often difficult to explain what Zen really is and what its significance is. The only true way to understand zazen is to practice. "The best way to communicate may be just to sit without saying anything. Then you will have the full meaning of Zen." That practice itself seems to be Zen in its simplest form. There are many complex, paradoxical and thought-provoking philosophies and Koans regarding Zen Buddhism, but the practice is very straight forward. There are very specific instructions on how this should be conducted.

As I said before, Zen does not advocate practicing to obtain anything. The practice should merely be just to practice. I try to clear my head of thoughts giving my mind a chance to rest. I don't necessarily force myself to stop thinking. I just let thoughts pass through. The easiest way to maintain a settled mind is to focus on your breathing; natural deep breaths in and out through your nose. Suzuki explains how breathing is important because it is the one thing that truly connects you with the cosmos. When you breathe, you are one with everything and an individual at the same time. This refers to non-duality. It is not two separate things. It is not one. It is like two sides of the same coin. The mentality of meditation seems very simple, but it's actually pretty difficult.

The physical aspects of zazen meditation, however, are where it gets real interesting. This was the part that I always saw on TV and in magazines: bald monks with nightgowns sitting Indian-style with their thumb and index finger tips touching while their hands rested on each corresponding knee. This actually isn't too far off from real zazen practice. If you were to ask me if I've ever truly meditated in the proper zazen form, I would have to respond with a "no." Not because I'm stubborn or because I think it's silly, but because the flexibility involved in the leg placement ain't hap-nin for me.

Posture/Practice

Suzuki explains how the right foot should go on top of the left thigh and the left foot should swivel around and sit on top of your right thigh. I made the attempt once. That's all I have to say about that. But the posture in this practice is essential. "Proper form," claims Suzuki, involves sitting in the full lotus position so that your legs have become "one." "The position expresses the oneness of duality: not two and not one." After your legs are situated, it is important to keep your back, or more specifically your spine, very straight. "Your ears and your shoulders should be on one line. Relax your shoulders, and push up towards the ceiling with the back of your head." Now, with your hands, you form the "cosmic mudra" by making an oval. Your right hand should lie in your left palm and your thumbs should touch with just enough force where you could potentially pull a piece of paper through them. This shape should rest right around your belly button supported by your forearms on your thighs. Suzuki explains that your arms should be close enough to your body to support eggs. There should be enough force to hold them, but not enough to break them. Your eyes should remain open and angled slightly down for comfort. Now that you're all pretzeledup, you can begin your 15-30 minutes (or however long you want) of silence and stillness. Is this comfortable? Not necessarily. Suzuki even mentions, "With your whole mind, you sit with painful legs without being disturbed by them." He then goes on to say, "At first you feel some restriction in your posture." Yes. For me, that restriction was the tendons of my groin being yanked like the chord of a crossbow. But, despite the pain, the posture is necessary.

Now, I took the time to explain, in great detail, the precise posture of the zazen practice for the same reason that Suzuki did. "This is not just form or breathing. It expresses the key point of Buddhism... If you want true understanding of Buddhism, you should practice this way." Zen Buddhism consistently refers to the art of living in the moment and doing everything you do with a clear mind and with 100% devotion and attention. "When you do something, you should be completely involved in it. You should devote yourself to it completely." Suzuki uses analogies like cooking and eating. To cook is not to prepare a meal for you to eat. When you cook, you should just cook. All your effort and all your attention should be focused on cooking the food. Then when the food is finally done, all your effort/attention should be on eating the food, nothing more and nothing less. The practice is no different. When you practice zazen, you just do it... and you do it right. To me, Buddhism sounds a lot like the things I would hear from my high school coaches. "Just give it your all. Stop thinkin' so much and just give it hell." Zen practice suggests that you carry this mentality with you in your day to day routine as well. True zazen doesn't really stop or start with meditation. It's involved in everything you do. "Usually we think, 'Now zazen is over, and we will go about our everyday activity.' But this is not the right understanding. They are the same thing."

Zen Rhetoric

Having made my attempt at explaining Zen Buddhism, Zen Rhetoric, the finale of my chapter, is easier to process. When we write, we are virtually taking our thoughts, our potential speech patterns and putting them in a standard form for all literate people to see and react to. When we read, it is as though we are listening to the author speak his/her mind. Since the beginning of my ventures of reading and writing, this concept has almost always been on making or validating an argument, agreeing or disagreeing with ideas and notions, and interpreting ultimate meanings through my own opinions.

In non-argumentative writing, these methods are useless, or more specifically, wrong. Suzuki explains that "when you listen to someone, you should give up all your preconceived ideas and your subjective opinions; you should just listen to him, just observe what his way is... We just see things as they are with him, and accept them." On the first day of class, Professor Syverson explained, quite accurately, that the notion of Non-argumentative Rhetoric in Zen was very similar to how one would raise a child. You don't necessarily urge them to involve themselves in specific activities. You simply encourage whatever their interests are. And when their interests change, you acknowledge the change and continue to support. Now, I said "when" their interests change instead of "if" because that change is the link between Zen and Non-argumentative writing. "The basic teaching of Buddhism is the teaching of transiency, or change. That everything changes is the basic truth for each existence."

Heraclitus says "you never step into the same river..." (Heraclitus of Ephesus) The constant flow of water, autonomic motion of the organisms, the mobile sediments on the river bottom all change, every moment.

This expression, however, does NOT mean that the world around you changes and you, as an entity in the world, remain static. Your physical make-up, the thoughts in your head and the emotions you are feeling may be different tomorrow or in an hour or a minute. They may even be changing as you finish the rest of this sentence... This notion helps shed light on the idea behind Non-argumentative rhetoric.

Argumentation and persuasion are meant to evoke a particular emotion or convince specific actions to be taken.

Sometimes this style can be effective, but not always. Typically, when I argue, I separate my listeners/readers into two groups: those who are heeding my information and those that aren't. By doing this, I automatically alienate a certain group. I've already established a black and white, winner-loser, positive-negative relationship. And unless my issue is indisputable, duality will exist.

Non-duality is indicative of non-argumentative rhetoric in Zen; the two sides to the same coin. How would you persuade a smoker to stop lighting up? Would you explain the health risks? Would you show them a list of receipts that add up to hefty totals? Maybe you'd just complain about the stink and hope you could coax them into quitting out of sheer embarrassment. But despite your valiant efforts, there's still a likely chance your argument will be ineffective and that they'll keep right on puffing the cancer sticks. Non-argumentative rhetoric, however, would state just that. Despite health problems, increasing cost and aroma, people remain persistent with their tobacco consumption. Some people smoke, some don't. Things are what they are. Though your intention might still be persuasion, you take on a passive role. In this way, you do not set boundaries for right and wrong activity. You simply state the truth. You allow the audience to consider facts and think for themselves. Often times, the truth is difficult when heard out loud. And since people, as well as everything around us, are constantly changing, you open up an opportunity for contemplation and consideration amongst your readers/listeners rather than pointing judgmental fingers.

Rebellion: My Zen "Rock Bottom"

Everything is in this state of constant flux. Even my opinions about this class have been in a state of flux since day one. When the class first started, I was simply interested in learning what Zen was. After a couple weeks into it, I became interested in the practice and started meditating. Well, I guess this was also because daily meditation was a requirement for the course. But I was genuinely interested and practiced regularly. After reading a handful of our assigned material, I started getting the idea that Zen was just a way to be happy. I was generally a happy guy in the first place so I assumed the rest of the readings would just be common sense information similar to a self-help guide. But then I ran across this passage in Joko Beck's *Everyday Zen*: "When we don't get something we want, we suffer. And yet when we do get it we also suffer, because we know that if we get it we can lose it." Whoa, whoa, whoa... What? Can I not just be happy? This angered me more than anything I've ever read. I usually judged whether or not I was practicing correctly on my current state of emotion. If I felt happy, I was probably on the right track. If I was upset, I needed to take a step back and assess what I was feeling and why I was really feeling it. Though I might still be upset, I could see the emotions for what they truly were and let them dissipate naturally.

But after reading that, it made me feel like there was no hope. It was at that point that I actually rebelled against the class, put down the Beck book before finishing it and never picked it up again. I think the most interesting thing about this was that I believed the quote. I could have easily shrugged off this idea as false and moved on, but I didn't. Everything about Zen seems to represent ultimate truth and this felt like a personal attack.

During that period, I convinced myself that I was happier NOT practicing Zen. I thought that if what Joko said was true, then I would rather live in blissful ignorance. I have been blessed with many good things in my life. I had a great childhood. I have a loving and supportive family, great friends, an incredible girl-friend, a decent job and zero debt. My life is pretty smooth and this is what I would think about when I started feeling down. I would just notice the positive things and my demeanor would pick itself right back up. Joko made me feel like I HAD to suffer because nothing is permanent.

This was my most memorable Zen experience. This state of suffering from Joko's words was foreign to me because I had refused to believe them for so long. I went through weeks of contemplation and recovery before realizing that the truth in that quote was, in fact, the source of the happiness that all good things create. If life was always good, nothing would be appreciated. The "good" things such as the loving family and great friends would just be normal. Only a loss of these would incite understanding of their necessity for happiness.

When I ventured into the next book, *Buddha's Brain*, I started getting the impression that I had the right idea all along. However, I was not living in "blissful ignorance" of happiness as I had suddenly thought. I was conjuring up good thoughts to drown out the often dwelled upon negative thoughts. The book explains how your brain ultimately controls your mind and therefore, if you change your brain, you can change your mind. A common practice includes "gradually replacing negative implicit memories with positive ones, just making the positive aspects of your experience prominent and relatively intense in the foreground of your awareness while simultaneously placing the negative material in the background." Now, this may seem like a Peter Pan method, "Just think happy thoughts and you'll feel better." But in fact, there are very specific neurological actions and reactions to this method of training your brain.

Applied Learning

Buddha's Brain gives account of all the neurological and chemical processes that occur in the brain and body during active Buddhist practice. The beginning focuses on the synapses in your brain and how they become wired together from neurons firing simultaneously. I really can't go into great detail about how this process works for two reasons. One, I don't want this paper to sound like a scientific research essay and two; I'm really not a hundred percent sure how it works anyway. But basically what the "happy thought" method refers to is training yourself to redirect your negative second darts into positive second darts. Second darts are the after thoughts from initial stimuli.

I was driving southbound on I-35 coming back from San Marcos, Texas. I was cruising down the left lane of the freeway when a guy passes me on the right with his middle finger pressed up against his window at me. The first dart I experienced was the realization that someone was trying to get my attention. Then the second darts kicked in and I immediately wanted to perform the pit maneuver on this tiny little Toyota. "Why would he do that?" "What would he do if I followed him wherever he was going?" "I think I could take that guy. He didn't seem that big." These darts were followed by others such as, "Was I driving too slow in the fast lane?" "Maybe I did deserve the bird." "I wonder if everyone else is mad at me too."

The more you dwell on these second darts, the more associated neurons fire and, thus, the stronger those synapses become. And the stronger the synapse, the more likely they are to be activated again when similar neurons fire. So every time I would pass someone on the left side, I would feel nervous and instinctively feel like I had to go 80 in that lane or instantly shift back over to the center. All those emotions naturally started to swell up again because I had hardwired my brain to do it.

The good news I found in *Buddha's Brain* is that this COULD be changed. Through constant practice, I could neurologically prune the old synapses and create new ones with positive emotions. When passing someone on the left, I deliberately thought of positive memories; a hug from someone I love, an exciting vacation I took, any thought that evoked positive emotions. This sounds silly, I know, but it was effective. By maintaining this practice, eventually my synapses of positive memories gained more strength than the previous negative ones and therefore, every time I was in that lane, the neurons in my brain followed the stronger path and provoked good emotions from the hug/vacation/etc. Now I'm not saying that I have to drive down the left lane to feel happy nor am I advocating driving slow in the fast lane. It makes me just as angry as Toyota guy. But, through that method, I was able to diminish that overwhelming stress I had felt before.

It's nice to know that I was unknowingly training my own brain in this exact same fashion when I was faced with my issue regarding the Joko Beck quote and my personal method to stay happy. Did I know I was physically rewiring my brain? No. I thought I was just trying to stay positive, which I was. But there was more to it than a simple decision to remain upbeat. A very natural and complex process was taking place in the fabric of my brain that was allowing me to live a happier life. I was therefore able to carry this skill over into my driving anxieties.

Now What...

I'm approaching the final portion of this course and have read and written pages and pages about Zen. The funny thing is, the more I read, the more questions I have and often times, the more confused I get. So after this class is complete, what's next? One thing is for certain, and that is I must simply keep practicing. I will continue meditation. I will continue attempting to be aware. I will continue to focus on each activity of my daily life with the utmost attention and effort. I will continue to see the world as it is and not as I feel it should be. The world and I are ever-changing both as individuals and as one being. Tracy Lawrence pretty much nailed it. "The only thing that stays the same is everything changes, everything chay-yanges..."

Works Cited

ThinkExist.com Quotations. "Heraclitus of Ephesus quotes." ThinkExist.com Quotations Online

1 Oct. 2010. 16 Nov. 2010 <http://einstein/quotes/heraclitus_of_ephesus/>

Lou Baker is a fourth year Rhetoric major and freelance drummer from Hico, Texas. He currently plays with Shane Smith as well as The Chris Morris Band and plans to continue pursuing his music career.

A Search for Truth
Alana Prant

I will begin by giving you a glance into the mind of a completely ignorant Zen student-poised to begin the journey, but without any formal training minus that of popular culture.

My naïve soul comprehends the state of Zen as a sense of tranquility, of peace, and of a newfound reality that is so daunting the average untrained mind cannot even grasp its basic understanding. I have always compared it to my understanding of the Kabbala, the Jewish mystical teachings. It is said that the Kabbala should be studied only by men of many years who have lived full lives and studied the Jewish traditions immensely. In addition, there are said to be many routes into the understanding of Kabbala and every person must find their unique route. Likewise, I have heard that there are also many paths to enlightenment. In my perspective Zen Buddhism is another mystical teaching, searching for the deepest human truths.

When I think of Zen Buddhism, various key words come to mind. Such as, peace, state of mind, enlightenment, reality, and journey. Each word's meaning becomes more ambiguous than the next. It seems that each word relates to this notion of finding truth in our lives. I equate most of these words with achieving happiness or being on the path to finding it.

In my understanding "peace" in terms of Zen, means to be content in ones thinking and current state. It is an acceptance of life that leads one to a happier place. One's "state of mind" is their current orientation in their mind and in their world, as far as my knowledge goes. I am most perplexed by the term enlightenment; it seems to me to be something only those who are enlightened fully understand. I have always wondered if enlightenment was a mental state or a physical experience, or both. In the study of Zen does everyone go about finding enlightenment the same way? And does being enlightened feel the same for every person? I would imagine it is similar to the exploration of the Jewish mystical teaching, in that many paths lead to the center. I would also assume that the feeling of enlightenment encompasses all the senses, and embodies both our mental and physical states. I find it interesting that one of the words I associate with Zen is reality, when in my mind the path towards enlightenment is something that transcends the physical reality of life.

I think of it as a pseudo reality, a perfect Zen garden lacking the natural chaos of life. It may be a way of thinking in an alternate reality that helps us find order in our own realities. Plus is this search for our reality the same as our search for truth? What differentiates truth and reality?

Lastly the word journey pops in my head. It has such a simple meaning, how to get from point A to point B, but somewhere in its meaning lies the "how" in Zen. It appears that achieving a state of Zen is wrapped up in the journey, a journey to enlightenment. Life is truly the ultimate physical journey, is Zen a person's spiritual journey?

I have always been fascinated by the way time and space interact with the spiritual workings of the mind. How a meaningful moment can almost stop time. Again connecting my beliefs of Zen with my beliefs of Judaism because I find them very similar, on the Jewish holiday of Yom Kippur you are suppose to be fully satisfied by prayer that your body is able to fast. I have heard stories of Buddha going long periods of time without food- surviving solely on meditation. The capacity of the body to feel full from the spirit is astonishing. Here our everyday understanding of fullness is challenged. When I think of full I think of something being filled to the brim, however in terms of spirituality I assume fullness is simply feeling content- it is the necessary amount to survive. This makes an important statement about our society today. We are searching for too much in our lives- an excess of perfection or sustenance. The Zen teachings are an attempt to bring our world away from these detrimental thoughts.

I often think of what are minds and bodies are capable of, and meditation is a portal to the amazing feats human beings can accomplish. I am still confused to whether meditation is a silent task or one full of thought? Does the act of silencing your soul bring you to some kind of nirvana? Nonetheless, this is truly difficult. I often feel my mind is moving in infinite directions, searching and searching for the correct path. Will discovering Zen help me find the right path?

In my ignorant understanding of Zen, my thoughts are drawn to feng shui. I think about the calculated placement of our valuables in our dwellings, and the energy they create. In this practice Zen focuses on our physical space to improve our spiritual space. This idea is absolutely beautiful to me; it brings the higher powers of the universe into our individual homes. It appears to be a practice that brings order to a person's world, while letting life flow freely through their space. It opens a person's soul to the truths of life; it is opening your physical space to let in spiritual truths.

Zen is a mystery to me; my ideas come from popular culture and little knowledge of the practices. Its whole essence is daunting to me. I see it as a world of spiritual exploration that takes years of study and concentration to penetrate. I also see it as a movement in feelings not actions. In some religions what you do is more important that what you think and experience. However I feel as though Zen Buddhism is based heavily on your emotional experiences. The human mind can create things the body only dreams of, therefore the possibilities of a thinking like Zen holds no boundaries. My physical body can only be so great, but my spiritual mind can do anything. Zen seems to tap into the fundamental nature of human beings and transcend our core with peacefulness.

I am excited to fill my mind with the teachings of Zen Buddhism, to experience spirituality unlike my own. I am curious to how the meditations will affect me, and possibly change me. I think Zen has the power to show you the world in a unique way, unlike any other religion or teaching.

I am eager to open my mind and soul to a tranquil peace. To find an order in my chaotic life-to find truth in my reality.

This section remains in the raw, naive state it was originally written in to show how my knowledge and understandings of Zen Buddhism evolved over time.

After some basic learning of Zen Buddhism I have grown in my knowledge and understanding of its practices. This is where my mental and physical grasp of the concepts is halfway through the course. Here I will explore the ways in which Zen teachers use rhetorical tools to convey meaning to their students.

In modern rhetoric, the rhetor often tries to convince or persuade the reader using an appeal to their emotions-or pathos. Throughout my early discovery of Zen Buddhism I have noticed that the teachers or rhetoricians of Zen use the physical body to evoke emotion. In the practice of zazen, Zen teachers use pathos to educate their students.

To my understanding, zazen is a seated meditation practice in order to open the mind and body. This process of aligning the body to match the mental and emotional sense of self becomes a metaphor for being more aware in ones life. The connection to the body becomes the rhetoric of Zen. By calling on the student to do something physically, it will force them to feel something emotionally. For example, in teaching a sense of duality, Suzuki explains that during zazen one must cross their legs in such a way that you cannot tell which leg is the right or left-whether it is two legs or one. Thus teaching the student a lesson of oneness, that our mind and body are neither one nor two parts. This appeals to the student's emotions because it is a physical reminder of their emotional dependence and independence. Many times small actions or practices can evoke strong emotions. Again relating my discovery of Zen to my knowledge of Judaism, I would compare the zazen practices to the Jewish practice of the mezuzah. A mezuzah is a small box that is mounted on all doorposts that holds one of our most sacred prayers, the Shema. Every time you pass through the door you are to kiss the mezuzah and touch it with your hand. This serves as a reminder, when you touch the box you are reminded of the prayer inside. Likewise I would imagine that every time people cross their legs in such a way they recall the teachings of oneness.

After crossing your legs, you are told to sit with your spine straight, shoulders back, and your chin up. Suzuki says, "This will help you maintain a physical and mental balance"(26). I love that Suzuki mentions that this position is hard to breath in at first but will eventually feel natural. Here your physical body is aligned with your Zen journey. As I have experienced, meditation is difficult, but like breathing, it is necessary for living. Learning to be truly awake is also necessary for living in this moment. Therefore one can conclude that further mediation will only make living easier. Once seated upright, you are to put your hands in an oval shape, as if you were holding something precious to your chest. This analogy relates meditation and its practices to something the student values. By equating something valuable with the hand gesture, the rhetor convinces the student of the practices' importance. By occupying my hands, this allows me to take my focus off whether or not I should be doing something with my hands, to doing something not with my hands.

It is apparent that the flow of ones breath is a key factor in meditation and in Zen. This teaching awakens my interest, for I have always felt that breathing was the portal to emotional strength. Suzuki talks about how are breathing is like a swinging door, always letting air in and out. He also talks about how this swinging door is the gateway to our "inner world" and our "outer world." I believe that our breathing can a mirror, reflecting our true emotions-letting our inner world appear as the swinging door flies open. When I am anxious I breathe faster and I am fully aware of every breath. When I relax I breath slowly and again focus on my breathing. However when I am at my normal pace, I am completely unaware of the breaths I take. The swinging door metaphor teaches the student to completely calm their mind and body, leaving only the swinging of the door- the inhaling and exhaling. To almost shut down your body and mind, while honing in on the one essential action to live. This type of serenity and simplicity is something truly profound in Zen Buddhism. In my meditation as I try to streamline my mind waves and move to a place of just being I find it impossible not to wonder if I am doing it right, which is doing something and not being absolutely awake in the moment. This I feel comes from practice and a devotion to Zen I am currently lacking.

In your body's ultimate rhetorical device, its ultimate sign of devotion: bowing, you are to give yourself in full to the Buddha. You are to give up all views of duality and become one with the Buddha. Unlike bowing to a king, where you lower your head to show inferiority or respect, you bow here in zazen to be enveloped by your Buddha nature. While reading about bowing in "Zen Mind, Beginners Mind," I wanted to experience bowing. As I bowed, alone in my room, I felt uncomfortable and exposed. The action of bowing put me out of my comfort zone and allowed me to feel vulnerable in my own space. This vulnerable state allows you to see your place in the world. Suzuki teaches us that bowing is meant to help us learn to not be self-centered. However I feel this is quite a daunting feat for the human race. How can one not think of their own well being constantly- even if it is in conjunction with the thought of others you are still always worrying about yourself in some way or form. In addition, I also feel that the path to enlightenment is a selfish journey. How could my meditation or practice of Zen affect anyone else? Maybe it is just my true nature to strive for these things, even if I may never achieve them, my attempt could bring greater peace to the world. As I continue on this journey to discover Zen Buddhism I will continue searching for how these practices can have a great affect of the world as a whole.

I have come to think that the literature of Zen is genius. Where many religions today try to persuade potential followers with comparison and well-crafted argument, Zen, without proselytizing, convinces the reader of their teachings, seemingly without effort. The rhetoric is not, "this is what Zen teaches," it reads like, "There is no other way of life than this way of life. Zen practice is the direct expression of our true nature"(Suzuki 47). This book is entitled "Zen Mind, Beginners Mind," meaning the intended audience is a beginner in Zen practice, however the book is written to someone who has knowledge of Zen, while the actual audience is most likely beginners.

Meaning that people who read this book may or may not believe all these teachings, but by using such rhetoric as "there is no other way of life than this way of life" makes a deep impression on the impressionable student. By stating what he believes as a fact, he is making a clever argument for taking on these Zen practices.

I sit in my college apartment reading about Zen and attempting the zazen pose, and as I try to follow the books' instructions to fitting my body into the perfect position for meditation the pose begins to tell me a story. Some people can feel when rain is coming in their bones, or feel the onset of sickness, but this pose tells me so much more. It tells me how I am feeling, what I am thinking, and awakens my soul. My own pathos is sparked as my back aches from being straight, I can no longer decipher my legs in their oneness, and my hands have a feeling of purpose about them. The physical movements have convinced me of their power, not only the words in Suzuki's book.

In this exercise the hands were the tipping point for me. My hands often move sporadically, mimicking the activity in my brain. I talk with my hands, and often find my hands nervously searching for the next word. Here in the zazen pose my hands have a job- they are forced to be still. This stillness is profound for me. It gives me the opportunity to feel vulnerable in my thoughts- for my need for a security blanket has been silenced. I am slowly realizing that every action in the practice of Zen has a thoughtful purpose. I would imagine that the deepest meanings of these practices slowly reveal themselves. I have just begun peeling away at the layers of understanding. Maybe someday the zazen hand pose will mean much more to me than a way to relax my mind through the stillness of my hands.

Giving meaning to minute gestures and poses leads into the idea of always being awake. I have learned to try to always be aware and present in everything I do. We are always doing something, even if we are thinking about doing nothing we are in fact doing something. What we do in every moment has profound meaning like I said before. This notion of "doing" when I am "not doing" baffles my mind. However the rhetoric of the idea is astonishing. I can't even fathom a sound argument against the statement "you are always doing something." If you are living you are doing!

Through the physical movements I have seen how Zen rhetoric can be extremely persuasive. The zazen position, posture, and breathing during meditation are truly eye opening, they convince me of their argument with the use of mere movements. The motions are their brilliant diction, and the actions write a narrative of rhetorical genius. The pathos in Zen rhetoric not only brings movement to your physical body but also helps move your mind to a state of peace, ideal for meditation.

This third piece of writing represents a deeper understanding of the material and shows my movement through the understanding of happiness and love. This section ties my new understandings with my current emotional state.

Zen teaches us about second-dart reactions, where you unknowingly overreact to something. This is something I have seen myself doing over the last few months. In the book Buddha's Brian we learn that there are four stages to becoming aware. The first stage is this second-dart reaction, where you are completely unaware of your anger and action. I have often noticed myself reacting to the people close to me in this way, but I believe I am currently in stage two. Stage two is when you realized you are being controlled by an emotion like hate but you cant help but react in the same way as you did in stage one. When I react in such ways, like lashing out to someone close to me, I am often aware that my emotions are fueling it, but unaware of which emotion it is or how to control those emotions. I feel that thus far in my Zen journey I have become more aware of my being but I am still blinded by so many emotions. And these emotions are still causing me to react. I hope to soon make it to the third stage that is where you are aware of your feelings toward the situation and you are able to stop yourself from reacting. I hope I can move to a place where I an aware of the feeling and the urge to lash out, but I have developed the ability to restrain myself. Lastly in the fourth stage, that urge to react no longer arises. Your underlying emotions no longer control the sensation to act out. In this stage your have learned to train your mind so greatly that it has grown to protect your emotional states. The way I understand it is that if our complex brains register unhappiness when these emotions cloud our judgments then over time as part of natural selection our minds will no longer allow those feelings to arise in that kind of circumstance. Thus our minds are the ultimate protectors of our hearts.

I feel that these reactions stem from not being happy in ones life. I have seen that many people seeking to practice Zen are searching for greater happiness. Zen talks about happiness as becoming aware of how your afflictions control you and then going through the four stages to learn to control them. Part of this is a viable option in my opinion. I think it is important to explore what is making you unhappy and work to eliminate it, however I am also a strong believer in ignorance is bliss. Over the last few weeks as I have been thinking about this teaching of happiness and looking in my personal life for what holds me back from being perfectly happy. In doing this I have become unhappier than I was before. Granted this is most likely a learning curve, I am skeptical if it is possible to completely eliminate all the bad and all the debilitating emotions in your life. New fears and hatred will always be coming up and yes you can learn how to deal with them better, but if you are always searching for a perfection that is unreachable you will spend your life disappointed- an emotion Zen practice works to eliminate. Though

I don't completely agree with this Zen teaching, my understanding of the four stages to awareness and of happiness have led me to my own twist on the teaching. If our brains control the feeling of happiness, and we can learn to control our thinking to be more aware then we can teach ourselves to be aware of what makes us unhappy and learn how to deal with it properly-not completely eliminate it or ignore it. This way the next time something similar comes up your brain will know how to bring happiness out of it without you reacting in a drastic way.

I believe that the reason I came to this conclusion about happiness is the fact that I have not only been searching for happiness in my Zen journey, but love. I believe this to be a common misconception among beginners on the path to Zen practice because I have heard my peers often compare and apply the teachings to their search for the romantic. The purpose of Zen practice is to obtain wisdom and compassion-not romantic love. Though at 22 years old romantic love consumes my thoughts.

Menzan Zenji says that "When, through practice, you know the reality of zazen thoroughly, the frozen blockage of emotion-thought will naturally melt away"(71). Joko Beck tells us that your emotion-thoughts are the self-centered things we worry about on a daily basis that prevent us from having genuine love in a relationship. She talks about how we create this perfect picture in our minds of how our partner is suppose to act and when they of course act differently we are disappointed and hurt. Reading this completely opened my mind, for this is something I am extremely guilty of. I am always feeling disappointment in my relationships because my expectations are blocking my ability to have a genuine relationship. This also turns the love in my relationship into hostility and anger. Beck reminds us that no human being is perfect and every relationship will have its difficulties, but she encourages us to move away from the "false love" that creates unattainable dreams and through practice develop relationships based on a genuine love.

I have begun trying to teach my brain to move away from my dream world like expectations of my relationships. In theory it is so simple, however the mind is still a mystery to mankind and my underlying desire for romantic perfection still seems stronger than ever. This to me is a perfect example to where I have come in the few months of Zen practice. I have become aware. Aware of my body, my presence in the spaces I inhibit, and aware of the emotions that fuel my actions. Though as still a true beginner, and only in the first leg of my journey, I am able to say that I have yet to get over the hump- to stop myself from causing unhappiness and disappointment in my life. At first I was discouraged that I hadn't progressed much more than my initial realizations, though as I process all the changes in my spirit over the past few months I am aware how monumental they truly are.

I began this journey searching for the truths of Zen Buddhism, asking countless questions and expecting definite answers. As the class comes to a close I realize I am still at the beginning. The beautiful nature of this practice is that it is something ever changing. I am certain that my ability to be awake in my life will evolve as I mature and experience the different stages of life. Zen is a rich spiritual practice whose rhetoric lives beyond the pages of its texts'. I have never experienced such prose that evokes actual physical movement and emotion. I am shocked at what these practices have brought out in me and the direction in which the journey has taken me. Therefore overall my final conclusion of Zen Buddhism is that it is not a search for Truth like the title of my chapter, but really a search for happiness.

I am in no way finished with this journey, for I have just merely begun.

Alana Prant is a third year Rhetoric and Writing major at the University of Texas at Austin. Alana is from Austin, Texas but spent a year living in Israel before attending college. She is currently the president of her sorority Alpha Epsilon Phi and hopes to intern in New York this summer.

Realizations through Writing; My Zen Experience
Barret M. Howell

Professor Syverson once told us the story of when she was writing her dissertation. She explained that after working for countless hours she wrote eighty pages and decided the dissertation was complete. Shortly after completion, she realized that what she had written was not what she wanted to say and that she needed to change the entire paper and start over. She began from scratch and wrote an entirely new dissertation. I had a similar experience with this chapter. It wasn't until after I had submitted it that I realized how badly I wanted to change what I was saying. This is the final product of my chapter following these changes...

Over the course of the semester I have written three separate drafts of this chapter. Although the drafts were all very different, they each revealed certain things to me about my writing and my experience with Zen Buddhism. In hindsight, it's obvious to me how the process of writing in drafts influenced my everyday experience with Zen. It changed the way I "practiced" because everything I did was in consideration of writing my chapter. While I don't necessarily think this is a bad thing given the context of the class, I do feel like it caused my practice of Zen Buddhism to be slightly skewed away from the ideal methods we learned about in the readings. Nonetheless, the writing process is what ultimately triggered a majority of my most meaningful realizations and moments of clarity. After writing each draft, it became clear to me where I needed to refocus my energy and how I needed to redirect myself onto a different path. Although I sometimes convinced myself to re-adjust in ways that were just as misleading as before, I never would have learned from those mistakes if I had never made them.

The First Draft; Memorizing Definitions

The first draft of my chapter set the bar pretty low in terms of making a lot of meaningful realizations or finding moments of clarity, but this was kind of to be expected. Before taking this class I had never studied Buddhism, much less actually tried to practice it, so it's easy to see why the first go-around was mostly investigative. Basically, the first draft began by trying to establish exactly what I already knew about Zen Buddhism, and continued by exploring the first two Noble Truths and a couple other basic Zen concepts. The process of writing the first draft led me to my first important realizations. The first was that I had almost no previous experience or knowledge with regard to Zen Buddhism. The second was that my default method for learning new material was a conditioned product of my experience in school. At first, I found my first realization odd because even despite my blatant lack of familiarity with Buddhism, I still had a mental block about practicing it, like I thought it was a hoax or voodoo or something.

Looking back, I now see how silly it was to think that Buddhism and voodoo were even slightly similar, but at the time I had nothing else to base my opinions on. The little exposure I had with Zen Buddhism at this point in my life had been tainted by some experience I had gone through along the way. In response to Chloe Chiang's Unquiz question on this topic I said,

"No matter how open-minded or unbiased we like to believe we are, we make judgments, decisions, and draw conclusions based on what we have already learned and experienced in life. Our personal experiences, and the lessons we have learned from them, are ultimately all we have as a tool to evaluate and analyze any new experience. Eventually, all the knowledge we gain through experience accumulates into a one single entity that is our psyche, our intelligence, our personality. So no matter how unprejudiced we try to be, our past history constantly influences us in the present. An example of this would be our experience with Buddhism. Before taking this class, most of us had never encountered Buddhism, so it was a new experience. Initially, each of us evaluated Buddhism entirely based on our past experiences. Some of us, including myself, admitted that our opinion of Buddhism had often been tainted by our exposure to pop-culture, media, religion, or some other personal affair. It wasn't until we actually experienced Buddhism for ourselves that we were able to break those preconceptions and develop our own personal understanding of its teachings. Now, Buddhism is just another part of our overall accumulation of experience, and it influences our interpretation of new ideas and experiences just like pop-culture had influenced us before."

This is an important example of a realization I made through the writing process and my experience with Zen Buddhism. When the class started, I had never really taken the time to think about how my past experiences shaped me as a person and also how they influenced my interpretation of new ideas. This seems like such a simple thing to realize, but for some reason it took me a really long time to wrap my head around it and let it sink in. If I had never written my first draft, I never would have looked back at it and realized my mistakes. It was my experience with Zen Buddhism that actually caused me to recognize my mistakes, see why I made them, and learn from their outcomes. My lack of previous knowledge about Zen Buddhism was the reason I was able to learn so much in just one semester, but it was partially responsible for my reservations against practicing Buddhism.

Earlier I explained that I made a second realization through the process of writing my first draft, and more specifically, that my default method of learning was actually a response conditioned in school. As early as elementary school, my classes and teachers always had a specific way they wanted us to learn the given material. The same basic format was consistent across almost every class I took. Basically, the teacher would introduce a new piece of material, then provide a definition or explanation of it, then show us how to apply and practice it, and finally they would test us over it before moving onto a new topic. Over the years, repetition of this progression conditioned it to be my default reaction to all new information. So, when this class started, I instinctively approached Zen Buddhism in this way, which was ultimately the only way I knew how.

The following is a selection from my original first draft:

For as long as I can remember, the way I have been schooled has taught me to research and practice new concepts until I am completely comfortable with them. As an example, in the seventh grade, I was first introduced to the Pythagorean Theorem. At the time, it seemed like an impossibly difficult concept to master. It took steady repetition, practice, a couple failed homework assignments and an excellent math teacher before I was ever able to consistently use $A2 + B2 = C2$ to solve for the hypotenuse of a triangle. Today, the Pythagorean Theorem is something I use with the slightest degree of effort, but this was not always the case.

I admit that comparing Buddhism to middle school math is a little unfair considering the differences in complexity between the two, but consider this... There are mathematicians who have devoted their entire lives to mastering the science of calculation, yet they continue to discover new formulas, theorems, and procedures. Is this so different from Buddhism? Just because someone invented a new way to solve differential calculus does not mean I am going to understand it. I have to take the time to learn it for myself, from the ground up, building on every concept until I reach the point that I can learn to solve the most difficult of equations. The same is true for Buddhism. I have to start at the beginning, learn the basics, then build on them until I can look back one day and say, "I get it!"

In my immediate reaction to Zen Buddhism, I began researching its origins, analyzing its demographic information, and identifying its key historical influences. I was systematically dissecting Buddhism as though I was preparing myself to be

tested over it or something. I tried to compare it to other subjects I had learned in school which didn't really work because
I had never studied anything quite like Zen before this class. I
had to rack my brain must to scrape together some really basic
information about the origins of Buddhism and some of its
basic concepts.

The following is a selection from my original first draft:

Having read Siddhartha in high school, I can say I vaguely
remember the story of how Siddhartha Gautama came to be
the first Buddha. I know that he had his "enlightenment" while
sitting beneath a tree and that his journey involved many hardships. I know that his teachings have spread to every corner
of the world over the past centuries. I know that Karma is a
Buddhist concept, explaining that there is a force of cause and
effect in the universe and that good and bad come to those
deserving. I suspect that the largest concentration of Buddhists
reside in Southeast Asia, where it began. Hysterically, that is
the extent of my knowledge about Buddhism. Sad, right? But at
least I can call it a clean slate.

After a little research, I discovered a more comprehensive
set of information and statistics about Buddhism. The religion
began in 520 BCE in Northeastern India. Behind Christianity,
Islam and Hinduism, Buddhism is the fourth largest religion
on Earth and is most prevalent in the Far East. In total, there
are around 360 million Buddhists on the planet. There are two
main branches of Buddhism, Theravada and Mahayana. Both
divisions have unique practices and beliefs, but are largely
based on the same values. Those values revolve around the
Four Noble Truths and the Eightfold Path. Ideas such as Karma
and Rebirth are also cornerstones to Buddhism. This general
outline of Buddhism's demographics, practices, and values is
adequate for now, but I hope to be able to continually expand
my understanding of Buddhism through the duration of this
class.

Looking back, my initial expectations for Zen Buddhism
were actually pretty impractical because they focused so heavily on achieving some degree of self-improvement through

my experience. I expected for my practice Zen Buddhism to somehow make me a better person. I expected Zen Buddhism to somehow help me find solutions for and solve my problems. I expected Zen Buddhism to give me a feeling of enlightenment by the end of the semester. In hindsight I see how ridiculous these kinds of expectations were, but it goes back to the idea that I had nothing else to base my expectations on. I made another realization once I recognized that Buddhism was not a solution to my problems or a ticket to enlightenment, but that it was more a way of thinking about life than anything else.

The Second Draft; Part I, Balancing Theory and Religion

The second draft of my chapter was essentially just a continuation of the first draft. I had yet to realize that my current approach to my writing and practice about Zen Buddhism was incorrect. The second draft went into much more depth about all Four Noble Truths, it explained the three forms of Dukkha, and it also addressed the issue of reconciling my Christian faith with my Buddhist experience for the first time. I think that the second draft of my chapter was where I first realized that I was focusing way too much on the literal, tangible aspects of Zen. The second draft showed me that studying Zen Buddhism would only take me so far, and unless I actually applied and practiced the concepts I would never make any progress.

Many times in class we made a comparison between practicing Buddhism and Cooking. We talked about how you can read cookbooks all day long and memorize recipes, but unless you actually try to cook you will never be able to become a master chef. It takes thousands of hours of practice to master the art of cooking, and Buddhism is no different. Honestly, I'm not entirely sure when it happened, but at some point I made this connection and I realized that my approach to Zen Buddhism in the first two drafts of my chapter had been completely misleading. I had spent the better part of half the semester trying to focus on the specific elements of Zen Buddhism that I was able to memorize and study.

When I signed up for this class I thought it would be a good way to expand my horizons. I remember saying to myself, "I should be open-minded and look at different people's perspectives. This will be good for me." I saw this class as an opportunity to expand my understanding of religion overall. I figured that studying different belief systems would help make me better-informed and unbiased person. Fairly quickly though, I realized that Buddhism didn't really fit the regular conventions I used to define a "typical" religion. "Buddhism is not a belief system. It's not about accepting certain tenets or believing a set of claims or principles... Buddhism is about seeing." (Hagen 4) I was shocked to learn that Buddhism was much more focused on a personal journey and self-experience, rather than on specific concepts like other religions I had learned about.

I never expected to actually practice Buddhism because I am Christian. I assumed that I couldn't practice because there was too much conflict between the two. While I wasn't really wrong about this, I wasn't really right either... You see, I now believe that the two can coexist within certain boundaries, but it took me a long time to feel this way. For most of the semester I struggled to commit to a lot of the "practices" we engaged in because of the idea I had somewhere in my head that Zen Buddhism was some kind of hoax or voodoo or something as I mentioned earlier. I had to constantly resist the urge to outright reject some of these practices for no other reason than that I was suspicious of them. It turned out that this was just another necessary road bump in my learning process because I eventually overcame my doubt. My suspicion went away once I found applications of Zen Buddhism that were comfortable for me given my existing set of beliefs. What I started to realize was that studying the theoretical concepts of Buddhism was causing my discomfort with it. Once I moved away from my approach in the first two drafts of my chapter, and began focusing more on my experience and practice, the objections I had to some Buddhist concepts were visited less frequently.

What caused me to make this realization was a point made in one of our required readings called *Buddha's Brain*. In the text, it is stated that "we evolved to pay great attention to unpleasant experiences. This negativity bias overlooks good news, high-lights bad news, and creates anxiety and pessimism." (Hanson 48) It was this fact from *Buddha's Brain* that helped me realize that my thoughts were focusing more heavily on negative, rather than positive, experiences.

Nonetheless, the differences between Christianity and Buddhism made it inherently impossible for me to fully embrace both religions. To be completely honest, I am still not willing to abruptly abandon my Christian Faith, which I have believed for my entire life, in favor of Buddhist ideals. However, I do believe that my practice of Zen Buddhism has been and will continue to be beneficial in my life. I feel like it is possible to achieve some degree of equilibrium between the two without compromising my beliefs.

The Second Draft; Part II, the Three Forms of *Dukkha* and Religion

In the original first draft of my chapter I explained that Hagen, one of the authors we read, describes the three forms of Dukkha but I did not explore them until the second draft. According to Hagen the respective order of the Four Noble Truths is Dukkha, Samudaya, Nirodha and Marga. Dukkha, the first truth, states that all existence has suffering. Hagen describes the dukkha as "suffering," but admits that this definition is not entirely adequate because dukkha also implies pleasure. He uses the metaphor of an out-of-kilter wheel to explain the first truth more clearly. He claims that human suffering is like an out-of-kilter wheel, "it bothers us, makes us unhappy, time after time, with each turn of the wheel, each passing day, we experience pain." (Hagen 26) I think that this is a hard idea for a lot of people to grasp because we don't want to admit that we suffer every day. I think that most of us want to believe we are truly happy but the fact remains that "No matter how hard we try to cultivate pleasure and keep it coming our way, eventually the pleasure recedes and the disturbance and vexation return." (Hagen 26)

The following is my explanation of the three forms of dukkha (pain, change and being) as written in my second draft...

"The first kind of Dukkha is straightforward pain, both physical and mental." (Hagen 29) Unfortunately for us all, there is no way to avoid pain entirely. We can numb ourselves with drugs, or try to prevent painful things from happening to us, but in the end pain always finds a way to creep into our lives. Regardless of whatever precautions we might take, pain will find us, mentally and physically, if not through injury or sickness, then through death. "Sooner or later, even if you're perfectly healthy now, you'll get injured, you'll get sick, you'll hurt, you'll die." (Hagen 29) Since we know that suffering is unavoidable, it would be advantageous to educate ourselves on the distinction between physical and mental pain. Hagen says that "Physical suffering occurs whenever something is out of kilter in our bodies. Mental suffering arises whenever we feel something is out of kilter in our lives, in others' lives, or in the world in general." (Hagen 30) Even though this may seem obvious, simply recognizing what pain is and how it arises will not help us rid ourselves of it. The only way that we can truly deal with pain is by confronting it, staring it straight in the face and accepting its inevitable existence.

"The second form of Dukkha is change. All aspects of our experience, both physical and mental, are in constant flux and change." (Hagen 30) Everything in our lives is constantly moving and nothing is ever completely stationary. In a literal sense, think about your body. You may lay down and try your very hardest to be still but your heart is still beating, your blood flowing, your cells converting oxygen into carbon dioxide. The Earth is always rotating, orbiting around the sun, so even in your stillest state, in death, your remains continue to move. As humans we try to address this problem by attempting to fix things in their places. "We attempt this externally through force, control, and manipulation. And we attempt it internally as well, by conceptualizing the world." (Hagen 30) Hard as we might try to hold things still, we will never be able to keep anything stationary which is exactly why change manifests itself as the second form of Dukkha.

The third and final form of Dukkha is much more difficult to understand than the first two. It cannot be summed up in one word because is it too intangible, but we can try to understand it by asking ourselves some very basic questions as Hagen suggests. "How did you get here? What are you? Where did you come from? Where are you going?" (Hagen 32) Hagen points out that even though we may believe we know the answers to these questions, we cannot truly be sure that they are right. We can only speculate, not know for certain.

Writing these three paragraphs helped me to understand how my suffering works. I particularly enjoyed Hagen's book because of its simplicity and matter-of-fact style of writing. His basic definitions for the three forms of dukkha gave me some much needed assistance when I most needed it. However, grasping the definitions opened up a countless number of other doors leading to even more questions without answers. In my case, many of those questions circled back to the conflict I had between Christianity and Buddhism.

I do not know if I am willing to part with the belief system I was raised to accept as true. As a Christian, I have been taught to believe that God is omniscient, that His existence is the reason for my existence, that there is a God. I will never be able to understand ideas like death or the universe, but I can always have faith and choose to believe in something more powerful than me and beyond my comprehension. I may not be able to explain how life was started but life did start, and something had to start it. I guess I just have a hard time thinking that humans happened by chance or coincidence. I think the fact that universe is so vast and incomprehensible makes me want to believe that somewhere there is a being more powerful and more intelligent than a human.

The Second Draft; Part III, the Four Noble Truths

The Second Noble Truth is "the arising of dukkha," which manifests itself in three separate forms, sensual desire, thirst for existence and thirst for non-existence. The first form, sensual desire, is a slightly deceiving term. When I first saw this term, I interpreted it as referencing physical and sexual desires. According to Hagen, this is an incorrect assumption. Hagen submits that sensual desires are in fact mostly mental cravings, including but not limited to things like good conversation, a balanced emotional life, and enjoyable art and entertainment. (Hagen 33) The second form of craving, thirst for existence, can essentially be boiled down to the fact that as humans, we don't want to die and would much rather live forever. The final form of craving, thirst for non-existence, simply explains that as humans we wish to rid ourselves of all our troubles and turmoil. Hagen explains that these three forms ultimately imply that our greatest pains are all self-inflicted as a result of our own desires. "Virtually all the woes of humankind stem from these three forms of craving... Name what afflicts you and you will ultimately find it linked to your craving, your wanting, your de-siring." (Hagen 34) Samudaya is the second of the Four Noble Truths and is described as the arising of Dukkha. Again, Samu-daya presents itself in three different forms... sensual desire, thirst for existence, and thirst for non-existence. In the previous chapter, I explored this subject in more depth than I am going to here as we need to move onto the third and fourth truths.

The third Noble Truth is Nirodha which can also be de-scribed as cessation. Nirodha states that "whatever is subject to arising is also subject to ceasing." (Hagen 44) By ending confusion, sorrow and loss, one may achieve nirvana, which the Buddha explained by saying "Were there not the unborn, ungrown, and unconditioned, there would be no escape for the born, grown, and conditioned. Since there is the unborn, ungrown, and unconditioned, so there is escape for the born, grown, and conditioned." What I think Buddha is trying to here is that because there are things in this world that have not yet come to be but we know will someday arrive, there has to be an equal but opposite phenomenon for things already in exis-tence. I may be wrong, but the only way I can try to rationalize this is through this scenario... I am twenty years old. I do not have a child, but I will someday. My child although he or she is not alive yet, already exists conceptually as an idea; they just have not gotten here yet. In the same way, I already exist in another state as well; I just haven't gotten there yet. I may be interpreting this entirely incorrectly but it is this exact type of difficulty that makes my studies, practice, and learning about Buddhism important. I cannot expect to understand Buddhism correctly the first time, just like the Pythagorean Theorem, but if I keep trying I might be able to eventually get there.

The fourth Noble Truth is Marga which refers to the path to cessation of suffering or the eightfold path. The eightfold path is a realization and practice for bringing about the cessation of dukkha. In other words, it is a means of ending our suffering. The eight aspects of the path are right view, right intention, right speech, right action, right livelihood, right effort, right mindfulness, and right meditation. Each of these aspects presents a different way that we partially rid ourselves of suffering, but when combined all together, we finally experience cessation and nirvana.

The Third Draft; Turning Point

Finally, the third draft considered my practice of To-Do-List Meditation, that I reached a turning point in my experience through it, and how it helped me identify the ways I cause myself unnecessary suffering.

All this time that I have been writing about "the foundation" of Buddhism has been an excuse to hide something much more significant. Although my practice and experience with Buddhism has not been perfect, it has exposed many things to me. Just as we have learned, suffering is all around us. Suffering is constant in our lives, it is everywhere, from the moment we wake up to the moment we go to sleep, we are always suffering in one way or another. What Buddhism has taught me, is to recognize my own suffering. Up until this point, I have avoided talking about this, mostly because I think... I was afraid to. But what Professor Syverson has shown me is that I have to confront the causes of my suffering and try to stop them. Identifying the ways that I cause myself to suffer and explaining how I think I can fix them will be the focus of the remainder of this chapter.

Remember when Forrest Gump said that life is like a box of chocolates? You never know what you're going to get... Yes, this is a fairly very clichéd quote from pop-culture, but I think Gump's observation can help me to illustrate my initial experience with Zen Buddhism. Looking back to the start of the class, I admit how oblivious and naïve I was about Zen Buddhism and its teachings. At some point during my lifetime I developed biased opinions about Zen Buddhism that were based on misleading inferences and false assumptions that couldn't have been farther from the truth. You see, we can always imagine and hypothesize what filling is inside a chocolate, but it is impossible to be positive unless you take a bite. I know I'm getting a little metaphorical, but what I am trying to say is that most of what I thought I knew about Zen Buddhism was actually inaccurate. It wasn't until I took a bite and began practicing and embracing Zen Buddhist concepts that I started to reveal certain truths to myself.

It is easy to look back and define a linear path of progress in my ability to practice Buddhism, after all hindsight is 20/20. But the truth is that my path was not at all linear, but jagged and zigzagging. I went through a separate and distinct process to discredit my inaccurate preconceptions about Zen Buddhism. I went through a separate and distinct process to rationalize my own religion with Zen Buddhism. I went through a separate and distinct process to develop awareness for the causes of my suffering. Each of these end-results is a representation of one, single point of progress on my path to practice Buddhism more effectively.

Over the course of the semester I have learned a great deal about Zen Buddhism and meditation, but most importantly, I have learned a great deal about myself. In all honesty, I never expected to personally benefit or learn so much from this class. This was partially a result of my assumption that, as a Christian, I had inherent moral and ethical objections to all Buddhist teachings. Again, I emphasize how oblivious and naïve I was about Zen Buddhism.

"To-Do-List" Meditation

About a third of the way through the semester I decided to change my method of approach with meditation to a technique that Professor Syverson said she had once practiced, a technique I like to call "To-Do-List" meditation. Most of the time we spent writing following our fifteen minute in-class meditation sessions, I would recap what I had constructed in my mind and try to put it onto paper. Usually what would happen is that I would end up with six topic-areas that each has specific items beneath it. The six main topic-areas that I have used throughout the semester are...

My girlfriend, Stephanie
School
Work
Family
Friends
Self

I arranged these topics sequentially in order from the most to the least important, although all six topics are still very important for me in my everyday life so don't put too much stock in the rankings just yet. So every time I would sit down to meditate, I would run through this list in my head, in the exact same order every time. I would then make sub-lists for each topic-area, these items could be anything, really they are just things that I need to remember to do. Here is an example of one of my lists, written on 10/13/10...

My girlfriend, Stephanie
School
    Unquizes/observations
    Econ quiz
    Paper 2.2 due
Work
    Symitar list
    I.P. Meeting 11/4

Family
    Margot's b-day
Friends
Self
    Laundry
    cvs

Ok, so this is a really typical example of what this list might end up looking like after every time I meditated. For the first couple weeks this technique seemed to really help me stay organized and on top of everything I needed to do, but what I started to notice after a while is that my lists were getting out of control. They were growing much faster than I was able to maintain or keep up with them, which caused me to get really frustrated. Without a way to relieve the mounting stress and frustration from all the things I wasn't getting done, I just let them all build up, and keep building up, more and more and more... Until finally something snapped in me.

Earlier in the semester we talked about the image that at first just looked like a man lying down but after a while your brain would flip and you could see a cow. The snap that I felt in myself was very similar to the sensation I got from first seeing that cow. What happened was that I realized that all this time I had been spending trying to make to-do lists and be more organized wasn't helping me to actually get anything accomplished. Just because I could rattle of my course schedule and due dates from memory or make a really neatly organized to-do list didn't mean that I was actually getting anything on those lists accomplished.

Essentially, the only purpose those lists were serving was to remind myself of all the things I hadn't gotten done already, what all I still had to do, and giving me justification for why I should be panicking, stressed and frantic. That's when it happened, when I felt the snap! It was a peculiar feeling, the snap; all that really happened was that my brain made a new connection between two idle pathways. All that changed was my perspective, I had never thought to look at my to-do lists as a potential source of my suffering because I convinced myself that they were only helping. I was too caught up in making the lists that I failed to realize how much time I was wasting! This was my turning point... when I realized the causes of my suffering.

Barret is a junior at the University of Texas. He was born and raised in Dallas and has lived in Texas his entire life. Barret enjoys watching and playing all sports, keeping in touch with his family, and planning his next ski trip to Colorado.

My Zen Journey
Clayton Gurley

Suffering Before Zen

In my current state, enlightenment seems like a pipe dream. Attainment of such a wonderful state would take a giant surge of willpower and strength to overcome. Perhaps, though, I will be able to come into my own, and into a higher state. Perhaps I can slowly build my willpower up.

As for now, I struggle daily with obsessions and compulsions, which often get the best of me. I have massive anxiety attacks on a regular basis, and get intimidated by the blankness of a page to be written. My ruminations are never ending, bouncing back and forth in my head uncontrollably. I was diagnosed with OCD recently, but I've known I have had it for a long time. I was also diagnosed with Gilles de la Tourette's as a child.

I think that Zen is the key. If I could learn to embrace such a thought pattern, I can train my neural paths mindfully, and possibly even redirect them to mitigate activity in my prefrontal cortex. It is something I worked on over the summer, but I never thought a class could help it. If there ever was one, though, it would be this one.

In my opinion, It is difficult to really know what enlightenment is. Enlightenment is an embrace of what you have currently, and this keeps you from perverting your own mind. Enlightenment is forgetting your fears and worries and going forth. I take that back—it is not forgetting your fears, it is embracing them as well, but not letting them chain you down from reason. Taking all of your current states and moving forward relentlessly. Not being emotionally tamed. This is the very tip of the iceberg, this is what I think enlightenment will bring me.

The other idea that I have about this class is, maybe it will help me get out of my own human condition. Maybe it will help unveil other's minds and their fears and concerns and conditions. I've been getting more outside of self lately, and it scares me hearing myself speak from an outside perspective. It makes me wonder what other people are thinking when I talk. This new experience makes me want to minimize my interaction, and almost disappear into the background. I do not know whether or not this is a Zen trait, but getting outside of my own perspective is something that is very new to me.

The most interesting part of Zen Buddhism that I have read so far has been that Zen is not a journey, or that is a journey that goes nowhere. It does not go outward, and it does not go inward. It is immediacy, characterized by our completeness, and our ability to be our own sanctuary. These concepts make little sense to me at this time. They are not completely foreign and incredible, but they are something that is difficult to wrap my head around.

Some days, I am so overwhelmed by the world that I do not even want to get out of bed. On some of those days, I don't get out of bed. I lay waste, thinking of all the possibilities and responsibilities. All of the things that could go wrong if I were to get out of bed. I think about what bad things and words could be done and said. I let myself wallow in the mire with my fears. Instead of embracing these uncertainties, I let them control me. Not only do I let them figuratively chain me down, but I am literally a part of the bed; inanimate. My fear makes me inanimate.

I even have a fear of graduating. I have a fear of working a 'real job,' because I don't feel real. It is like everyone else has something I do not have. It is as if they are not chained down by the human condition all the same. I get lost in my inward search for perspective. I get scared, because it seems anything, directing inward or outward, is vast and infinite. The only thing that seems small and understandable is the immediate. The 'now' that Zen is guiding us to be in.

The scariest thing about Zen Buddhism is embracing the change, the cycles of birth and death, whether it be relationships, needs, thoughts, our own lives, the lives of the ones around us. Instead of being held down by these cycles, learning to admire them while they're here is an immensely difficult task. It reminds me of Porphyria's lover, how he wrapped her beautiful hair around her head and ended her life, just to preserve that moment in time forever. Even though he accomplished nothing more than a sick act of pain and asphyxiation of another, he saw it as a way to hold on forever.

Recently my mother and I talked about how I've developed. I spent part of the summer writing short stories, and she told me that they were very good. My mother holds me in the highest, and always supports everything I do. She lauded me for my attempt to read The Divine Comedy for pleasure, even though I struggled immensely, especially due to the periodic structure of the sentences. As a thinker, she noted that I had a better grasp on my obsessive-compulsive disorder, even though she always lets me know how frustrating my obsessional ruminations are (of which I am completely aware). have to hear and process every sentence, and cannot let things go, which frustrates myself and those around me. She is amazed at what I have learned in my Computer Science studies, and even though she is the most avid reader I know, she still praises me for my reading abilities (even though I think reading is a weakness of mine). Over the summertime, I wrote some short stories. It was nothing tremendous, just ideas bouncing around in my head. I then had a hectic work schedule of 40-50+ hours a week, and had forgotten that I even wrote them. I went back and read the stories 2 months later, not knowing what to expect. To my surprise I actually enjoyed my own writing, instead of thinking it was hackneyed, like I had in the past.

Listening is another trait that needs much improvement in me. I am trying hard to listen more thoroughly, especially at class time, when it is the utmost importance to pick up on everything that the professor says in order to do my best within the class. I guess since I was so uptight in high school, hinging on the teacher's every word, I wanted to change that and escape that by doing the exact opposite in college. Instead of taking the good and throwing out the bad, I just polarized, completely undermining my past character. Research has been a major factor over the summer. I have delved in head first into Linux, trying to find out everything about it and becoming a much more skilled and competent programmer. My biggest struggle is speaking in thoughts clear enough for others to relate to. I hope eventually I will be able to clarify and voice my opinion so rationally that everybody would find it easy to understand.

Practice of Zen

A lot has changed in such a short time. I feel metamorphosed, as if my life is coming together finally. I am aware that this is just a cycle, but I am capitalizing on it while I have the chance. I will elucidate as accurate as possible four of these major changes in my life that have come about since embracing Zen.

Firstly, I have much more spare time. Being in the moment, being "sincere to make [my] full effort in each moment" (Suzuki 46) has given me a much more immediate appreciation of time. I'm able to accomplish much more, while not being burdened by overly complex thoughts. In Suzuki's informal talks, he mentions that "when we do something with a quite simple, clear mind, we have no notion or shadows, and our activity is strong and straightforward" (62). This approach to my conscious thoughts have calmed my aforementioned obsessional ruminations, and allowed me to be a much stronger person in current situations. This can be illustrated by my newfound ability to keep cool under pressure. Yes, I still go off every once and awhile, but lately my thoughts have been a lot less turbulent and destructive. My thoughts before were "with a complicated mind, in relation to other things or people, or society," and because of this, my activity had become very complex (Suzuki 62). "Mind" in this sense, it must be clarified, means "xin" (sheen).

This translates as close as possible to "the heart / the mind / conscience / moral nature / intention / idea / ambition / design / the core / the middle, center or inside / one of the two." So now, the core of my thoughts, the very design and structure of my thoughts, is so simplistic and modular, that they can connect and form together, and all of the negativity is washed away. Now, there is much room for improvement, but this foray into zazen has already had sufficient results.

Secondly, I have the ability to gauge myself much better, and to track my progress. This way, instead of being bogged down, it's like I have a direct comparison of who I was, to who I am becoming. I can see my skills increasing, and I can learn more fluently, without having to be nagged by the excess baggage of failure and the over inflating ego caused by accomplishment. I am living "from achievement to non-achievement," and learning to do things in the "spirit of non-achievement" (Suzuki 59). It's as if I had only the goosebumps on my skin and the popping of my ears to determine the temperature and the pressure, and now I'm given the blueprints for a thermometer and barometer, and liquid mercury and apparati to construct it with. This, I believe, is due to the ability to keep a "quiet and stable mind [in the midst of noise and change]" (58). Instead of forcing my wills and desires, I let the patterns emerge naturally, and just learn to mold them slightly. The best example of this gauging process is in my ability to stay task-oriented. Instead of letting the infiniteness of this world distract me, I let it center me, and make me more aware. Any distraction can be turned around and enhanced if it is used to keep you focused instead. Meditation has brought this insight to me, by keeping me still and aware, without following Disorder down its rabbit-hole of confusion and distraction. For instance, instead of letting a project bog my mind down with doubt, I can now reward myself at the intermediate steps with slight distractions, such as Facebook or a flash video game, and then get back to work. Eventually, the innate reward in the intermediate steps themselves will surpass the rewards from the distractions, and my mind will have a greater focus on the task at hand. This gradual training mirrors the zazen concept of "pull[ing] the weeds and bury[ing] them near the plant to give it nourishment" (Suzuki 36). These weeds in my mind, these distractions, can be utilized to sate my overactive sensory palate, while at the same time with careful guidance, can be the very thing that grows my xin's spiritual awakening. This also is very Zen-like in its gradual progress, instead of trying to abruptly change a part of the mind, and then failing just as rapidly. "Even though you try very hard, the progress you make is always little by little," which may seem painful and tedious, but if you use your weeds to nourish your garden, it is a much facilitated process (Suzuki 46).

Thirdly, I am not lackadaisically and imprudently wasting my energy. Instead, I am investing what energy I have left each day towards my future. I am aware of what I am doing, and what needs to be done in the future, and reserving energy accordingly. I am still honing this skill, and while it is difficult to take such an active part in the restructuring of my life, it will be worth it in the end. This, to me, is an example of "imperturbable composure" (Suzuki 34). From this concept, I can see that "those who attain perfect wisdom are forever inspired by the conviction that the infinitely varied forms of this world, in all their relativity, far from being a hindrance and a dangerous distraction to the spiritual path, are really a healing medicine" (Prajnaparamita). This approach lets "every single being in the interconnected world [be] a dweller in the boundless infinity of love," which is exactly what this type of thinking makes me a part of. Instead of being separate, I can utilize my energy to bring this interconnected world to the people surrounding me, filling them up with the love that their soul innately desires.

Interest in my studies has increased at least three-fold. I am reading more in-depth, instead of skimming over pages, and I'm thoroughly enjoying the learning process, as opposed to dreading it as I have done before. My reading abilities have increased, as well as my writing abilities and my ability to convey coherent thoughts to my colleagues and peers. I am able to express myself in a truer form, and am that much closer to my "Buddha nature," my "true human nature" (Suzuki 48). I can see concepts clearer, and I can understand the path on which I am walking, the path of time, past, present, and future. This is soothing to me.

Even still, I struggle with some of the concepts in the reading; for instance, the idea of "no subjectivity or objectivity" (Suzuki 37). I feel that when everything is removed, objectivity is left. It is the remains that cannot be removed. The only possible link that I could see is that this could be an intrinsically paradoxical sense of the word; for instance, one that follows the stage of "form is emptiness and emptiness is form" (Suzuki 41). In this sense, all that exists is our "xin," which seems to be in the vein of Plato's ideology. It follows on page 37, that we should "make an effort up to the last moment, when all effort disappears." The fact that we are trying to find a higher awareness, but we're staying calm and trying to reach a state of unawareness is still very perplexing to me, but hopefully as we continue to learn, this obfuscated technique will become apparent.

Some other ideas that I struggled with before became more elucidated upon further reading. Before, I did not understand how we could have the "innate power to purify ourselves and our surroundings," but now that I've been reading how to practice zazen, as well as practicing meditation and free-writing, I am starting to grasp this technique, and it indeed is causing me to be "friendl[ier] with others" (Suzuki 37). This seems to be something that is inherent in zazen, and inherent in our human nature, because I have not had to try very hard to attain at the very least a step in the right direction towards such an ability to purify. It is a possibility that the more that you yourself become organized, the more you are able to re-organize, and help others order themselves as well, much like a seed crystal increasing the growth of all of the crystalline structures around it. "It is impossible to organize things if you yourself are not in order," and since I am gradually increasing in order, I am slowly seeing my surroundings increasing in order as well (Suzuki 27). I am not my problems; I am merely sitting in the middle of them.

The most pivotal point of my practice will be once I have finally grasped the spirit of repetition, without letting my awareness wane. This has proven to recurrently be the most difficult task that I have faced in all of my years. Suzuki says that "this will not be difficult if you are full of strength and vitality," but I simply do not have enough of these traits to follow through persistently (56). "You should be very observant, careful, and alert" while repeating tasks, yet it seems that such repetition dwindles your ability to be this careful, and to be this alert (56). In this treatment of such practice, however, it is clear that you avoid idealistic gaps. If you train your mind so carefully, such that repetition does not become tedious, and that everything is carefully inspected, you gain a good understanding of your abilities, based on performance while practicing. This performance, however, has no negative or positive connotation. It is simply a reference point, not something which is either considered a success or a failure of your abilities. As much as I can think about this, though, I still have yet to put it into effect in my daily life, which is something that must be consistently worked upon. This shortcoming must also be noted, so that I will be able to consciously be aware of it on a daily basis.

The most notable trait that has been gained so far is the recession of my fears. These techniques have mitigated them, and let me be more at ease inside my surroundings, as a part of a whole. I feel the completeness that is talked about, and I finally feel like I am starting to see myself as a whole being. This has caused much happiness on a day-to-day level, whether the day is filled with conflict or accord, and has helped me remain centered. Though I know this journey is long and difficult, I believe that these first steps are great strides towards the form I would like to someday exist as; a form of continual peace, prosperity of xin, happiness, and good nature.

Suffering with Zen

Practice in Zen in the last half of this semester has gotten a lot harder. I am actually attempting to meditate daily, for at least 15-30 minutes. I have always known that Zen and Buddhism would be an invaluable practice, but I never realized how crucial it is until this class. "No more cutting corners," I tell myself. But it's precisely this mentality that has gotten me to my current state of awareness. I am in a state that is not unwelcome, but so novel that it is difficult to deal with. More aware than normal but frustrated at what I am aware of. The reason being, I think, is the same reason illustrated in *Buddha's Brain*, the second stage of growth. To quote the book—"stage two: you realize you've been hijacked by greed or hatred (in the broadest sense), but cannot help yourself: internally you're squirming, but you can't stop grumbling bitterly [about your problems]." (39) This squirming has proven to be more stressful than I would like it to be, but it is better than the overall stress of life, which is more indifferent about my plight than this stress that I am bringing upon myself.

My viewpoints from the "Practice of Zen" section have not changed dramatically, but the way I see those viewpoints in reality has. A simple anecdote of this effect can be represented by myriad programming tasks that I've encountered in the past 5 years. When I first start an assignment, I think, "Wow, this is a simple program. It shouldn't take that long to complete." However, as time passes by, I realize that there are all of these subtle nuances that were not first accounted for; skipped over, because I understood the concept and the underlying theory about what I was programming and assumed that application would be just as easy. I could voice it, but that didn't mean I could actually accomplish it in the physical realm. This sort of bottleneck is now what I am facing in Zen. It is different, but not dissimilar, from the "bottleneck of fear" that Charlotte Joko Beck talks about in *Everyday Zen*. For instance, Joko talks about "the limitations of life [that] are present at conception" (*Everyday Zen* 17). These limitations and fears have a lot to do with the limitations I am facing now, and they may actually be one and the same, but I picture them differently. I do feel a "false identification with a limited self" (19), and I do not have an "open and spacious response to my life" (19). While I feel that I am subjected to this "bottleneck of fear" as well, my main bottleneck stems from my inability to see from a realistic point of view; these bottlenecks are from my lack of focus. The way that these two things operate on me, the bottlenecks of fear and delusion are in a homeostasis inside of me. They feed off of one another, and propagate my current state of confusion. I lack the ability to determine something clearly, which therefore causes me to have a false identification, and therefore I become conditioned improperly. Once the next determination point arrives, I call upon my conditioning, which is already wrong from previous delusions I have suffered. A caveat to mention to the reader trying to understand this is that all of this is happening at a very microscopic scale. These delusions, this error margin occurs within each firing of the neurons in my brain. Granted, they sometimes do conceptualize into a greater delusion, but overall it's just a constant incorrectness that is tacked on to every sensory input that I receive. I think the only way in which this can be mitigated is through much greater and more focused meditation.

Speaking of sitting, I have mentioned that I have been sitting more. In my last sitting, I noticed several things. I saw a lot of my past emotions that were being dragged around through the mire in my mind. A lot of the events where the failures of my past occurred started springing up, wanting to be put to ease. I started counting them, then dismissed them, knowing that I did not have enough time to sit with them in mind at the present time. I noticed that none of my successes came to the surface of my consciousness. They were all sitting peacefully with me, inside of me, fueling my momentary enlightenments. But I also noted that my consciousness's one-sidedness can be troublesome if I get stuck too deeply in these conscious thoughts. This also fits in with the aforementioned delusions and fears in that this also attaches a negative bias to the stream of incoming sensory input. The positive thoughts just sit below my subconscious, only triggered by actions which remind me of them, while the negative thoughts crop up interminably, never ceasing unless I make the effort to consciously halt them. Through all of these thoughts, however, I can see an enlightened state peeking out, only to recede again quickly. The most wonderful point to this bittersweet realization is that I can see my journey ahead more clearly. I can see what needs to be done to achieve no-self, and my pathway, the middle path, the Eightfold Path, starts to be visible inside of my mind. This is a discovery that makes the painful act of sitting much more enjoyable to me.

Still, the benefits mentioned above still hold true; I do not want to downplay them in this section at all. I would just like to present a more accurate state from which you can relate to me. I am still flawed, I am still "I," and while people around me have noticed a change, a friendlier demeanor, a more caring persona, deep down, I am still selfish, self-conscious, and self-centered. It drains me to listen to others, because my mind absorbs their problems as if they are my own. I want to live their life for them, while still maintaining (and thereby cluttering) my own life, instead of being an ear for them to mouth their frustrations to. This is all they really need—someone to listen to them, and possibly point them in the right direction, but not a problem solver. I still take on the persona of an Oracle, someone who tries to impose their supposed absolute viewpoint on others. This is problematic in very many ways, and something major that I cannot even touch yet until I reach a further point in my zazen.

The few Zen practices that I am able to hone currently are simply mindfulness, task-completion, and sitting. I am more mindful of what I eat, what damages I am doing to my body when I don't listen to its needs, what my friends need, what annoys my friends, what is annoying a complete stranger (that I can control). I have started to develop the desire to go to class, because I realize that my grade directly correlates. It is no longer desirable for me to lie in bed and sleep all day, so in that regard my willpower has increased. I am more inclined to do my homework on time, simply to have it done and out of my mind. Any extracurricular tasks are handled promptly as well, and then stored in my iPhone as a completed task, and quickly forgotten. This mindfulness comes from the idea that if I simplify my mind's current state, I can be in a higher state of awareness, thus have a higher chance to be enlightened from fleeting moment to moment. The idea of storing my completed tasks into my iPhone works in practice for two reasons. First—if I ever have to recall it, I can simply sift through the completed

tasks around the date that I think this event occurred. Second—
this way, if my obsessive-compulsive mind ever tries to recall
an event, and fails to do so, I am not thrown into a panicked
state. My parasympathetic nervous system stays in control,
and my sympathetic nervous system is never called into action
(as mentioned in *Buddha's Brain*, chapter 2). Sitting ties into all
of these things. Sitting increases my ability to focus on a task,
whether it be doing the dishes, going to the bank, going to get
groceries, because it helps me deal with any frustrations, fears,
and confusions that are floating around like ghosts unneces-
sarily in my conscious mind. Essentially, it works to push them
back down to my subconscious, where they do not require so
much energy and attention from my brain.

All in all, this foray into Zen has piqued my interest of Buddhism, and given me an exciting glimpse into what makes Zen
practice so unnerving and difficult, yet so rewarding. If I can
learn to take what I have done in this class and apply it to every
facet of my life, I shall continue to crystallize and use my obses-
sive weaknesses as my strengths.

Clayton Gurley is a senior in Computer Sciences at University of Texas Austin. He is from Houston and is seeking a long-term position as a software developer. He is interested in going to graduate school eventually, to pursue Artificial Intelligence and Natural Language Processing to his full extent.

Right Mind? Right Effort? Right On.

Sean Kamperman

Suffering

Right view, right intention, right speech, right action, right liveli-hood, right effort, right mindfulness, right meditation.

In my mind, there's a right way to look, a right way to sound, and a right way to act. There's a correct way around every task, commitment, and relationship: whether discussing the impli-cations of disguise in Shakespeare's Twelfth Night or writing a press release that will stimulate interest in my nonprofit's fundraiser, there is, most decidedly, a right way for the words to fall together; there's a right way to write my thesis, a right way to research the Glenn Beck Program, and a right way to check and make sure that I am, in fact, doing it the right way. There's a right way to joke and carry on, a right way to talk on the phone, and a right way to feel about everything from my relationship with my parents to my taste in cereal, TV dramas, and mid-70s AOR. And of course, in any given interaction on any given occasion—a lunch date with the girl from TC 660, for example—there's a right way to relate. Did you say enough interesting things—enough funny things, enough right things? What about your choice of restaurant—Thai—or your order, the weird green bean soup with the peanuts and the hard boiled eggs? I mean really, was that the right thing for a discerning menu-reader such as yourself to get? And when you arranged to go dancing with her on Friday night, what were you thinking? Sure, it's the 'right' thing for young people such as yourselves to do; but really now, you can scarcely lift a toe without tripping all over yourself. Think for a moment of her toes, and cancel— spare them from squashing while you still have time.

The thinking part of my brain has got me pretty much convinced that "right" is a matter of perspective. After all, claims about right and wrong are by nature controversial—and at this point, I've learned enough about rhetoric to know that, no matter how convincing or authoritative the claims, there will always be disagreement. So I don't consciously nail every piece of information that infiltrates my brain to a rigid code of dos and don'ts. No: my code is flexible—fluid even. I at least try to keep the stock arguments at its parameters in sync with the changes around me, and I'm perfectly willing to update it given a newer, better set of data. But that doesn't change the fact that, deep down inside, I want my papers, commitments, and relationships to feel right.

So it's Sunday night, and I'm standing alone in what precious little personal space I've managed to carve from the crossroads of my house, a ramshackle little dump whose unlucky lot it is to be the temporary abode of about four and a half twentysome-things, predominantly male and all quite dirty in some or other respect. My space is a little plot of dirt beneath the oak tree by my bedroom window, a place littered with cigarette butts and broken citronella coils and other evidences of my regular self-harangues. On a bad night, I'll step out back and smoke not one square but two (or three, or four), pouring over the same, unanswered questions, staring hard at the same, gaping hole in my being: Are you on the right track, Sean? Are you living your life as it ought to be lived? The day is done, and its events lay unfurled at your fingertips, ripe and ready for analysis. So how about your responses to these events? Were they adequate? Consider, if you will, any intelligent being capable of passing judgment on your naked actions. An admissions officer at the law school of your dreams, perhaps. Would the day's actions suffice to indicate to this gentleperson that you're on the path

you'd like to think you're on—that you're slowly but surely realizing that lovely little scene in which you play the ambitious but
grounded ADA, the exemplary husband and passionate lover,
the near-perfect father of two terrific little ones, the man of his
community, inspired writer and player of keys at weddings and
nursing home holiday parties and such? Are your thoughts,
habits, attitudes, and actions, his right thoughts, right habits,
right attitudes, and right actions, or are you slightly off the
mark? Is it all falling together, or are you still missing some vital
piece? Well?

Insofar as this future Sean's ways are right, my own—though
not necessarily wrong—are radial at best, always skirting the
edges of his model, his example. And thus, the answer to these
questions is always no. No, it's not all falling together, and yes,
there is most decidedly something missing from my life.

Though I could be asking different questions—questions
about squirrel mating habits, for example, or about the chain of
contingencies that led my roommate and best friend Tyler to his
decision to pursue a career in clinical psychology—my singular
obsession with determining right from wrong as a precondition
for action has led me away from such "trivial" concerns, turning my inquiry instead toward matters internal. And boy has
the inquiry ever grown tiresome. It keeps shining its flashlight
on the same old data—the same old perceptions, ideas, and
experiences that, when stowed away, picked apart, and spliced
together in a certain combination, lead me to the same old conclusions about life and how to live it. In the operating room of
my imagination, questions like the ones enumerated above act
the part of a team of surgeons, cutting open my conversation
with a professor or peer and retrospectively analyzing it for cor-
rectness, perspicuity, ingenuity; carving into my volunteer work
at the Austin Clubhouse and checking my interactions there for
kindness and sincerity, humor and humility.

You didn't do this. Good grief, Sean, you should've done
that.

And so the haranguing goes. In my own little corner of the
world I stand surrounded by a grim chorus of traveling com-

panions—fellow passengers whose never-ending arguments pull me every which way but now, entreating me to choose and choose wisely or perish. On a bad night, I'll keep their company in a cloud of smoke from not one square, but two (or three, or four). On a really bad night (as it often falls, the night before a due date), I'll find myself jabbering right along, adding my voiced disproval or assent. And nearly every bad night's the same, and has been for some time. I confront my companions—my problems—alone, searching desperately for that missing piece.

Practicing

I suspect I'm not the first to concern myself so assiduously with the distinction between right and wrong. Nor will I be the last. Forsaking chances to enjoy the here-and-now for the realm of regret and shoulda woulda coulda is simply a part of the human condition. While some of us—myself included—have a stronger inclination than others to get frustrated with ourselves for wrong speech, wrong action, and wrong livelihood, we're all inclined toward normative thinking, toward seeing things in terms of right and wrong; and each and every one of us, no matter how well fortified, occasionally succumbs to crippling feelings of stress and anxiety when we sense that there's something wrong with what we're doing or worse yet, with who we are. Life's unexpected twists and turns have a way of forcing us to fall back on normative coping strategies, particularly when the twists are painful. I've been very fortunate in that I've yet to have to deal with the loss of a loved one, but I certainly have no trouble understanding loss; and how often is grief compounded by the confusion that ensues when we start evaluating our reactions against what we perceive to be the right way to grieve, the proper way to say goodbye?

When confronted with life's most painful experiences, our expectations to think and feel a certain way in response to them are thus routinely confounded by the reality of what we actually think and how we actually feel. And sadly, the same applies in matters trivial as in matters great: given the right disposition, spilling coffee on one's blouse can seem as calamitous as getting a C on a term paper, and getting a C on a term paper can be as painful as the death of a favorite pet. I generalize, sure. But if my generalizing offends, please view it for what it is: as a testament of faith, not an exercise in specious armchair philosophizing. Having experienced so little, sometimes the faith that my own experience is not so different from everyone else's is what pulls me through the rough patches, the brutal, backyard brain-wracking sessions that always leave me empty and answerless. And as uncomfortable as I am with religion, Zen has taught me that there's nothing wrong with having faith in the fact that we're all connected.

Which brings us to the point. There's something about Zen that speaks to our natural experience. As a systematic approach to life, its extraordinary appeal rests in the sheer ordinariness of the questions and concerns that have shaped its transmission from one culture to the next. We all experience pain and suffering, and we would all like to know where that suffering comes from and what we can do to avoid it. We all hunger to connect, and we would all like to know how to really do it.

Going into the semester, I had no answers. I was hungry, but above all I was tired. I had just gotten back from a trip to my grandparents' in New York, where I was given leave to run around the city for a couple of weeks and live as the natives do. This scheduled reprieve from my routine gave me just the perspective I was looking for. Soaking in the city's otherworldliness gave me a fresh, invigorated sense of life's possibilities, bequeathing on me a powerful feeling of conviction. I, Sean Kamperman, had spent enough time engaged in sundry navel-gazing pursuits to know I'd had enough. I was—or so I thought—quite through with self-examination; what with being a senior in college and having a million little ships to launch, the time for hand-wringing was most certainly through, and the time for action—hard, firm, aggressive action—was nigh. Real nigh. So when I got home from our first class meeting, right jazzed and ready to get on with all that Zen had to teach me, a little part of me was nevertheless reluctant. Study Zen all you want, it said to me. But whatever you do, don't let it slow you down. Don't think for a second that religion or philosophy or anything like it has a spot at the top of your priorities list. You, Sean, have everything you'll ever need to move forward from here. You've got your inner-resources, you've got your corner— by gum, you're fully equipped.

This conviction went a long way in shaping the contours of my first encounter with Zen. I was all for trying; but at the end of the day, it was just another game. My inquiry was as much a practical necessity for the purpose of getting good grades as it was a means to greater self-awareness. And so, eyes on the prize, I resolved to begin with an open mind and a nice reserve of personal distance. I'd go to class and patiently endure our fifteen minutes of silence and stillness, doing my best to keep the demons and tracks two and five of Michael Jackson's Off the Wall at bay as I concentrated on pulling my whole being into awareness of my breath. But the breathing proved just another distraction (Breathe deeply, Sean. You call that deep? Your diaphragm, man, engage the diaphragm!). I'd record these things in my meditation journal and wonder wide-eyed at our class discussions, cooking like mad to come up with contributions of my own but never managing to bring my thoughts to a question or point. Fearing as I did the rod of rebuke—and regretting this fear with as much hatred and loathing as one can regret with—I consistently failed in my attempt to find the right words, the right things to say. And so, the bell would ring and I'd head to the bus at 4:45, stewing over my timidity and vowing that next time, next time, I'd do the right thing—the expected thing—and speak up.

If this doesn't seem like a particularly enlightened way of reasoning my relation to Zen, it's because it wasn't. The walls were up, and they were getting in the way. Sure enough, as the semester progressed, my resolution to keep a partition between the realities of my personal life and my encounter with Zen started to seem more and more counterproductive. How could I ever add something meaningful to class discussion if I continued putting my practice at arm's length, resolved as I was

to embrace the grander aspects of Zen's philosophy while re-
jecting its prescriptions for daily living? Fortunately, the farther
along I got in the reading, the more these resolutions started to
chafe against the actual experience of my encounter. Reading
the teachings of Hagen and Suzuki felt uniquely satisfying, not
unlike drinking a tall glass of water—plain, refreshing, utterly
ordinary. I was enthralled by the beautiful concepts they elucidated with their poetic imaginations, drawn in by the patience
and humility they showed through their dedication to remaining in the moment. These guys were in it, and they were in it
for others—their friends, their families, their pupils and peers.
This Zen stuff, it seemed, was for real. It showed me how action
was to be had: via a mindset swimming in spacious awareness
of reality and the current moment. All I had to do was practice
and practice right, and the gap between Zen and my personal
experience would disappear with a poof, freeing me from the
criticisms of my fellow passengers.

But problematically, the practice wasn't coming easy. My efforts at meditation felt middling at best; if I wasn't distracted by
risk of ankle fracture in an ill-conceived attempt at the full lotus,
I was always distracted by one thing or another—the pitter
patter of rain, the roaring of diesel engines emanating from
I-35, the clear and present danger of being discovered sitting
Indian-style on my front porch by my judgmental neighbor and
her Great Dane Lola. At every turn, I was frustrated.

Truly, the distinction between my Zen mind and my ordinary
mind—the mind I brought with me to my first encounter, the
mind always caught up in rights and wrongs, dos and don'ts—
did not become clear to me until I sat down to write the second
part of this chapter. Rifling through my meditation journal, I
started to notice a pattern of rebuke. Even in free-writing, I was
constantly questioning whether I was on the right track with
this meditation business, constantly wondering about how I
might improve my practice. I must've come across a hundred
'should' constructions in my journal, some explicit ("Where
should I direct my eyes, my hands, my conscious thoughts?")
and others implicit ("Next time, I'll focus only on this kind of

breath, that kind of sound or sudden occurrence."). Reflecting on these things in the context of my ordinary, preferred way of seeing, I suddenly realized the truth of Suzuki's words in relation to my own experience: the secret of zazen is that it serves no purpose. It isn't about outcomes; rather, it's about effort. Right effort. There is no should or shouldn't—there is only thus. Reading Joko confirmed my realization, contributing the idea that, just as there's no right was to meditate, there's no right way to do or think or say anything. There's only doing, thinking, saying. In constantly fixating on an amenable outcome, I'm missing the mark of reality: I'm always a step ahead. And in continuing to stand night after night in the ashy vestiges of my self-imposed isolation, countenancing the harsh judgments of my grim fellow passengers and allowing them to determine my value in relation to some storybook version of myself in faraway future land, I'm in reality a step behind.

Emptying Out

What studying Zen has given me, then, is a way of understanding myself that's both strictly scientific and decidedly relational. This understanding is scientific in that it's based on observation; it's relational in that refuses to see any piece of data or information as anything but connected. Reading through my journal, I observed a pattern that told me something about the way I see the world. I never once consciously set out to create patterns in my writing—the patterns simply came to be. Truly, the grandiose notions of my own self-concept that I brought with me to this class pale in comparison to the clarity I've gained through simple observation of my habit of mind and its relation to the world around me.

So the questions I've been asking for as long as I can remember may very well have no answers. Right and wrong are tied to outcome—groundless, afloat, with little basis in seeing. Effort, on the other hand, is real. It's here and now. It seems to me now that asking about the difference between right and wrong really isn't good for much. Nevertheless, I take comfort in knowing there are still many questions to ask.

My days of fighting myself in an endless contest to determine do from don't are far from over. Indeed, they'll never be over, as pain, or duhkha, is like the unpleasant experience of "a wheel out of kilter," arising again and again with the turning of time. The next question, then, becomes one concerning practice: if our goal is to get to know the turning of the wheel and thereby fortify ourselves against unnecessary suffering, what's our recourse when we can't surmount the pressures of our ordinary minds on our own? To whom or what can we turn when the task of seeing becomes too great and we find ourselves returning to old ash heaps and still older habits? For me, the answers to these questions have been predictably hard to come by. Even in the midst of my willful reorientation from outcome to effort, I felt I was still getting stuck on the same old points, the same old deference to my conditioned perception of the distinction between wrong and right. In a nutshell, I was still afraid of reaching out to others with my interest in Zen for fear of exposing any shortcomings in my thinking on the matter. And a big part of me still is.

But having read Dale S. Wright's expositions on knowledge and understanding in *Philosophical Meditations on Zen Buddhism*, I feel I'm getting close. What Wright has shown me is that trying to figure out the right way around every task, commitment, and relationship is truly a pointless enterprise. What we can try to figure out is how other people's various definitions of right speech, right action, and right livelihood "originate dependent" upon the people, places, objects, and ideas that have shaped them—and how, in turn, those people, places, objects, and ideas connect them to everything else. Because every thing, being empty of independent nature, is by logical necessity connected. And when you start thinking about how this is so—as Wright has helped me to do—the illusion that we are anything but related to each other fades away, as does the fear of rebuke. What becomes precious, then, is not our commitment to right goals and right ideals, but rather our commitment to each other.

I am grateful for Zen, and I am grateful to Professor Syverson and my peers in RHE 330E for nurturing my encounter with Zen's elegant and often surprising take on life and how to live it. I am grateful for David Hagen, Shunryu Suzuki, Joko Beck, Rick Hanson, Richard Mendius, and Dale Wright; each of these individuals has, through his or her dedication to unraveling the mysteries of life through attention to the moment, furnished me with profound teachings that have and will continue to influence my thoughts, actions, speech, and livelihood. I am grateful for Huang Po and for John Blofeld, for the monastic and secular communities they ministered to in medieval and modern China, respectively; I am grateful for the Buddha, and I am grateful for everyone who has ever committed themselves to the task of transmitting his wisdom from East to West, from India to Austin.

Please forgive me if my cheesiness offends. I didn't intend on turning the final section of my chapter into an acknowledgements page; but given my current understanding of "dependent origination" and its implications for the "great matter" of life, I can't think of any better way to demonstrate what I've learned this semester. Zen has taught me how to see my pain and my petty quandaries in the round—how to note them when they vex me, and how to note the feelings of vexation as well; how to see both preoccupation and emotional response as mere activities of my anxiety-addled mind, and how to let them be when they threaten to pull me away from the feast. And for that I am grateful.

So this is my new, end-of-the-semester conviction: not to do the right thing, but simply to do. Far from being a peculiar effect of debate and logical demonstration, conviction is in reality had via experience—via seeing things. Not via worrying about things. That's something else I've learned. For me, breaking out of the realm of worrying and into the realm of seeing is going to take some work. Some right work. But to shun my fear of Suzuki's rod and let others teach me what they will—to fully embrace the truth that Buddhism, like life in general, isn't about going it alone in your own little corner—will be well worth the effort.

Sean is a fourth-year Rhetoric & Writing major at the University of Texas at Austin. He is from Waco. After graduating in May 2011, he plans on pursuing either a JD or a PhD in Composition. Long-time loves include music, Mexican food, and a good jog.

Wake Up and Smell the Zazen

Lili Serfaty

PART I: In the beginning, there was Zen.

My initial encounters with Zen Buddhism have led me to be-lieve that the ultimate goal of Buddhism is awareness. I am not aware. Through *Buddhism Plain and Simple,* along with our meditations and free writing sessions and group discussions, we begin to head in the direction of awareness.

When I first look at Buddhism I see it as a religion; however, when examined from a neutral perspective it appears to be an interesting approach to life. As we come upon Rosh Hashanah, the Jewish New Year and Yom Kippur, the Day of Atonement, I am reminded of my devotion to my religion but at the same time I am intrigued because Buddhism offers teachings that seem to be compatible with Judaism, setting aside the cultural traditions and rituals that have become associated with Bud-dhism. From my understanding at this point, our ultimate goal is to achieve awareness. This sense of clarity in being able to truly see our surroundings can be invaluable in all aspects of life.

My first true encounter began with meditation at our first class session. Overcoming anxious feelings of being completely still and silent in a new environment with unfamiliar people, I slowly began to realize how fidgety I was, both in my mind and my body. Rather than succumbing to the temptation of using the precious time to think about my many commitments and responsibilities, I closed my eyes and attempted to focus on the sounds I heard in the room. When I was a camp counselor at a Jewish sleep away camp, one day we had an activity in place of morning prayers. My group went into the woods and we recited the daily prayer the Shema, which literally means "Listen." Following the short prayer we had ten minutes of meditation in the woods in which we focused on clearing our heads and listening to the many sounds we could hear in nature. While meditating in class, I recalled this experience, and the peaceful feelings associated with it. I began to count all the sounds I could hear in the classroom (5, in case you were wondering) and this focus cleared out all the unnecessary thoughts. I tried to become aware of my thoughts and direct them rather than let them follow their own path. I'm not sure if this is the correct way to face my thoughts during meditation, but once I became aware of my thoughts I was able to control them.

Additionally, once I reined in my thoughts, I became more aware of my actions. I had been fidgety, scratching every itch and readjusting constantly to find a slightly more comfortable position. I found, however, that after I had corralled my thoughts, I became more aware of my physical movements. I noticed that I was constantly moving, and then I attempted to correct it. When I felt that I had to scratch an itch, I was able to resist the urge by recalling something my father had told me. Living in New York, winters are bitterly cold, and yet, he rarely wears a coat when we go out to a restaurant or store. Walking from the car to the restaurant one day I was shaking uncontrollably and squealing and complaining about the frostbite overtaking my toes one by one, and I yelled at my father, "WHY AREN'T YOU WEARING A COAT? HOW ARE YOU NOT FREEZING?!" He simply replied, "It's only temporary." At that moment I dropped my arms from their stiffly tense position wrapped around my torso and realized my father was right; I would be completely fine walking outside in the cold for half a minute, and after processing that rational logic, I was able to withstand the cold, and many other uncomfortable states from that point on. During meditation I called on that moment of minor discomfort and re-alized that this, too, was just temporary. I simply acknowledged the itch and accepted the fact that I would not be scratching it, and eventually it passed.

Similar to the meditation, I also notice the importance of free writing following our brief meditation sessions. I don't know if this is a formal part of Buddhism, but the free writing is an opportunity to externally process the thoughts and ob-servations I have during the meditation sessions. It allows me to become more aware because rather than having a fleeting thought, writing it down creates a more permanent observa-tion. Later on I will hopefully be able to follow my observations to see a progress in my self awareness during meditation. During elementary and middle school, I dreaded the notorious "Free Write" but as I have grown up, I now see it as a valuable opportunity for thought and reflection. As someone who can process thoughts much more efficiently when I have written them down, I find free writing to be a helpful tool. If my un-derstanding of the importance of awareness in Buddhism is correct, each free writing session goes one step further in the right direction. While I can see many things, as *Buddhism Plain and Simple* explains, we rarely actually see what we're looking at. I find a similar situation when playing the game "Mad Gab." The objective of the game is to read the words on the card and figure out the phrase it is trying to convey. The difficult part is that the words are not written in the typical recognizable way, but rather they're split up into random words that are some-what similar in sound but not meaning to the original words. It is extremely difficult to discern any coherent phrases from the mash up of words; however, if you read them all aloud, you are able to see the true meaning of the phrase. I feel a similar phenomenon during my free writing session; even though I look at occurrences in my life and I see them and I think about them, it is not until I externally process them on the paper and read them again from this new perspective that I can actually see what I am talking about.

Admittedly, this is all very difficult to follow because my

mind is flooded with thoughts and questions and insufficient understandings of Zen Buddhism. As time progresses I am eager to learn more about the teachings and how to incorporate them into life and enrich daily experiences. I am not aware, and I do not claim to be; but on rare occasion think I see the briefest moments of clarity without understanding, and this adventure into Zen Buddhism is an exciting opportunity to dive below the surface.

PART II: Mid-Semester Zenophobia

Claiming a better understanding of Zen Buddhism after three weeks would clearly show a complete misunderstanding of Zen. At this point I have become slightly more aware of my unawareness. As we engage in more class discussions and read materials regarding the subject matter, I continue to be perplexed by the paradoxical theories that seem to define this school of thought. As we move on from *Buddhism Plain and Simple* to *Zen Mind, Beginner's Mind* and learn more about the practices and how they support the core beliefs, I am even more confused by the contradictory nature of these lessons. I appreciate the use of analogies, as they bring me slightly closer to at least the most basic level of understanding; however, the complexity discourages me from further pursuing Zen at this point.

Recently, however, I have been suffering from a severe case of Zenophobia—an irrational fear of waking up. A newly emerging restlessness and skepticism invade my initial willingness to participate and learn more about Zen. In the beginning of the semester, my schedule remained fairly open making it easier to devote time to meditation and feeble attempts at understanding these intricate theories. Unfortunately, as life picks up, uninhibited free time reserved for contemplation gets pushed to the back burner in order to make room for spontaneous nervous breakdowns and crisis management centered around vague post-college plans.

I was talking to a friend today who is a flight attendant for a living. She is chronically late, and yet, somehow she has been a flight attendant for twenty or so years. I asked how she has lasted this long in a profession so dependent on timeliness, and she said it's a balance; "I'm late in my personal life and on time in my professional life. I have a perfect balance, and if I try to be on time for a hair appointment, it'll mess things up." An important lesson that I've gathered from the text that seems to be easily applied to life is the importance of a balance. *Zen Mind, Beginner's Mind* is full of lessons for one seeking a life of awareness; however, all the many teachings seem to be centered around a foundation of balance.

Whether it's the swinging door or oneness of duality, I believe they are all rooted in balance. In *Zen Mind, Beginner's Mind,* Suzuki says "When we lose our balance we die, but at the same time we also develop ourselves, we grow. Whatever we see is changing, losing its balance." During my meditation I have noticed that my life is becoming characterized by an unsettling imbalance. Life presents itself in a pattern similar to that of waves hitting a shore; the strength of these waves is unknown, but I am becoming familiar with the pattern. I stand just where the waves break. For some period of time, I am able to stand upright and enjoy the calm, uneventful low tide. I can feel the sand between my toes and the cool sea breeze blowing in my hair. The calm of the water lulls me into a false sense of security, and immediately, I am bombarded by a wave that knocks me off my feet, and the water rushes over me, and tumbles me around as I stumble to recover the position of safety and peacefulness I had. Eventually, the wave passes and I regain balance. From that wave, I learn to adapt for the next.

Returning to the "oneness of duality" mentioned in the section of *Zen Mind, Beginner's Mind* on Posture, I almost understand this concept but not quite. This near-understanding feels similar to a word on the tip of my tongue, or an itch on my brain. Suzuki says, "Our body and mind are not two and not one. If you think your body and mind are two, that is wrong; if you think that they are one, that is also wrong. Our body and mind are both two and one." I don't understand this, but at the same time it makes sense. Perhaps in simpler terms, the other day a friend of mine said, "Sometimes I see myself from the outside, and then I go back in," which I believe is in some way connected to the "oneness of duality." Occasionally we have out-of-body experiences, but for the most part, our mind and our body seamlessly and independently coexist. Each is a fully capable, separate entity, however, if one was not functioning properly we would notice, and if it was missing all together, we would be incomplete. Clearly, I am unable to articulate this notion, most likely because I do not have a full grasp of it.

Even though the meditation led me to realize the imbalance, the imbalance in turn distracts from the meditation. Every session becomes a little bit more difficult to sit still. In the beginning of the semester, I attempted to control my thoughts during meditation; I wrongly thought that I should clear my mind. After several class discussions I learned that the more appropriate way to deal with thoughts is to follow them, because they have a story they're trying to tell me. If I refuse to listen to them, they will become persistent until I give them the attention they deserve. The difficult part of the meditation then occurs at the point in which I follow the thoughts to where they want to take me, and would then like to act on them. It almost feels like my thoughts are Lassie and they're trying to tell me that Little Timmy fell down the well. After I follow Lassie to the well, I desperately want to save Timmy. My thoughts, however, are not as dire as saving a small child from drowning in a well, and the true control and restraint comes from being able to recognize these thoughts as they pop into my head, see them through to the end, and withhold immediate action.

Unfortunately, I am now having trouble remaining completely still for an entire ten minutes. When I say it, it sounds like "only ten minutes"; however, when I will myself to stay still and silent for ten minutes, it truly becomes "an entire ten minutes." My restlessness brings me back to when I was a child. As a little girl, if my mother told me to wait five minutes before I could have her complete and undivided attention, those five minutes felt like an eternity.

According to my two semesters in Astronomy, I'm fairly

certain that this is only possible in black holes, and yet time definitely slowed down, and five minutes lasted at least three hours (if not more.) It's a little unsettling to think about it, but recently when I sit down to meditate, I once again become that little girl who can't sit still for an extended period of time, and I get this physical discomfort and anxiety when I try.

I am unable to hold correct form for the full time, but Suzuki has encouraging words regarding this subject in the section on the Marrow of Zen in his book *Zen Mind, Beginner's Mind*. Suzuki explains, "When you feel disagreeable it is better for you to sit. There is no other way to accept your problem and work on it... Everyone can practice zazen, and in this way work on his problems and accept them." I need to push through my feelings of physical and mental discomfort while sitting, and this persistence will help me to reach a more aware and awakened state. While I am encouraged by this, I am still concerned that my inability to sit has a negative effect on my thought process while meditating. However, I think that simply making the effort to sit and put myself within the problem I am thinking about sets me ahead of where I would be without meditation. Suzuki explains later in the section the Marrow of Zen, "When you are sitting in the middle of your own problem, which is more real to you: your problem or you yourself? This awareness that you are here, right now, is the ultimate fact." I need to place myself in the present to be truly aware. Clearly, this is easier said than done.

Sadly, not only is my meditation suffering at this point, midway through the semester, but I find that my free writing is also going downhill. While it still acts as a recording of my thoughts, when I have less important thoughts to recount, my writing becomes less useful in tracking my progress. I suppose that in recording these thoughts of grocery lists and fencing footwork moves to use at practice I am still tracking my progress, although it is unfortunate that this progress happens to be taking steps backwards rather than forwards.

Perhaps though, this development is not necessarily a regression. During my semester of Management, we learned about the Four Stages of Competence that a manager faces when training new employees. The first stage is Unconscious Incompetence, followed by Conscious Incompetence, then Conscious Competence, and finally Unconscious Competence. We all begin at the stage of Unconscious Incompetence in which we are terrible at a new skill or practice, and we have no idea. We all strive for Unconscious Competence, and if we devote enough time and effort, we eventually gain the ability to perform a certain task without great effort. This was a concept I was easily able to translate into other aspects of my life, most obviously being my growth as a member of the Fencing team. When I first joined the club, I enjoyed the sport, and occasionally I got touches on my opponents or even won a bout. Overall, I didn't think I was all that bad, especially for a beginner. As time passed, I took lessons, practiced my foot and blade work, and participated in my tournaments. Eventually I became extremely discouraged because I realized how terrible I was. When I discussed with my coach what had seemed like a huge decline in my skills, he assured me that I was improving. Had I known about the stages of competence at the time, I could clearly label myself as Conscious Incompetence at that point.

Similar to my experience labeling my position with the stages as it applies to fencing, I believe I am becoming discouraged as I am slowly moving into the stage of Conscious Incompetence. As we discuss most topics in class, and delve into more texts, I begin to realize just how much I don't understand. However, if I place myself within the Competence Stages, I can be encouraged by the thought that maybe this is just my path to growth and understanding. Before I can become better, first I need to locate where I currently stand in order to track my progress.

PART III: It's Raining Zen (Hallelujah)

There are two things that I really dislike—quitting, and being bad at something. Obviously, I can't be good at everything, but I can sure as hell try. It goes without saying that not everyone reaches an awakened state, and most of us never will. Ideally that would make a nice little goal, but I don't possess the drive and dedication to fully integrate Zen into my life. I can, however, label success as gaining a fuller understanding of Zen Buddhism, and implement it on a regular basis in the way that I have up until now: daily meditation and free writing. By simply shifting the focus, I will not quit, and with enough effort, I can become somewhat proficient.

Up until now, I have had a very limited view of things. As we discuss in class, every thought and emotion we have tells a story, and to understand the significance of the thought, we must trace the story back to its inception in our minds. I have had a particularly difficult time viewing these thoughts from different perspectives; my first realization of this came when I was unable to view the cow. At this point in the semester, I have become slightly more adept at understanding different perspectives by simply taking the time to think things through in meditation. A more literal, scientific explanation, as I have learned in my Introduction to Cognitive Science class, might call this Binocular Rivalry. I'm sure scientists hate when we common folk apply scientific theories to somewhat irrelevant human behavior, but I'll go ahead and do it anyway. Binocular Rivalry is when we are presented with two different visual stimuli, and we first perceive one, and then the other. We then slowly alternate between the two. In my case, I am really putting in a concerted effort to see the different perceptions, and my mind tries to wander back to where it is comfortable, and I continuously try to push it beyond its typical capabilities.

Sometimes, however, I don't even need to make that effort, but rather the practice seamless integrates itself into my life. I was just sitting downstairs with my roommate as she got ready for class, and at 12:15, she realized that she would never make it in time for her 12:30 class that was on the opposite side of campus from us. Prior to my Zen study, I may have said (or hopefully just thought) something along the lines of "You didn't budget your time, so now you will be late to class." Today, however, I thought "Perhaps there was a reason she was late—wait, there doesn't need to be a reason. I am her friend and her roommate and I will offer to drive her to class." I didn't say to myself that I am her good friend or her good roommate because as Suzuki explains in his section on the Marrow of Zen in his book *Zen Mind, Beginner's Mind,* "One who thinks he is a good father is not a good father; one who thinks he is a good husband is not a good husband. One who thinks he is one of the worst husbands may be a good one if he is always trying to be a good husband with a single-hearted effort. I observed my thought, followed it to back to its origin, and dealt with it accordingly by acting in the present and putting my effort into be a good friend and roommate. I chose to give my roommate the benefit of the doubt because there was truly no need for me to stress about the way she chooses to budget her time.

Even if I am able to see the different perceptions, as we discussed Dale S. Wright's chapter on Language in *Philosophical Meditations in Zen Buddhism,* perception can only be realized in language. Dr. Syverson explained that we connect new information to previously attained knowledge; throughout my chapter I tried to translate my encounters with Zen concepts into experiences that I can understand and relate to. This is an effective technique when learning any new skill. Most notably in my life I use this to put fencing into a language that I understand. I like to think of myself as having a quick wit and good comedic timing. A major strategic tactic in fencing is using timing to your advantage; initiating an attack can be seen as setting up a joke and then delivering a punch line. I can't deliver the line too soon, because the audience won't be ready, but if I wait too long, I'll have lost the moment, or someone else will have interjected some lame, but mildly amusing one-liner. In fencing, ideally, if I get my timing right, instead of my audience laughing, the phrase ends in me stabbing my opponent; in my use of language, the phrase ends with my conversational partner understanding the point I am trying to communicate. We learn though comparisons and associations, so we use the culture we know to broaden our understanding of new concepts.

As a beginner student of Zen in this course, I have had invaluable experiences that bring me closer to truly understanding who I am, my relationships with others, and the way I act in different situations. While I do not see myself fully committing to Zen practice, I am confident that I will continue to integrate these lessons and concepts into my every day life long after I have completed this course. Most importantly I will continue to make an effort to live in the present moment and strive to understand the full scope of language as the most powerful tool for communication. I do not anticipate myself to continue with formal zazen; however, as sitting has become a welcomed and relaxing part of my routine, I will try to carry on my meditation as it will help me to be aware of myself in the present, and I'm sure I will continue to play around with the concept of the oneness of duality.

As unpleasant as it is to step out of my comfort zone, it is crucial in my growth in understanding. Right now I am in this confined space of my knowledge and lack of awareness; as I keep learning, reading the texts, sitting, and having thoughtful discussions both in and out of the classroom, I continue to push out the walls of this small space. Thanks to my distaste for quitting and failing, I continue to make an effort. Occasionally things click, which is so rewarding that I continue to push. Relating this back to fencing once again, these small successes encourage me to keep working. When I make a particularly clean parry-riposte, I can feel my entire body say "that's the way it's supposed to be!" and it's so satisfying that I strive to make that move consistent and then exceed it. My Zen practice moves in a similar way as I take baby steps toward proficiency in certain areas. Whether it is during meditation, being able to better perceive a situation, or anything else related to practice, these brief "aha!" moments are so satisfying that I am driven to learn more.

Lili Serfaty is a fourth-year rhetoric and writing major at The University of Texas at Austin, originally from New York. She is a senior member of the University of Texas Fencing Club. Lili loves creatively crafting language and hopes to work as a copywriter with an advertising agency after graduating.

Zen

Mary Parsamyan

Zen

I became interested in this class because of its name.

I stress myself out a lot. These past few years have been crazy and college has been a major reason for that craziness. Every time I am stressed, I tell myself "to think Zen" as in to relax. I really have no idea what Zen means. I just know when I think of Zen I think of waterfalls and relaxation. I don't know where it comes from or how I got this idea. It has no link to any knowledge whatsoever. There is no reasoning behind this. The only thing I know about Zen is the word itself.

When I think of Zen, Buddhism comes to mind. I don't know what Buddhism actually means. I recently found out that it was not a religion and that fact interested me since I always believed Buddhism to be a religion. I am familiar with the Buddha figure and have seen many versions of it sold in various stores across the U.S. I have heard that if you rub a Buddha's belly it brings good luck. I have no idea if this is true. I am curious to find out. I'm sure this has nothing to do with the actual practice itself and is not related to Buddhism.

I have recently started reading Hagen's book and it has interested me in this indescribable way. I wasn't expecting Buddhism to be this interesting. I hate using that word "interesting." I mean, what does that really mean? I found that I agree with a lot of what Hagen says in his book. This is a great introductory book because it's easy to read. At first, I thought there was going to be a catch because generally I don't get that interested when reading assigned books. However, there is no catch; this book is made that way because it's for beginners. It's easier to read and is engaging. It didn't fail to interest me.

Buddhism is about being awake and being in touch with reality. A Buddha is not a figure to worship; he is just a person that is awake. There could be a million Buddha's walking among us. I agree with this idea of being awake. For instance, when people around me watch too much T.V., I feel like they are tuning themselves out from the real world and escaping reality. People could be doing something with their life rather than wasting time. I'm not saying anyone who watches T.V. is not in tune with reality. A little T.V. is fine, but too much is excessive and we should do everything in moderation. When I talk to someone while their consumed by the television, it's like I'm talking to a wall. I feel as though they are not paying attention to me and not fully present as I am speaking.

A Buddha figure is someone who is aware of what is going on at all times. They are active and are hands on with their life. For instance, Hagen says that to read about something is one thing but to experience it is another. I completely agree with this. Experiencing life and living it out will teach you more in a much more powerful way than anything else. A book cannot give you the experience you get by actually doing whatever it is that you want to do. I have moved around a lot in my life and so this idea of experience as opposed to knowledge means a lot to me. It's a powerful statement because I'm a college student who is close to graduating and so I have read a lot of things. Looking back, I would say my experiences have shaped me more than any knowledge or book could ever have.

In class, Professor Syverson mentioned that there was a past teacher who said something along the lines of you can't always get what you want but you can always be the person you want to be. I thought that was an interesting statement that was thought provoking. It's true and that's why it's something she mentioned. Generally statements that last for a long time have a truth to them and apply to life. This statement makes me wonder: if I work hard why can't I get what I want? Don't I deserve to get what I want? If I can't get what I want by working hard then why am I working in the first place? I understand that you can't always get what you want and that's the real world for you but that's still a discouraging statement. I guess that goes in line with Buddhism and the whole being awake to the reality of the situation idea. It's difficult to think this way sometimes.

Buddhism to me is being at peace with yourself. It is about finding the person within you and being able to focus on that. It's about accepting the reality of the situation. It's about seeing what is in front of you and understanding that simple fact. It sounds easy and may be simple for some but I doubt that it is that simple. Sometimes things that seem simple are some of the most complicated things to do for me.

In chapter 1, Hagen talks about the human situation. He mentions that most of us believe that there is something missing in our lives. However, we don't see that problem. Everything we need to get rid of this dissatisfaction is right in front of us but we don't realize it. All this apparently comes out of our hearts and our own confusion. This ongoing dissatisfaction is the first truth of existence. I believe a lot of Buddhism has to do with one's self. All problems can be resolved within us. However, this is one of the hardest things to do because we, as humans, usually blame others for everything.

I realized the three realizations from Hagen have a truth to them. "First, you must realize that life is fleeting. Next, you must understand that you are already complete, worthy, and whole. Finally, you must see that you are your own refuge, your own sanctuary, your own salvation."

I think the three realizations describe Zen and Buddhism in the best way possible but certainly not the only way. If one comes to reality with these terms they will understand the meaning of Buddhism. Once you see it and get it, it's simple and is not that complicated. Understanding what I need to do is the most complicated part for me sometimes.

Hagen compares us to a flower when he says "like the rose, our bodies and minds are fleeting. We die in each moment and again, in each moment, we are born. The process of birth and death goes on endlessly, moment after moment."

I believe this description is a good example of life in general. There is nothing else that describes life more accurately than this to me. The point of Buddhism is to help people understand and accept the truth. In my opinion, Buddhism is something a lot of people should read about today because many don't want to accept the truth and want to get away from reality. Many people actually make their situations a lot worse by trying to ignore it in the moment that it exists in. I tend to do this at times because it's the best way for me to get away from it all. However, I have to realize that getting away from my situation is only temporary and not permanent.

Meditation is a huge part of Buddhism. The first time I meditated I was confused as to what I was to be thinking about while I was meditating. I know we were supposed to look down and think but it couldn't just be that simple. My mind was racing and it wouldn't stop. I didn't know if I should be thinking about calming thoughts or even if I could because of all the other crazy thoughts racing through my head. After our first meditation period, I was left with many questions.

Ever since our first meditation, I have meditated a number of times. After talking to some students and the Professor I realized that you didn't really need to think. You shouldn't try not to think, you should just let each thought come and go. This explanation has helped me understand meditation a lot better. It doesn't require a lot of effort; it requires you to just be.

There is a lot more room to learn and the most important thing is that I find this class interesting which means I actually want to learn as opposed to being forced to do it.

Part 2

In *Zen Mind, Beginner's Mind* Shunryu Suzuki provides "informal talks on Zen meditation and practice" which are relatable to everyday life.

In this section, I've listed the quotes that have most impacted me and my thoughts in this class.

Part 1 Right Practice "Zazen practice is the direct expression of our true nature. Strictly speaking, for a human being, there is no other practice; there is no other way of life than this way of life."

This explains the reality of the situation that we live in. Whether I choose to accept it or not, it is what it is. I shouldn't try to make it something that it's not. Zazen is just that. I don't have to pretend to be doing something that I'm not already doing.

Part 1 Posture "These forms are not the means of obtaining the right state of mind. To take this posture is itself to have the right state of mind. There is no need to obtain some special state of mind."

This is the most important thing in Zen meditation to me. If I don't have the right posture, I can't sit still and it interferes with my whole period of Zen meditation. Posture is one of the most important things that I have learned about in Zen. It has helped me in all other aspects of my life. After I read this book I started being aware of my posture the majority of the time. Keeping a straight posture helps me focus on what I'm doing at that very moment. I would never think that this would have a huge impact on overall activities that I performed in my daily life but it has made a difference. Since I am able to focus better I am more productive at doing my school work.

Part 1 Control "To give your sheep or cow a large, spacious meadow is the way to control him."

This is humorous in some sense because it's true. Some people might assume the opposite but that would just make the sheep mad and uncontrollable. Giving people a lot of room and space allows them to grow into whatever it is they are going to grow into without any force. The majority of the time people will make the choice to do the right thing without outside influences. I can think of many good examples. For instance, I had friends whose parents were extremely strict and friends whose parents gave them freedom. The kids who grew up with many rules left their parent's home and went crazy because they were given such rigid barriers. The kids who had the freedom didn't have this urge to go out and do anything that was crazy, at least as a result of leaving home. This explains the above quote to me in a more practical way that makes sense.

Part 1 The Marrow of Zen "In the zazen posture, your mind and body have great power to accept things as they are, whether agreeable or disagreeable."

Many people who start out meditating automatically think they are not doing it right when they can't sit still or don't do it "the right way." It's nice to know that there is no "right way" and that everyone struggles at the beginning. For instance, when I just starting meditating, I struggled to do it the right way and am sure I'm still not doing it the right way. It's all about if you feel the right way when you're doing it as opposed to what you think the right way is. When I'm meditating, thoughts come and go and even though the bad ones don't go away, it makes me feel better to notice that they are there. I can choose when to think about them and this means I'm in control of my bad thoughts which is a good thing.

Part 1 Nothing Special "If you continue this simple practice every day, you will obtain some wonderful power. Before you attain it, it is something wonderful but after you attain it, it is nothing special."

When I first started meditation, I felt the same way. I felt as though it was this special thing but after I meditated a couple of times, it became normal. However, the "wonderful power" should not ever go away. It should be special at all times. It loses its meaning when it's not special. To think of it as going away makes it uninteresting for me. I always want to know that I can get the same excitement every time because that motivates me to want to do it again. If the experience isn't exciting, I might want to do something else that interests me and is exciting for me. Something that's going to keep me coming back for more.

Part 2 Right Attitude "The point we emphasize is strong confidence in our original nature."

This is true and pertains to everything that we do daily. If I'm not confident it is difficult to get through any activity. Confidence helps me focus on the activity that I'm doing. I like how this quote is general and isn't just talking about meditation but could refer to many aspects of life. Confidence makes a huge difference for me in my daily life. When I leave my house and am not confident, I don't have as good of a day then if I am confident. Being confident makes me feel good and if I feel good my interaction with others is positive. However, if I'm not confident, I could say something that could come off as a negative statement and that could result in a number of other unfortunate events.

Part 2 Repetition "If you lose the spirit of repetition, your practice will become quite difficult."

This idea seems negative to me. Repetition is not something I strive for all the time. This makes life boring and expected. The human mind needs challenges and surprises otherwise it's not experiencing life and that's losing out. For instance, if I meditate expecting to get the same thing out of it every time I do it, it seems a little un-motivating. I know the principle is the same but thinking about it as being repetitive makes it sound boring and not challenging. I'm someone who likes to take on a challenge so I strive for change all the time.

Part 2 Zen and Excitement "Zen is not some kind of excitement, but concentration on our usual everyday routine."

I understand this because I practice some meditation but cannot say I practice Zen all the time. I feel as though it doesn't work that way. I either have to accept it as a full lifestyle change or not practice it at all. It's hard to just partially do something for me. I'm either fully involved with it or don't want to do it. I like to give my best in every situation so when I have too much going on, I can't do that. When I have a few things that I can fully immerse myself in I am much more satisfied.

Part 2 Limiting Your Activity "Usually when someone believes in a particular religion, his attitude becomes more and more a sharp angle pointing away from himself. In our way the point of the angle is always towards ourselves."

This idea seems a little confusing for me because I thought Zen was about not focusing on us but taking the focus off of ourselves. I know I have to focus on myself to some extent while I'm meditating. If I think about doing a million other things my mind won't be focused on the practice itself. To burden myself with too much only distracts from meditation.

Part 2 Study Yourself "To have some deep feeling about Buddhism is not the point; we must do what we should do, like eating supper and going to bed. This is Buddhism."

When I learned more about Buddhism, I realized that I should just be living my life as honestly as possible. I should be doing the things I normally do and not try to fit into some form I think is best for me. I shouldn't try to be anything other than what I am. Buddhism doesn't distract from any of my daily activities. The practice itself may add to my life but won't take anything away. I believe it's only there to help me whether I accept it or not.

Part 2 To Polish a Tile "When you become you, Zen becomes Zen. When you are you, you see things as they are, and you become one with your surroundings."

I believe this is similar to the previous quote above which discusses one of the key aspects to Buddhism and that's about just doing what you already do. Being myself and doing what I need to do and what I have planned for my schedule is how I become one with Buddhism. I don't have to go searching for something spectacular that's not there. This ties in to being "awake" and knowing what is going on so I can fully experience life the best I can.

Part 2 Communication "Without any intentional, fancy way of adjusting yourself, to express yourself as you are is the most important thing."

I know that I already do this in my daily life. I try to be as honest as I can be with myself as well as with the people around me. I feel as though I could easily adapt to Buddhism if it was something I chose to practice wholeheartedly.

Part 2 Nirvana, the Waterfall "Our life and death are the same thing. When we realize this fact, we have no fear of death anymore, nor actual difficulty in our life."

My interpretation of this is that we have to experience freedom of mind in order to truly practice Buddhism. If I'm free the practice will flow a lot easier and I will be able to live like this and apply it to everything I do daily. If I'm not free, my mind is blocked off from the reality of the situation and that creates a problem within me to accept the truth. If I'm not free, my mind is tied up with something else that is preventing me from being free. I was closed off to the idea of Buddhism because I didn't know what it was but now I have a much clearer sense of what it is and so am more open to it.

Part 3 Right Understanding "Our understanding of Buddhism is not just an intellectual understanding. True understanding is actual practice itself."

This is explainable but is difficult for me to do because I feel that I understand it to a certain extent but do not actually practice it. I have an issue with meditating but I agree with a lot of what the books have to say that we've read so far. For instance, I understand a lot of concepts that the books talk about and agree with them but cannot apply it to my meditation. I guess I haven't been able to properly meditate and I agree with the above statement so feel like I don't truly understand Buddhism because I haven't been able to take on the practice of meditation in my opinion.

Part 3 Traditional Zen Spirit "If you are trying to attain enlightenment, you are creating and being driven by karma, and you are wasting your time on your black cushion."

The other day, I told myself I was going to meditate because I had so much going on. After I finished meditating, I really didn't feel any better. I thought meditating would help me but it didn't, it made me feel the same way I felt before I meditated. That doesn't happen every time, however setting expectations is only going to disappoint me.

Part 3 Transiency "We should find perfect existence through imperfect existence."

You can't keep running in this crazy whirlwind of speed because eventually you're going to burn out. That's what happened to me in my life. I use to speed through everything always trying to do then next thing when I wasn't done with what I started. Eventually, I realized that I need to slow down and walk because I was missing all the things around me when I was running. Once I realized this, my life changed dramatically. I was a lot more calm and relaxed with everything that I was doing. It just made my life make a lot more sense overall.

Part 3 The Quality of Being "When you do something, if you fix your mind on the activity with some confidence, the quality of your state of mind is the activity itself. When you are concentrated on the quality of your being, you are prepared for the activity."

This makes sense completely, especially since I have been able to apply it to my own life. If I'm writing a paper, like this one, and am not fully present and focused, the quality of my work will not be as good. For example, if my friend calls me on the phone, I can't continue to type and think about what I want to say while listening to her. I probably could, but what I type onto the computer screen is not going to make sense. In order for me to give my best, I need to focus on what is in front of me at that one time.

Part 3 Nauralness "Moment after moment, everyone comes out from nothingness. This is the true joy of life."

I know what I want and if I want to do something it is hard to stop me if I've already set my mind on it. If the argument is good, it might work but generally, just like with everyone, it's hard to change people's minds. I have many ideas come to mind and sometimes I don't know how I thought of them. These ideas are an accumulation of many past experiences and just life in general.

Part 3 Emptiness "When you study Buddhism you should have a general house cleaning of your mind."

I actually want to try this myself. When there are a lot of things around me, it is distracting. I don't like to have a million things around the house and in my room that are unnecessary and useless. I'm always thinking of ways to clear up the space around me. Things that take up space that I don't use don't need to fill the area around me that I'm in. I hope Buddhism can give me a general house cleaning by giving me a new perspective.

The concepts and the knowledge in Buddhism have opened up new ways of thinking about things for me. Nothing bad can come from added perspectives and a broadened view of the world.

Part 3 Readiness, Mindfulness "It is the readiness of the mind that is wisdom."

If I don't want to learn or am tuned out I'm not going to absorb much. Everything that comes in will go right out. Being a college student for the past four years and just a student my whole life, I can truly agree with this statement. If I don't want to do my H.W. and I'm forced to do it, I'm not going to learn anything from it. I might do it just to get it done but it's not going to benefit me because I won't take in the moment in time. When I'm ready, I know and that's when whatever it is I'm going to be doing will feel right.

Part 3 Believing in Nothing "In our everyday life our thinking is ninety-nine percent self-centered. Why do I have suffering? Why do I have trouble?"

I, as a human, don't intend my thinking to be like this but it is. Is there something I can do about it? Obviously life would be much better if I naturally didn't think like this. How can I control how I'm supposed to think? Someone else told me once that if you stop focusing on yourself so much life will be a lot better for you. It's really hard to stop focusing on myself though, when our society emphasizes that so much. America is the richest country in the world, but isn't the happiest. Those countries that are happier probably don't focus on individualistic self-centeredness and that's why they are happier. I don't know if the United States can change its people by changing its self centered way of thinking but I know that people can change themselves. It's hard to change where you grow up in a country that makes you believe that being self-centered is a good thing. I don't know if it's a bad thing either. I would say that I'm a little self-centered but if I wasn't I don't know if I would be able to survive in a society like ours.

After much thought and realization, Buddhism has come to mean something more to me than the word "Zen." This word doesn't just mean relaxation and waterfalls to me anymore. There is much more behind its meaning and isn't as simple as I thought it was. There is still a lot I can learn about Zen and so many other books I could read. Some people who practice this have said that it took them years to get it right. If I'm dedicated to something and my heart is in it, there are no boundaries. I will focus and give my all towards something that I'm passionate about.

Mary Parsamyan is a Sociology major and is graduating this year. She is interested in writing and the film industry. School has kept her busy but soon she'll have the time to pursue her true passions in life.

Unquizzes

Students created questions based on their present moment experience in the class, reading, practicing meditation, writing, and discussing the work in class. Each student was responsible for one question during the semester, and two questions per week were posted on the class wiki. The other students in the class responded to each question. The student who created each question selected the response that seemed most interesting or resonant for this curated collection of unquiz questions and responses.

Question 1. Inquiry Question: In Hagen's book, Buddhism Plain and Simple, on page 28 there is a picture that we are supposed to look at until we see what it is. Who saw it after a while and who had to go look it up in the back of the book? What does being able to see this picture mean to you in terms of Zen philosophy?

MYSTERIOUS FIGURE - REVEALED !

Like many of you said, I also didn't see the cow right away or even after looking in the back of the book. I also only saw the cow after reading _____'s post. [A student's post explained how to see the cow in Hagen's picture] I then experienced the moment of clarity Hagen talks about. Where suddenly what seconds before troubled you, was now something that empowered you. I suddenly had the feeling that I knew something other people wanted to know. In terms of zen I think this picture is to teach people to open their minds in ways they are not used to. I compared the inability to see the cow to the way we read. Our eyes can see and comprehend every word on the page at once, however we have trained our minds to only see and comprehend one word or phrase at a time. I believe we have trained our minds to only see certain things and not bring in every possibility at once. This exercise truly opens your mind to reaching clarity or enlightenment as Hagen says happens when you finally see the cow.

Question 2. Based on the discussion in class last week, following our meditation time, what did you experience or observe during meditation?

I read a comment that Charlotte Joko Beck writes in "*Everyday Zen*" and it has stuck with me through meditations. When discussing the idea of "letting go" during meditations, Beck goes further into detail about what that idea really means. She says, "The best way to let go is to notice the thoughts as they come up and to acknowledge them." In other words, she's saying don't look for a place where thoughts don't occur—because that doesn't exist—rather acknowledge the thoughts as they enter your mind and then return to the experience of the current moment.

So during meditation, I literally acknowledge every thought as it comes to me. That way, I am not stuck thinking about it over and over again, and it doesn't get to the point of stressing me out or making me feel anxious. It usually goes away, and then I'll think, "Well, glad that's gone. What's next?" I know it probably sounds so weird, but it's the only way for me to sit quietly and calmly during meditation.

Question 3. In Hagen's book, he tends to encourage "seeing" a situation through frequent use of the second person "You" or the inclusive "We." In your experience, did this strategy significantly impact your experience of the text? Is this a representation of any of the non-argumentative strategies we are observing in the class? Do you think that the text would have significantly changed if it was more reflective (I noticed, rather than You notice) or used more parables (Tom noticed)? Was this a "good" introduction to the rhetoric of Zen Buddhism?

I hardly even noticed Hagen's use of 'we' rather than 'I' until I read your question. It's not that I didn't notice because I wasn't paying attention while I read, I think it's rather because 'we' is generally used when teaching someone else or participating in some type of practice. I use 'we' like this all the time when I teach guitar lessons to my students. Rather than say 'you play a G-C-D progression,' I'll say 'let us play the progression.' I guess it's the way my music teachers always approached it. It seems to give the student confidence, especially when learning something new for the first time, because it's a mutual activity as opposed to student feeling individual pressure. I wonder if Hagen is doing this purposefully? Or if he just prefers the more relaxed language.

Question 4. Pg. 54, Hagen:

This is right intention, right resolve.

You cannot actually learn Truth from anyone. It's seen only through your own resolve. If you do not resolve to awaken, there's nothing a teacher can do for you. Right resolve is likened to a person whose hair is on fire. When your hair is on fire, you're not going to weigh the pros and cons of putting it out. If your hair's on fire, there's no waffling. You see no choice. You act.

Pg. 73, Hagen:

Right intention, the second aspect of the eightfold path, is what most distinguishes a buddha from those of us who are not awake. Why? Because in the moment we are awake, for all practical purposes we're without intention. We could say that the intention of an awakened person is just simply to be awake.

If we want to break the chain of suffering and confusion, our intention should only be to awaken. If our intention is partly to get something from being awake, however, this is already delusion. We don't get anything from being awake. If you're awake, you're just awake. And if you're awake, you'll act and speak in a way that doesn't do injury to yourself or to others...

Thus right intention is simply the intention to come back to this moment—to be present with no ideas of gaining whatsoever. You cannot be here and hold a gaining idea at the same time. Just becoming here and now is enough.

Pg. 76, Hagen

The mind doesn't only lean toward the obvious- fame, money, sex, and such- it can lean toward anything. It can even lean toward putting an end to leaning. "Oh yeah, I want enlightenment!" But, of course, this is to lean once again.

The thing you really want is for your mind not to lean. So what are you going to do about it? You may say, "Okay, I'm going to straighten up my mind!" And then you struggle to straighten up your mind.

But that is leaning!

QUESTION:

These three passages, quoted directly from Hagen's book (my own emphases added), give a perspective on what "Right Intention" looks like. What sense do you make of this? You can interpret what he means if you wish, but the real question is more how you are personally affected by these sentiments.

To me right intention, in these cases, is coming from a viewpoint that we ultimately live in a zero sum universe, or Buddhism's parallel to the first law of thermodynamics (matter can not be created or destroyed). In the system of our home planet this is obviously technically false, but I believe all might stand to benefit from the viewpoint regardless of technicalities. Essentially, that to gain is to take from someone else. So if we are to minimize the suffering we cause others, ultimately, we have to stop trying to gain privately. This focus on the minimization of suffering, if practiced by enough, would result in a net lowering of overall suffering, even in the individuals no longer trying to gain, as they would have no one adding additional suffering beyond what nature already provides.

To stop from leaning or having intentions altogether is certainly an astonishing task in my view. What is so easy to imagine, is much harder to put in to practice, I've found. Personally I find it very hard due to the immense social pressures to strive for the various goals listed in the third selection quoted. It seems like many people are interested in having us strive for each of those things, and simply in advertising alone, invest massive amounts of time and money to keep us constantly wanting more, wanting better, wanting new, etc. How we are to combat this, short of dropping off the grid altogether, is not something I have answered for myself.

Question 5. In the beginning of the book Suzuki states, "Actually, when you say, ' I should not do this,' you are doing not-doing in that moment. So there is no choice for you." Do you agree with this? Is it possible for a person to realize that an action is not in their (or someone's) best interest and yet still choose to do it? Does the practice of Zen always have to go with the right choice, assuming there is one? He talks about 'living in this moment' as the only point of importance. Can Zen practice support evil or 'not-to-do' acts?

I think that it refers to the whole "not leaning" aspect of Zen. If you think to yourself, "I don't want that chocolate sundae," then you really do want it. If you truly had no desire for it, why would you feel the need to even bring it up? When you say "I should not do this," you are just affirming the fact that you want to do this. You are actively not doing the thing, which is different than passively not doing the thing.

In the case of the smoker trying to rid himself of all cigarette dependency, we tell him "great job!" for every day or week he succeeds in not smoking a cigarette. He is actively "not doing" a thing. Does it make sense to laud a person who has never smoked a cigarette in his life for going another week without one? No, that's silly. This is the difference between active and passive not-doing.

"Is it possible for a person to realize that an action is not in their (or someone's) best interest and yet still choose to do it? "

Of course! The more interesting problem is harmful in regards to the self. In the case of the cigarette smoker, he knows that it harms him. Why then does he continue? Is there an internal cost-benefit analysis carried out within his mind? This seems plausible. Strictly speaking, one would have to define beyond a reasonable doubt the meaning and implications of "in x's best interest." In the short run, or in the long run? The Zen answer would be simple- the right answer is always changing with the situation at hand. One must only see the situation for how it really is and the right answer shall be quite obvious.

Whether it's possible to do something that one knows will harm oneself in the short run, however, is a very interesting question. Undoubtedly the thought process would be something like "well, it may hurt me now, but it'll be better for me in the long run somehow."

Question 6. In Zen Mind, Beginner's Mind, Suzuki frequently points to the gap between language and communication. The meanings behind many of his words are distorted by translation, and those that do make the jump from Japanese to English are subject to seemingly endless equivocation. The concepts of "emptiness" and "nothingness" come to mind; his meaning by these words seems to be very different from our own, and yet it is imperative for our understanding of Buddhism that we try to see what he's getting at.

To remedy this problem, Suzuki often turns to analogies, evoking striking images of waterfalls, bonfires, and singing birds to help explain the Buddha's teachings. Which image or images made the strongest impression on your understanding of Buddhism, and why?

The room comparison helps me understand buddhism a little better. I like to keep my room organized, just like my thoughts. I have to writ down my thoughts though- and prioritize. I like redecorate my room sometimes. So in comparison I like to change things up- break up order a little bit. I like to toss out old stuff and replace it with new things. Sometimes I find a better way of thinking about things or a different way of thinking that causes me to throw out the old version. Sometimes

I hold onto somethings for too long. For example I have a lot of bad memories that I keep in the back of my head and don't ever think about. Same as the old pictures and shoes that I keep in the back of my closet. Some of those things remind me of bad memories and some good. Sometimes you just need a new perspective- some of the worst things that have happened to me have actually turned out for the better. So slowly those old pictures that were once bad memories are now good. Some of the clothes that I had to throw away because they didn't fit- gave room for new clothes that I like better. Everything is all relative and changes with time. Just because you think one way doesn't mean you will think that way forever. Just because I like the room one way doesn't mean I won't get tired of it tomorrow.

Question 7. How does the Zen literature that you've read, differ in terms of rhetorical construction from other philosophical or religious texts? Have you noticed the way you construct arguments, or just use language in general, to change in a similar way during meditation?

In the fundamental structure of Zen though is a strong sense of actively overcoming biases one brings to discussion. No other philosophy or religion I know of touts that as a core belief. Typically, in western philosophical method, the assumption of the author is that he's right, and the reality he describes is static. It's decipherable through the schema he lays out. These are pragmatically useful to a very little extent. The same is true for religion, typically, with the exception of Jewish Mysticism; but even in this case, the non-didactic nature of the texts is replaced with unclear exposition. On the one hand, there's a clear narrative laid out, but at the same time this narrative is riddled with oft unexplained contradictions. The Zen literature we have encountered so far (which I agree with Logan excludes Hagan in favor of the Zen-directed audience of Suzuki) gives at least somewhat of an explanation of the contradictions that they give rise to. For example, saying "Form is form; emptiness is emptiness" and all of their iterations makes sense in context of the greater Suzukean exposition. The biggest difference between Zen literature and Western philosophy and religion, though, is that Zen literature claims to be talking about something that ultimately you can't talk about. The expository function of the teaching is only meant to supplement the most important part of the tradition: the practice. Zen thought acknowledges the dynamic face of reality, and therefore offers no hard-fast rules by which to abide. There's no universals in Zen. There's only the situation presented to you, and the only way you can be sure that you deal with it in the correct fashion is to be in touch with yourself, with reality, and with others.

Zen has affected the way I construct arguments inasmuch as it has reified the sentiment that I should always remove my biases when listening to another. I am oft guilty of not listening to others so much as waiting for my turn to speak, a decidedly un-Zen frame of mind.

Question 8. Have you discovered that meditation has helped you with a problem? If not, what is one problem you hope meditation can help with?

During the recent weeks, the father of a good friend of mine(whose family has really adopted me in a way) has really taken a turn for the worse, health wise (he is 84). He is a lifelong alcoholic and in response to depression brought on by illness he went on a two week bender which has hospitalized and nearly killed him (which is, incidentally, why I missed class last week). I find that during my daily meditations though, I am able to really be with my grief, confusion, anger and sense of urgency. Because I take the time to just be with myself, I have found, conversely, that these emotions seem almost to back off during the time when I have to be there for the family, or with the man in the hospital. It is like my emotions know that at some point in the day, I will sit with them, and so they seem less agitated. Its really a surreal sort of experience. Its almost like each of the emotions I feel are actually tiny people, who act like children. And as long as they know that I will pay attention to them, they stop begging for my attention. In the meditation, I find that I can be with those parts of me without having to shove them away or fix them, and in doing so, they really seem to begin to "fix" themselves. I look forward to seeing the long term effects of this all as I move forward.

Question 9. On Monday, we discussed how zen is supposed to help us notice that a lot of our problems are derived from our own actions. Professor Syverson used the analogy, "It's as though we notice our hand is burning and then realize that we have it held over a candle." If this is so, why do you think zazen enforces daily meditation that can cause pain and discomfort?

I think the pain and discomfort in zazen is to help us understand what real pain and discomfort is, so that we do not mis-attribute pain to something that is not actually painful. Essentially, by being grounded in what we know is pain arriving in the now, if we are being mindful, we can cease from being confused about other things in our lives which we may symbolically attribute as being painful, but may actually be beneficial. The better we actually understand what will pain us, the less likely we are to leave our hand above the candle, as we know what will happen because of it, is pain.

Question 10. Each author we've read, especially these first three, emphasizes the way we handle comfort and discomfort, pleasure and suffering, joy and sadness, etc.

We learned that Buddhism describes life in terms of the manner of our acclimation to suffering. That's not to say simply that "life is suffering," but that the way humans respond to and form behavior/habit around suffering (be it desires, fears, appetites, basic survival necessity..) is the 'crux' of our identity and agency within society.

Think "Verbs."

It's accurate to say much of what we "do" is in response to some form suffering, be it thirst, desire, fear, sadness, not-enough-money-ness, etc.

Now, the aspect of Zen which has been difficult to understand for many of us is the notion that pursuing goals/achievement is something of a losing battle. Joko attempts to clarify this by emphasizing aspiration over expectation. SHe says aspiration is something that comes naturally, while struggling for achievement is often an effort to hide from a dissatisfaction (some kind of suffering) with our lives. She says aspiration is always satisfying; expectation is never satisfying. I'm curious about how others view this field of issues.   How, if at all, has this course influenced the way you view practice, aspiration, expectation, and suffering?

I think that merely separating the ideas of aspiration and expectation have already had an influence on the way I view things and my feelings toward accomplishing goals. This can be most easily and recently applied to a fencing tournament that I had this weekend. The event on my first day led me through a roller coaster of suffering, starting out with greatly exceeding my low expectations which subsequently raised them too high at which point they were completely shattered when I lost, leaving me with a great feeling of suffering, dwelling on what I could have done and what mistakes I made. During my event on the second day, however, I took a different approach of taking each bout as it came to me, rather than planning ahead of how I thought the event would pan out. I found that when I went into the event without any expectations, but rather took each "phrase" (point) one at a time, I was much more relaxed, and afterward pleased with how I had done, rather than disappointed in what I hadn't been able to accomplish.

Question 11. In addition to practice and concepts, we have discussed the rhetoric of Zen throughout the semester, and I think we have come to some general agreement upon what rhetorical techniques are used in Zen. To name a few things we've observed, Hagen uses inclusive words like "I" and "we" to engage the audience, and many Zen teachers use paradoxical statements backed up with analogies to convey Zen practices and concepts. In the texts that we have read and discussed the authors use "non-argumentative" rhetoric, as the course title suggests. I was wondering, do you think that this type of non-argumentative rhetoric predominantly found in Zen could be effective if used in our western culture?

I honestly think for the most part "non argumentative" rhetoric would NOT be effective in western culture. Especially when discussing Zen, I think most people will need solid, clear explanation. While Zazen really is solid, and ultimately very simple, it is only so when the student or seeker ceases to want something from it. I feel most people would want an answer or some special advice from Zen, which they most certainly would not attain- at least not at first. So, for instance, when I try to explain my Zazen practices to some members of my family many of them respond with questionable looks and doubt. Zazen seems like such a weird/crazy concept even though it really isn't because so many people are caught up the whirlwind of emotional life. The teachings of Zazen, particularly stepping out of one's self is so foreign in the western world, that a lot of people immediately shut down rather than being receptive to new perspectives. So, in this way, because one would have to 'argue' to convince someone of Zen's benefits the practice and ideology would be lost in the process. I think Zen rhetoric is only effective with people who are willing to learn and cope with their own suffering.

Question 12. I have shared my learning in Zen with a variety of people, including my co-op, family, and friends. Most people are very critical of the notion of Zen, because they think it is unrealistic or contrary to other philosophies they treasure. Do you discuss your learning with others? How do they react?

I've discussed Zen with my mom and a couple of friends. My mom (being my mom) was very interested to hear what we've been learning about. She was especially intrigued when I told her about the class's emphasis on non-argumentative rhetoric. Non-argumentative rhetoric? What's that? Likewise, my friends more so than anything were baffled by the seemingly exotic mixture of eastern religion and rhetoric, as they're used to associating rhetoric with the West, not the East. In short, the people I've shared my learning with have been less interested in the Zen part and more interested in the paradoxes presented by the course topic.

On the other hand, I have found opportunities to share my learning with others in a slightly more indirect fashion, talking about the limitations of our understanding and the value and benefits of simply being aware of what's happening right in front of us. These ideas really seemed to resonate. This could have to do with the fact that, in explaining them, I focused on their applicability to our everyday life rather than their association with Buddhism.

Question 13. Buddha's Brain by Rick Hanson provided us with a different take on Buddhism: the relationship between science and contemplative practice and meditation. Does having a scientific understanding of the relationship between Buddhist meditation practice and philosophy and the neurological functions of our brain help your own understanding of Buddhism and/or yourself? For example, did it clear up any confusions you may have had? Were you surprised by any findings revealed in this book?

I am continually blown away by the extent to which Buddhist philosophy seems to converge with scientific discovery. For me, it's somewhat relieving to think that traditionally unscientific concepts like wisdom and compassion can now be shown to have a real, fundamental basis in neuropsychology... just goes to show that our knowledge doesn't have to be perfect for our practice to be sound. Loved the exercises, too.

Furthermore, it's interesting how the goals of Zen and psychological science seem to be the same: using the rhetoric of observation, both seek to know as much as possible about direct experience. The union between the two hinted at in this book could give us a way to embed Buddhist principles in a cultural vernacular that Westerners seem to understand—namely, that of positive psychology. So I guess the rhetorical differences between this book and the others are what interest me the most.

Question 14. I'm really interested in Zen because I often feel consumed by little problems in my life to the point that I can't focus on the task at hand. Zen has been great for helping me stay in the present, keeping a positive attitude, and making practical decisions regarding my schedule, but I'm worried that my productivity-related interest may be limiting my experience in Zen.

Do you find that you use your Zen practice to reach certain aims or goals? If so, in what ways, and do you think that your motivations distract from, or are counter intuitive to, the true goals of Zen?

Well, I think that surmising I understand the true goals of Zen would be a little arrogant at this early stage in my study. And yet, from another perspective, I would say that the beginner sitting their very first zazen understands Zen fully. I guess I try not to be too anxious about how I am relating to Zen. If Zen has taught me anything, it is that what there is to do is merely to be with what is arising. So, for instance, I remember sharing in class one day that I had been unable to keep my thoughts quiet and had found if very difficult to stay present to the physical world around me during my meditation. The professor responded, "Great! So you really observed that." And I thought to myself, "Oh... yea... I guess I did." It was then that I realized something new had become possible for me out of Zen. But I only reached that "goal" because I was reaching for something else. I think it is naturally human to try things out in our lives. So, even though it might not get you enlightenment, I think seeing what becomes possible for you out of using Zen or Zen rhetoric to move towards a goal is entirely appropriate. How else will you figure out whether it is valuable or not?

Question 15. "Ultimately, happiness comes down to choosing between the discomfort of becoming aware of your mental afflictions and the discomfort of being ruled by them."—Yongey Mingyur Rinpoche (pg. 49, Chapter 3)

Now that our understanding of Zen is more evolved, do you think this is an accurate depiction of happiness? If not, what is it lacking, or what has it missed? Can you see yourself being happy while still aware of mental suffering? Does the concept of happiness seem to be only a choice between the lesser of two mental sufferings?

Seemingly. For me, this quotation evokes the idea that happiness cannot be got at except through suffering. Breaking any kind of attachment is painful to some degree, even if it's an attachment to something bad, such as a delusion, habit, or addiction. So the means to happiness can cause some serious discomfort, and we have to be okay with that. Personally, I feel like this definition is complete—I can't really think of a better one. Perhaps the reason it seems inadequate is that we tend to associate the state of being happy to its corresponding feelings. What we leave out of our definitions is the means by which a person attains happiness—which, according to Zen, is a matter of choice.

No Question 16.

Question 17. Is there a situation, teaching or reading that you have "tested against your own experience" (today's lecture)?

Did it lead towards well-being, happiness or waking up?

If not, can you think of an example that you could test against experience?

Yeah, I have directly applied the things we're learning in class particularly to my pursuit in improvisational comedy and acting in general. The biggest problem you can have as an actor is getting caught "acting." This happens when someone perceives you calculating your next action. Being in the moment helps with that.

In improvisation, I have a problem with expecting a scene to go a certain way. When I do, it invariably goes counter to how I expect it, leaving me wondering what it is I can possibly do to remedy this "broken" scene. Applying zen concepts has helped tremendously in this realm. There is never a "bad" scene. The scene is always as it is; it is always "thus." Thinking about it in this way has led me to approach each scene as an exciting adventure where I didn't know any more than my scene partner where it was going. The same applies for social interactions on any scale.

Question 18. In Philosophical Meditations on Zen Buddhism, chapter 2, Huang Po's disciple, Lin-chi, calls texts "dung clods" and "worthless dust," but Huang Po's knowledge of the texts seems to be in contradiction with this approach to Buddhism. This polarization has baffled many Zen scholars, but the same dichotomy can be examined within our small amount of experience with Zen within this class.

My question to you is, how has gaining insight by reading the material differed from actually experimenting with Zen practice within the class and the meditations outside of class?

I have experienced a number of differences between when I read about a certain zen practice and when I actually try to practice it. At some point, just like almost every other discipline, there is only so much you can gain from reading a book. The other day in class we used the "cooking" metaphor to describe this. You have to study cook books to become a master chef, but unless you actually practice cooking, all the time you spent reading cook books will be wasted. You have to get out there and practice... After all, the saying is "practice makes perfect," not "reading makes perfect." Basically in this example, cook books are just a helpful tool to become a better chef, but studying books alone won't get the job done, you have to actually practice cooking. The same idea applies to us in our practice of Buddhism. We can read all the books we want, but unless we actually make an honest attempt to practice, then we will never gain anything from all the reading.

Question 19. "All sentient beings developed through natural selection in such a way that pleasant sensations serve as their guide, and especially the pleasure derived from sociability and from loving our families." – Charles Darwin

"The story of the Two Wolves in the Heart suggests that we each have the ability to encourage and strengthen empathy, compassion, and kindness while also restraining and reducing ill will, disdain, and aggression... Love and Attachment evolved as a way for hominid bands to keep their members connected for many years in order to sustain and thus pass on the band's genes. As a result, the human brain acquired powerful circuitry and neurochemistry to generate and maintain both Love and Relationships. Romantic love is found in almost all human cultures, suggesting that it's deep in our biological – even our biochemical – nature." - Buddha's Brain: Chapter 8, ~pp.. 121-127 (with some slight tweaking)

I am interested to see what kind of impact the ideas of love and relationships have in our book chapters. It seems to me that evaluating love and relationships is an essential part of our experience with Buddhism yet most of us, including myself, have focused mainly on other topics. Now let make sure I am being clear, I am talking about much more than just love and relationships via a "significant other," although that is certainly relevant. But what about the love you have for your parents? Or the relationship you have with your best-friend? Do you love your best-friend? How has your experience with Zen Buddhism changed the way you label love and relationships... has it changed anything at all?

This is a great question. Learning about Zen has definitely given me a fresh perspective on love and relationships. For me, the trigger was reading Wright and thinking about the concepts of emptiness and dependent origination. To say that we're empty is simply to say that we depend on each other in more ways than we could ever fathom. No one is disconnected; no one is independent; no one is in any way separate from the people around him/her. It's easy enough to see how certain people in our lives shape us—our parents, our siblings, our closest friends, our "significant others." But what concepts like emptiness and dependent origination invite us to do is to look into how we are shaped, period. This has led me to a greater appreciation of the people in my life I've hitherto taken for granted, as well as to an awareness of the possibilities inherent in my interactions with others, "significant" or otherwise. If love is an abandonment of self for the "reward" of establishing a deep, lasting bond with another, then the Zen teachings would suggest that the place of spacious awareness and the state of being in love are essentially the same thing. The more aware and "awake" we become, the greater our capacity for love—for celebrating rather than denying our mutual connectedness.

Question 20. Throughout the semester I have been fasci-nated by the unique rhetoric used in the Zen texts we read in class. Wright says that "...when language... function{s} as an instrument in Zen, it is a tool of considerable power and preci-sion."(82) In your opinion how does Zen rhetoric convey this power, and what about zen rhetoric makes it so effective?

In addition does everyone think zen rhetoric is powerful?

I think the power of Zen rhetoric lies in the uniqueness of

Zen's "ends." How often do we encounter speech whose goal is not to convince the listener of some truth, but rather to enlarge his or her awareness of the rhetorical situation? What do you say to a person when your intention is to give them a novel sense of their role in the conversation, or to show them how they fit into a bigger, more expansive picture of reality? Such discourses and interactions are rare, at least in our experience. This could help explain why Zen rhetoric is so powerful; it is by necessity highly specialized to fit unique ends.

Question 21. Wright says, "Every experience arises out of what came before it and shades off into whatever comes after it, forming the continuum of past, present, and future that shapes the mind's awareness. Aside from relations to "before" and "after," the presence of the present moment would not appear as it does. Each element of time is embedded in the others as their presupposition" (173).

I read from this that every element we have learned in class is interconnected and leading us into the future as well as giving us better introspection into the past. Being that the present state is the conclusion of our course, what have you learned and how does it connect to your past and future? In so many words, how does your learning in this course relate to your own individual past, present and future path? Will you use what you learned; and if so, how?

This is an interesting question. I would say what we've learned connects to my past in that I am by nature pretty introspective and have up to this point spent a lot of time trying to figure out where I fit in relation to the people, places, ideas, and objects around me. In the past, this habit has resulted in more self-consciousness than anything else. In a sense, what the class has taught me, then, is how to refine my methods of self-examination in a way that yields greater self-awareness—and even more significantly, how to connect this broadened sense of self-awareness to an awareness of the world around me. Having been exposed to these ideas and having tested them out against my own experience, I feel strongly that pursuing awareness is the best possible course for me.

So this is the present course. As of now, I fully intend I learning more and continuing my practice. But I can't say with any certainty that I will, because I simply don't know. It's kind of weird when you think about the gap between our fixed conceptions of where we are at a particular point in time and what we *actually* know about the future. I have these plans now, so I feel like I have a pretty good idea of what the future's going to look like. But in the end I can't know. What I do know is that, even if I eventually get distracted from or lose interest in my study of Zen, I'll never forget its strong suggestion that there is no 'self'—that what the 'self' *actually* is is nothing more than a bundle of relations to the outside world and everything in it. For me, this one thought skirts the foundations of everything I've learned in this class, and it's a lesson that I'm sure will stick with me.

Question 22. Now that you know how impermanent, dependent, and empty everything is, what has changed within your life?

For example, are there any things that are now more important to you and your life? Are there any things that now seem trivial?

Relations are definitely more important to me now than they were at the beginning of the semester—specifically, understanding how things relate to one another. It gives me a way of studying and learning about the world that never biases one perspective, but rather takes as many perspectives into account as possible. For me, when I think about how one, single node in a network of relations—a person, an object, an idea, whatever— fits in with and influences all the other nodes in that network, I get a deeper, more satisfying appreciation for that node, that network, and, in general, the nature of life. In this respect, I have trouble viewing anything in my life as trivial—but for what it's worth, I definitely grant my 'self' a lot less authority than I did a few months ago.

www.ingramcontent.com/pod-product-compliance
Lightning Source LLC
Chambersburg PA
CBHW022115080426
42734CB00006B/145